# Rethinking
## CONSCIOUSNESS

# Rethinking

# CONSCIOUSNESS

Extraordinary Challenges
for Contemporary Science

John H. Buchanan
Christopher M. Aanstoos
Editors

Foreword by Stanley Krippner

PROCESS
CENTURY
PRESS
ANOKA, MINNESOTA 2020

*Rethinking Consciousness: Extraordinary Challenges for Contemporary Science*
© 2020 Process Century Press

Process Century Press
RiverHouse LLC
802 River Lane
Anoka, MN 55303

Process Century Press books are published in association with the International Process Network.

Cover: Susanna Mennicke

Acknowledgements
Chapter Six, "Revision and Re-enchantment of Psychology," by Stanislav Grof, is a condensed and revised version of an article from the *Journal of Transpersonal Psychology*, which generously gave permission for its use in this collection. *The Journal of Transpersonal Psychology*, 2012, Vol. 44, No. 2, 137–63)

VOLUME XX
TOWARD ECOLOGICAL CIVILIZATION SERIES
JEANYNE B. SLETTOM, GENERAL EDITOR

ISBN 978-1-940447-43-8 (pbk.)
978-1-940447-45-2 (e-book)
Printed in the United States of America

## SERIES PREFACE: TOWARD ECOLOGICAL CIVILIZATION

We live in the ending of an age. But the ending of the modern period differs from the ending of previous periods, such as the classical or the medieval. The amazing achievements of modernity make it possible, even likely, that its end will also be the end of civilization, of many species, or even of the human species. At the same time, we are living in an age of new beginnings that give promise of an ecological civilization. Its emergence is marked by a growing sense of urgency and deepening awareness that the changes must go to the roots of what has led to the current threat of catastrophe.

In June 2015, the 10th Whitehead International Conference was held in Claremont, CA. Called "Seizing an Alternative: Toward an Ecological Civilization," it claimed an organic, relational, integrated, nondual, and processive conceptuality is needed, and that Alfred North Whitehead provides this in a remarkably comprehensive and rigorous way. We proposed that he could be "the philosopher of ecological civilization." With the help of those who have come to an ecological vision in other ways, the conference explored this Whiteheadian alternative, showing how it can provide the shared vision so urgently needed.

The judgment underlying this effort is that contemporary research and scholarship is still enthralled by the 17th century view of nature articulated by Descartes and reinforced by Kant. Without freeing our minds of this objectifying and reductive understanding of the world, we are not likely to direct our actions wisely in response to the crisis to which this tradition has led us. Given the ambitious goal of replacing now dominant patterns of thought with one that would redirect us toward ecological civilization, clearly more is needed than a single conference. Fortunately, a larger platform is developing that includes the conference and looks beyond it. It is named Pando Populus (pandopopulous.org) in honor of the world's largest and oldest organism, an aspen grove.

As a continuation of the conference, and in support of the larger initiative of Pando Populus, we are publishing this series, appropriately named "Toward Ecological Civilization."

-John B. Cobb, Jr.

ACKNOWLEDGEMENTS

THIS BOOK would not have come into existence if it not for the seminal conference, Seizing an Alternative, which took place in Claremont, California, in June of 2015. As envisioned by John B. Cobb, Jr., this conference explored the many possibilities offered by process thought for reimagining our civilization in light of the manifold threats that now face humanity and the planet. Our thanks go out to the hundreds of people whose hard work made this gathering possible, and especially to John Cobb, Andrew Schwartz, and Vern Visick, who were the backbone of this enterprise.

Next, our great appreciation to the contributors to this volume, most of whom were part of the "Extraordinary Challenges" track at the Seizing an Alternative conference, but several of whom were unable to participate directly in our track discussions. They were persuaded to contribute chapters to this book nonetheless, and the essays by John Cobb, David Ray Griffin, and Larry Dossey have strengthened and deepened the general view being developed in these pages. Thanks to the track participants for their additional efforts to turn their conference presentations into the chapters you will find in this book, and for their patience and goodwill during the editing process.

For their diligent help in the initial editing of the chapters, a tip of the hat to Gina Picard and Nancy Walter at the University of West

Georgia. Our particular thanks go to Elizabeth Stemen, who coordinated the final editing of the chapters and the assorted details involved in preparing a book for publication. Finally, this project would not have even gotten underway without the encouragement of John Cobb on the front end and Jeanyne Slettom on the publishing end. Jeanyne's labors at founding and managing Process Century Press have created an important venue for process-related books, something we feel is of great value.

A special note of thanks to the *Journal of Transpersonal Psychology*, which generously gave permission to include in this volume a revised version of an article by Stanislav Grof. Also, we would be remiss not to acknowledge Catherine Keller for her helpful suggestion regarding the title for this book.

# CONTENTS

# Foreword

*Stanley Krippner*

THIS BOOK IS REMARKABLE. Its chapters propose an "ecological civilization," one that reflects the impending climate changes of the twenty-first century. These have been discussed since the establishment of the "greenhouse effect" in the 1800s and the subsequent predictions at the turn of the twentieth century. In recent years there has been a plethora of books and articles on this topic, as well as some dissenting voices. However, the latter objections do not deny that the climate is changing, but claim that human activity has little to do with it.

What is new about this volume is its link to exceptional human experiences, especially those anomalies that cannot be easily reconciled with mainstream science's understanding of time, space, and energy. On the one hand, we have mainstream science's contention that an ecological crisis is impending, and, on the other hand, we are told that it can be prevented (or at least managed) by data that contradict the constructs of that same science. This type of dialectic is not uncommon in postmodernity dialogue, but here the consequences are more than an intellectual exercise. Personally, I recall the philosopher Alan Watts, a pioneer ecologist, discussing these portents with me and my friends on his houseboat in Sausalito, California.[1] At the time we had no idea how prescient he was!

i

The extraordinary suggestion of the chapter authors is that the concepts and data from transpersonal psychology and parapsychology, long rejected, ridiculed, or ignored by mainstream science, are the very resources needed to reorient this endangered world and its tattered societies. None of this would come as a surprise to Alfred North Whitehead, the visionary philosopher whose process philosophy easily encompasses both quantum physics and the anomalous experiences enumerated by the chapter authors. Indeed, such physicists as Henry Stapp and such cosmologists as Bernard Carr have accommodated these phenomena within their models. Further, it was not so long ago that seminal physicists such as David Bohm, Niels Bohr, and Wolfgang Pauli expressed an open-minded attitude to parapsychological data. I was fortunate enough to be present when Bohm presented his "new theory of mind and matter" to an appreciative audience in New York City.[2]

The anthropologist Jeremy Narby has expanded this discussion in his landmark book *Intelligence in Nature,* pointing out that intentional behavior is not limited to the human species.[3] Self-deterministic decisions, behaviors, and activities can be found not only in other animals but in many other forms of life—not only the proverbial birds and the bees but in microscopic organisms as well. Abraham Maslow, a founder of transpersonal psychology, once told me that there was a need for a "transhuman psychology," one that would recognize these uncanny dispositions of other forms of life. I responded that, for me, psychology is the scientific study of experience and behavior, and that humans are not the only organisms that experience and behave.

Maslow's ideas constantly ran counter to those of his fellow past-presidents of the American Psychological Association, many of whom modeled cognitive neuroscience after the natural sciences.[4] However, the celebrated "hard problem" in psychology argues for human subjectivity and doubts that it can be explained by current paradigms.[5] Susan Gordon has proposed a solution, replacing materialistic cognitive science with a nondualistic neurophenomenology informed by Indo-Tibetan Buddhist philosophy.[6] Julia Mossbridge and Imants Baruss go a step further by proposing a "post-materialist" science of consciousness in a paradigm-shifting book published by the American Psychological Association.[7] These authors build their case on data from parapsychology, transpersonal psychology, and associated disciplines that have spent decades waiting for an opportunity to join the discourse that finally seems available to them.

Over the years, it has been my great pleasure to visit the University of West Georgia, where Chris Aanstoos and his colleagues have developed a pioneering but rigorous curriculum in transpersonal and humanistic psychology. He and coeditor John Buchanan, an alumnus of the West Georgia graduate psychology program, are the perfect shepherds for this stimulating series of essays, thought-provoking probes into implementing a platform for a civil civilization, one that is uniquely appropriate for the twenty-first century. It calls for a recognition of the connectedness not only of humanity but of all life forms. The recognition of this connection could forestall ecological disasters and nuclear catastrophes as well. Let us hope this vision can be incarnated before it is too late.

Stanley Krippner
Alan Watts Professor of Psychology
Saybrook University

# Introduction

*John H. Buchanan & Christopher M. Aanstoos*

In June 2015, a large international gathering met in Claremont, California, to explore the possibilities offered by process thought for reimagining civilization. Titled *Seizing an Alternative: Toward an Ecological Civilization,* this conference articulated the need for such a reorientation in response to the catastrophic threats currently facing our world. The subtitle's focus on "ecological" was meant to indicate that this reorientation requires a more holistic vision of reality, as well as effective ways of preserving and restoring the planet. Among the more than eighty tracks that explored these issues, one focused on *extraordinary experiences,* that is to say, experiences that cannot be fully accounted for by the dominant scientific paradigm of our times. The subject matter of this track included the evidence for parapsychological, transpersonal, and other anomalous phenomena. If such experiences could be truly understood, on their own terms, they might offer real insight into the more holistic workings of an intrinsically interconnected universe. This kind of understanding of deep interrelatedness truly "seizes an alternative" to the modern Western worldview that still relies too uncritically on old notions of insentient elements connected only by extrinsic causality.

This volume contains essays based on most of the presentations from this track on anomalous experience, as well as three additional papers contributed by individuals who were unable to participate directly.

These essays explore experiences that present significant challenges to the modern scientific worldview, in particular, to its insistent refusal to reconsider its underlying commitment to a materialistic, mechanistic, atheistic metaphysics. Philosophically, Alfred North Whitehead's process view of experience is described as being more congenial not only to extraordinary experience, but to the current state of scientific research, which has revealed that activity, selection, and response are facets of every level of reality from the quantum event to the neural cell. Ironically, the only part of our world whose synthetic responsiveness—whose "subjectivity"—is regularly called into question by the academy is the human subject. And the primary reason for this most peculiar situation is modern science and philosophy's largely unconscious metaphysical allegiance to one-half of an abandoned Cartesian dualism, which in practice is no longer accepted by any scientific discipline. Nonetheless, try to assert some idea that does not cohere with this assumed notion of reality and prepare to be informed it is "impossible," while at the same time being told that this response is not related to any preexisting metaphysical sentiments.

The area of scientific research that challenges the modern paradigm most head-on is parapsychology, which has for decades churned out careful study after study supporting the existence of extrasensory perception, especially telepathy, clairvoyance, and psychokinesis. The reasons why this research has been doubted, challenged, and sometimes vilified are several, but underlying all of them are certain philosophical and, surprisingly, theological choices made about the nature of reality during the formative period of the scientific endeavor. Descartes' mind/ matter metaphysics on the philosophical side, and the denial of action at a distance—partly in order to preserve the unique quality of Christian miracles—on the religious side, still haunt the foundations of modern science, even though "mind" (and God) have been exorcised, while action at a distance remains a shrouded constant in scientific theory (e.g., gravity and electromagnetic attraction).

Transpersonal psychology, which studies all types of extraordinary experience—mystical, psychedelic, near-death, out-of-body, and psychical—presents an even greater challenge to the modern paradigm's materialist-mechanical worldview: the notion that the universe is composed solely of bits of inert, insentient matter in motion. While the phenomena studied by transpersonal psychology offer more dramatic anomalies for the modern paradigm, especially in its most recent atheistic incarnation, the phenomena researched by parapsychology are far more amenable to experimental investigation and thus present a challenge on science's home turf. This may also help account for the vehement reactions often elicited by the mere mention of parapsychology as a credible science.

But it is important not to oversimplify the reasons for the widespread suspicion of psychical "powers," especially in academic circles. If they exist, why don't we see them regularly in action? Or if only certain people are significantly endowed with these abilities, why aren't *they* at least able to provide clear-cut demonstrations of their existence? Beyond these valid questions, there is the more complex issue of *how* telepathy or psychokinesis might operate, that is, what is a possible explanatory mechanism for how they function? The essays in this volume provide coherent—and, to us, persuasive—answers to these excellent questions by offering important new ways of looking at the nature of reality and the basic structure of the universe.

It should come as no surprise, given the context of the conference from which these papers originated, that the primary philosophical framework being drawn upon here is that of Alfred North Whitehead. Whitehead's metaphysical vision is especially important and useful because of his wide-ranging expertise in mathematics, logic, physics, history of ideas, and the philosophies of science, nature, and religion. Particularly important here is Whitehead's incorporation of both quantum theory and relativity into his mature philosophical synthesis. Thus his efforts to "fuse" religion and science within one encompassing vision of the nature of reality and the universe is one that still holds import for us today and is uniquely suited to addressing the issues raised by parapsychological research and the findings of transpersonal psychology.

While, to some, talk of metaphysics, truth, and constructive philosophy may seem out of touch and behind the times—several hundred years behind, if Kant's critique of metaphysics is taken to be the final word—just the opposite may well be the case. Whitehead might have been so far *ahead* of his time that the world at large is only now starting to catch up with his ideas. In his conference-closing lecture, David Griffin outlined trends suggesting that Whitehead's ideas are making important gains in many parts of the academic and scientific community around the world, especially in Europe and China. Since these ideas offer vital possibilities for a new way of organizing our civilization in order to confront the enormous environmental and societal challenges that face our world, we truly hope that Griffin is right in suggesting that we may be witnessing the beginnings of a "Whiteheadian Century."

The essays in this volume are concerned, in their various ways, with not only pointing out the limitations of the modern scientific and philosophic worldview, but also revealing a richer and deeper way of understanding the universe and ourselves. John B. Cobb, Jr. starts off this exploration in chapter one with the provocative question of whether subjects have any efficacy at all. Do human actions really count? While the answer may seem obvious, this universally shared experience has been more or less denied in scientific theory, if not in practice, for much of the modern era. Since Descartes, the notion of purpose as causative has slowly been replaced by efficient causation based on matter in motion. Through a historical review of how subjectivity has been exorcised from the Western academic worldview, Cobb also reveals what its disappearance has meant for our civilization. In the inexorable advance of modernity, subjects became persona non grata in science and the academy; all reality was to be studied objectively, thus reality became synonymous with objects. The fact that this study is carried out by subjects is held to be irrelevant, rather than ironic.

Using the field of economics as an example, in particular the theories of Adam Smith and Karl Marx, Cobb exposes some of the negative impacts that favoring this objective worldview has had on society. Viewing society instrumentally inevitably diminishes the intrinsic value of human beings. This process has been resisted with relatively limited success by the Romantics, the existentialists, and, most recently, through language studies. But it has been an uphill battle, given that the triumphs of the physical sciences and technological advances have been the primary drivers of Western civilization.

In order for our society's general orientation to change, Cobb argues, philosophy must change. It needs to become radically experiential— based on *all* experience, not just the world of objects as revealed through visual perception. We must start instead with the *act of seeing*, rather than the objects given through sight, that is, start with the act of experience itself. This, Cobb argues, will lead us to a radically different understanding of perception, of reality, and of subjective/object relations. After offering a nontechnical description (at least, as nontechnical as is possible) of the alternative worldview offered by William James and Alfred North Whitehead, Cobb shows how paranormal phenomena become "normal" when considered through the lens of process philosophy. Broadening science's view on what is considered valid evidence concerning the nature of reality in this way provides a starting point for reclaiming the importance of the subject and, paradoxically, the value of the world as well.

In our second chapter, David Ray Griffin expertly diagnoses the reasons for the rejection by most scientists of the possibility of parapsychological phenomena. Their underlying suspicion arises from a fundamental conflict between the modern worldview and the very existence of psychical powers. In order to locate and contextualize this decisive clash, Griffin traces the pertinent developments in philosophy and science from around the time of Descartes through their latest modern incarnation as mechanistic, materialistic atheism—which is now held to be *the* scientific worldview. While science claims to be truly empirical, a special version of empiricism has come to dominate. This *sensate* empiricism privileges the data of visual perception above all else, although other conscious sensory data may at times be recognized. Like Cobb, Griffin suggests that a *real* empiricism is needed: something like the *radical* empiricism advocated by William James, or better yet, Whitehead's panexperientialism, which draws heavily on James's insights.

Modern science's commitment to its brand of materialism, which denies any inner activity or sentience to "matter," along with its belief that mechanical causation is the only efficacious form of causation, make parapsychological phenomena inherently impossible, since psi requires some sort of action at a distance or direct communication between feeling individuals. Whitehead's metaphysics, on the other hand, opens the door to things like telepathy and psychokinesis through his revisionary theory of perception and his understanding of nature as composed of active, synthetic events. Griffin reviews the evidence for these types of parapsychological phenomena and also explains why it is so difficult to refute charges that parapsychology is a pseudoscience: basically, because circular logic is employed to discredit it. Finally, Griffin argues that "true" precognition—exact knowledge of a *settled* future—belongs in a different category than other hypothesized psychical powers, in that it is *logically* impossible. Thus parapsychology might strengthen its standing by ceasing to advocate for the existence of *literal* precognition, which Griffin sees as generating the strongest resistance in the scientific and philosophic communities.

Chapter three provides an overview of parapsychology by John Palmer, one of this field's top researchers and theorists. Palmer's subtle analysis of the debate over the reality of psi phenomena reveals that employing meta-analysis techniques to assess the validity and power of parapsychological studies is not as simple as advocates or opponents might hope. Palmer also offers some helpful suggestions on how to reframe the general controversy over psi by changing the question from "does it exist?" to "how does it work?" Focusing on the issue of mind-body relations in the latter part of his paper, Palmer considers medium-ship and near death experience as possible evidence supporting the idea that mind can exist apart from the body. His essay concludes with some observations on quantum mechanics and its possible implications for parapsychology.

In chapter four, James Carpenter directly answers Palmer's call to shift the fundamental question about psi from "Does it exist?" to "How does it work?" Picking up the gauntlet tossed out in his essay's title, "Parapsychology Needs a Theory," Carpenter offers a novel and surprisingly Whiteheadian-friendly approach to psychical experience that synthesizes his decades of research and study in the field of parapsychology. After setting the stage with a breezy summary of a bit of the history of the study of psi phenomena, Carpenter pithily encapsulates the current state of the field of parapsychology: decades of excellent experiments combined with a lack of clarity about often inconsistent results, and continued skepticism in the scientific community as a whole. To move beyond this stalemate, parapsychology requires a general psychological theory: a system of coherent ideas that can effectively guide research through an intelligible description of the processes and variables involved in psi phenomena. Carpenter argues that this kind of improved conceptual understanding is necessary to move psi experiences out of the realm of curious "anomalies" and into the world of recognized empirical phenomena. Carpenter's First Sight Theory shows how this step forward might be taken.

John Buchanan's essay, the focus of chapter five, builds upon James Carpenter's discussion of parapsychology through First Sight Theory.

Buchanan's goal is to demonstrate how a Whiteheadian framework can help ground and enhance Carpenter's ideas, as well as better connect First Sight Theory to psychology and the wider scientific community. This task is simplified by the great similarity between Carpenter's and Whitehead's understandings of the nature of experience, especially their theories of perception. In particular, Carpenter's use of Whitehead's revolutionary notion of *prehension* for the basic mechanism of psi stands as one of the clearest and most effective implementations of Whitehead's metaphysics to a particular scientific field of inquiry. Buchanan highlights some ways that this interface might prove even more beneficial for both sides, as well as for constructing a more encompassing worldview that includes transpersonal psychology and the scientific community as well.

Stanislav Grof, one of transpersonal psychology's preeminent researchers and theorists, summarizes his lifetime of explorations into nonordinary states of consciousness in chapter six.[1] Grof is concerned especially with the type of nonordinary experience he refers to as *holotropic*—"moving towards the whole." These are experiences that might be classified as spiritual or mystical, and which have the greatest potential for healing and transformation.

Grof's "cartography of the human psyche" serves as a matchless compendium of the varieties of spiritual and extraordinary experience that he has observed during many decades of supervising sessions involving nonordinary states of consciousness. Significantly, Grof's cartography is almost identical to the range of human experience reported across cultures and throughout history by shamans, mystics, psychics, and everyday individuals in extraordinary moments. Of course, the mere existence of such experiences does not directly challenge the modern worldview. The crucial question is: Do these extraordinary experiences reveal actual data and insights into the nature of reality and the universe at large, or are they merely subjective impressions and fantasies with no greater significance? Grof argues vigorously that the former in the case. If so, the realms perceived in his cartography suggest that major changes are required in our current scientific and philosophical models, changes that cohere with a more Whiteheadian or Eastern understanding of reality.

In chapter seven, Leonard Gibson takes a multidisciplinary look at the transpersonal realm, and the psychedelic experience in particular, exploring the roots and fruits of psychedelic/mystical experience from a

Whiteheadian perspective. Gibson first presents a brief historical survey of the important role played by nonordinary and psychedelic states, and then turns to his main theme: explicating how psychedelics function in the human psyche by amplifying aspects of the subjective process. His "ontology" of the psychedelic experience involves an analysis of how "disruptions" in processing may occur at the neurophysiological level, the significance of trauma and cathartic healing at the level of the psyche, and finally the metaphysics of the psychedelic experience as a whole. The latter includes Whiteheadian-based insights into the relativity of time, the presence of the past, our psychological birth and death in every moment, and the deep realization of the intrinsic importance of each instant of reality.

Rudolf Steiner began his career as a philosopher, but soon turned his primary attention to the spiritual realms, which he probed at least as deeply as any other modern Westerner. Along the way, Steiner also managed to do important work in many other fields, though only his ideas in agriculture and education (Waldorf schools) are well known today. Robert McDermott examines Steiner's wide-ranging and prodigious thought in chapter eight, especially in regard to where Steiner's theories are similar to or different from Whiteheadian philosophy. McDermott's chapter is in part a response to a paper written by David Griffin a number of years ago on this very topic, a paper that McDermott believes, like Steiner's writing, has not received the attention it deserves.

McDermott starts with the contrast that, while Whitehead was most concerned with *truth*, Steiner was devoted to *transformation*; he then proceeds to show that this difference is more nuanced than it might first appear. Moreover, Whitehead's often highly abstract metaphysical approach is in need of just the kind of support and fleshing out that Steiner's system, and transpersonal psychology in general, can offer. The intricacies of spiritual realities and methods of psycho-spiritual transformation were not a major concern for Whitehead, so if these areas are to be usefully developed within a process approach, it makes sense to turn to those individuals and disciplines that have studied them most closely. On the other hand, Whitehead's novel philosophical synthesis provides a framework for integrating spiritual practices and theories with our scientific and practical understanding of reality. McDermott's essay advances this project of exploring how these two systems of thought might mutually inform and enrich each other, and the world at large.

In chapter nine, Christopher Aanstoos presents a newly emerging answer to that most ancient of questions: who are we, really? In light of the findings of contemporary ecology, this answer must now take most seriously the deeply interconnected relationality of person and world. Allied with this ecological perspective, twentieth-century currents in philosophy and psychology that have taken interconnectedness as cornerstones for understanding the meaning of human being now become strikingly relevant to the development of this newly coalescing vision. These include phenomenology, especially as developed by Husserl and Merleau-Ponty in the twentieth century and by Abram and Adams in the twenty-first, and in the holistic philosophy of Whitehead. These very closely aligned approaches offer a keen analysis of our interrelatedness as it is lived, or experienced, most concretely. Such analyses are crucial for any deep understanding of psychological life, but are especially important in light of the current ecological crisis. This crisis is not merely the expression of the need for a new technology; it is most of all the expression of the need for a new way of understanding ourselves and our relation with the world. Aanstoos presents this new understanding of the self as specifically an "ecological self," whose intrinsic involvement with the world discloses that deep interconnectedness—thereby decisively challenging the old paradigm's image of the self as merely mechanistically related to the world through causal, extrinsic relations.

Although Larry Dossey's entertaining and provocative chapter ten essay might well have launched this volume's exploration into rethinking the modern paradigm, it serves equally well for tying things up. Dossey takes the modern worldview to task for failing to adequately account for the full range of scientific evidence, and, more generally, for failing to provide a system of values and way of life that is sustainable for humans or nature. Dossey makes the case that quantum entanglement is much more than a strange aspect of post-Newtonian physics, and is rather an opening into a new, and old, way of seeing the world as an interconnected whole. One of the important possibilities suggested by quantum theory is a much more *subjective* view of our universe. His exploration of quantum reality includes of course the anomalous phenomena of entanglement and nonlocality, but Dossey is primarily concerned with some of the intriguing implications these ideas hold for consciousness, interconnectedness, and for how these things might be manifesting around us, for example, in animal behavior and parapsychological events. Dossey concludes by examining some key turning points in the history of science that help explain how and why it became cut off from a universe of value, meaning, and subjectivity.

## CHAPTER ONE

# Denigration of the Subject in Late Modern Thought

*John B. Cobb, Jr.*

ABSTRACT: *René Descartes established the modern scientific study of nature on the basis of considering only what is objective. He denied to nature, including animals, any feelings or purposes. Darwin showed that we are part of nature, and scientists began to study us in the same way. They have gained a vast amount of accurate information. Although the social sciences have not excluded human purposes totally, they have overall emphasized the objective and marginalized the subjective. They have sought exhaustive explanation but the exclusion of the subject has rendered causality mysterious. If, instead, we consider experience comprehensively, we can discover causal feelings of our past experience as it flows into the present. We can then understand all causality by analogy to the way past experiences determine much about present experience. If we continue to examine our experience we discover that it includes the influence of the conceptual aspects of past and remote experience. Whitehead clarifies the distinction between purely physical aspects of experience that are deterministic and the influence of other aspects of the past that are not.*

IN THIS BOOK we are focusing on remarkable aspects of subjective experience and their effects in the objective world. This places us well outside of late modern thought. The hypotheses we would like to have investigated are not considered at all. Evidence in their favor is not taken seriously, however carefully it is attained. Although scientists like to claim that they are interested in evidence, their commitment to objectivism is stronger than their commitment to evidence.

For example, many moderns view the evidence for telepathy the way I would view evidence that ships had fallen off the edge of the world. In my view no "evidence" for this would count since I am convinced there is no edge of the world off of which ships could fall. For those fully socialized into late modern thought, "subjects" are not the sort of things that could have an effect on anything, much less anything that is not contiguous.

This late modern assumption is, of course, counter to common sense. For this reason, there remain many people who agree with me that the world has no edges, and who are quite sure that subjects act. They are glad to learn that there is evidence that subjects do quite marvelous things. And since they cannot learn about that in our educational system, they are attracted to a less controlled literature. This has the disadvantage that people who become focused on the things that the late modern world leaves out sometimes have difficulty distinguishing the reliable wonders that actually fill the world from idiosyncratic fantasy.

Instead of concentrating on the objection of moderns to claims about unusual things that subjects do, I will focus on their objection to the efficacy of subjects in general. For one who thinks of reality as consisting of objects, subjects are inherently mysterious sorts of things. When those of us who take the reality and efficacy of subjects for granted undertake to explain, we realize that indeed subjects are truly wonderful things. Just what and where they are is worthy of serious reflection.

The late modern worldview is so strange that we need to reflect about how it came to control the content of our education. Of course, the story is complex, but a simplified sketch can meet the needs of this essay. The first chapter in this story took place at the outset of modern science.

Although a variety of worldviews were associated with scientific inquiry in the sixteenth and seventeenth centuries, the two most important for our study are the Aristotelian one which had dominated the Middle Ages and the mechanistic one which has dominated modernity. Aristotle thought that explanations of events or objects took four forms. One was material. That is we understand something better when we understand of what it is composed. A plate may be made of wood, or clay, or metal. We can then ask of what does the wood, or the clay, or the metal consist. The alchemists sought answers to these questions, and modern chemistry developed out of this work.

A second is formal. What distinguishes the plate from other things made of wood, or clay, of metal? That is: What is its shape or form? This becomes scientifically interesting when we go to the next level and ask: What distinguishes the wood, the clay, and the metal from one another? In Aristotle's day "forms" were used chiefly to classify things. But today the forms as shapes play a minor role, and the forms proposed are mathematical formulae. A modern book of physics or chemistry is likely to consist largely of such formulae.

A third is efficient. What made an event occur or brought an object into being? This was the primary focus of the new science. Today the word "cause" functions almost exclusively to refer to efficient causes. This shift shows the prominence of this concern in modern science.

The chief difference between Aristotelian science and modern science has to do with the cause Aristotle called "final." This was prominently appealed to in the Middle Ages. In considering a human action, we can ask why a woman acted as she did, meaning what was her purpose. Scientists could study animal behavior with the same question in mind. Or they could study the human body to discover what purposes were served by different organs.

Modern scientists, of course, note that various organs do fulfill certain functions in the body. But this is not considered a scientific statement. Of course, the heart pumps blood around the body, and it is possible to learn how that is essential for bodily life. But the scientific question is that of the efficient causes of that pumping. The goal of modern science is to provide an exhaustive explanation in terms of efficient causes. These are to be found objectively in the events leading to the outcome. Evolutionary theory can explain how efficient causes led to the development of specialized organs. The end actually served or attained is not now considered a "cause" at all.

Purposes are inherently subjective. They are not necessarily conscious, but they are in continuity with the conscious. Sometimes we become aware that we are acting purposely and of what the purpose is, although we were already acting before we were conscious of the purpose. Psychiatrists may help us become conscious of our purposes. We normally attribute purposes to animals, especially to our pets and to those animals that are most like us.

Modern scientists thought that asking about final causes blocked their inquiries. Modern philosophers, and specifically René Descartes, encouraged us to view the nature studied by science as lacking final causes. To make this clear, he taught that nature consisted entirely of material things. Some things act as if they had properties other than purely material ones, but this is a deception. For example, animals seem to have feelings like ours and to behave purposefully, but Descartes taught that they are really machines that produce objective phenomena that we falsely attribute to subjective purposes. These thinkers pointed to the dancing figures on the Strasbourg clock that appeared lifelike but were entirely material.

In the early modern period, emphatically, it was not supposed that human beings were part of this nature. The human soul was viewed as an important subjective agent. It had purposes and rational abilities and the freedom to act according to its will. It was morally responsible. And it would survive death, since death applied only to the material world. The human soul engaged in the scientific study of nature, but there was no scientific study of the human soul. Reflection about that was left to theology and philosophy.

There were obvious problems with this radical dualism. Although there was no scientific study of the human soul, the human body was an important topic for science. But the boundary between the two was hard to draw. And the correlation of human purposes with bodily behavior made it difficult to maintain the dualism.

Most people thought that the explanation of the existence of this very remarkable material world required positing a rational Creator with purposes favorable to human beings. The Creator was also the lawgiver. There were natural laws, which were unbreakable, and moral laws that human beings were called on to obey. This "deism" was the default position for thoughtful people.

Although deistic dualism has not actually disappeared, this dualistic worldview collapsed in principle in the middle of the nineteenth century. Charles Darwin showed conclusively that we human beings, body and soul, have evolved from simpler forms of life. The dualistic view could not be maintained within science, and the human soul, now understood as part of nature, could no longer be understood to be beyond investigation by science. The complex world whose creation had led almost everyone to posit a divine Creator could now be explained as a gradual development from a much simpler world. Most scientists concluded that God was no longer needed to explain either the existence or the specific order of the world.

With respect to the world, thinkers had two choices. One was to call for rethinking nature. If the human soul is part of nature, they thought, then nature includes soul-ish qualities, such as subjectivity and purposiveness. Science was wrong in viewing its subject matter as purely material. At least some of the entities that make up the nature studied by science have subjective aspects including purposiveness. If this choice is taken, final causes can be explanatory after all.

However, by the mid-nineteenth century modern science had preeminent status. Darwin's work heightened that status. Science could explain even more than previously supposed. Accordingly, most scientists refused to revise the worldview into which they had been socialized in a way that would require drastic revisions of science. They moved in the alternate direction. If the human soul is part of the nature to be studied by science, then it is to be studied as all nature is to be studied—purely objectively.

Among the cultured elite and in the educational system, both of these possible directions were discussed for a while, but by the twentieth century, universal materialism was in the ascendancy and by the middle of the century, it determined the methods and contents of education. Subjects were not allowed an explanatory role. Questions of purpose and value were excluded from education.

The early modern dualism could never solve the problem of how nature and the human soul are related. Modern materialism can never solve the problem of how the subjects who study the world scientifically and develop new technologies to manage it can coexist with the denial to subjects of any explanatory role. The adherents of this successful choice are virtually asserting that we are all zombies.

Neither the early modern worldview nor the late modern worldview can meet the most elementary requirements of common sense. But we have seen how the former dominated the scene for two centuries and collapsed only as its own successes destroyed it. I suspect that the latter also is immune to common sense or philosophical criticism. Since so much has been learned by it, and it has helped in the production of such wonderful technology, the fact that it doesn't make sense is unimportant to those who control education and sophisticated culture.

The denigration of the subject has profoundly affected the human situation far beyond the natural sciences. The field of economic thought will serve as an example. The single most influential book in the shaping of economic thinking is Adam Smith's *The Wealth of Nations*. It is common knowledge that Smith wrote this as the second volume on moral philosophy. The first explains that morality is based on sympathy. The second shows that self-interest also has a place and that it can also serve the common good when individuals behave rationally.

However, Smith assumed that the sphere in which self-interest could serve was contained within the larger sphere that was formed by morality and community. He showed that market transactions based on self-interest work well in a community, partly because people know each other. If someone acts deceitfully, that is likely to be found out and damage that person's future success in the market. It never occurred to Smith that the positive potentials of self-interested activity would be taken to indicate that the morality based on sympathy is unimportant or even unreal.

However, a culture that considered the objective more real than the subjective quickly undertook to detach the operations of self-interested rationality from the context of community. Laws might be required to prevent distortions of the market, but these belong to the objective sphere. Something as subjective as sympathy is not considered.

A central element in the transformation of Smith's ethics of sympathy to support of an ethics of self-interest was grounded in Smith's statement on one occasion that "an invisible hand" turns the many self-interested acts into a benefit for the whole society. The point was that when two men exchange goods, let's say $20 and a pair of shoes, both gain. The man who parted with $20 did so because he preferred the pair of shoes. The man who parted with the shoes did so because he preferred to have $20. The market is the sum of all these transactions. The more transactions take place, the more people are benefited. "An invisible hand" turns the self-interest of each into the benefit of all.

Smith really believed this. He did not believe that the "invisible hand" thereby dealt with all questions of morality, such as the distribution of the increased good that takes place through exchange. Certainly for Smith there are many questions of human relationships in home and community that are not reducible to market transactions. Markets are good, and if one has a really free market with plenty of competition, the market is the best determiner of prices. These prices will then lead to a good allocation of resources. But Smith never supported giving primacy to the rational self-interest of the market in relation to the community relationships established by sympathy. The global markets largely controlled by large corporations that are destroying communities all around the world certainly do not have Smith's support, although his economics is often appealed to as their justification.

I believe that something similar could be said about Marx. He was deeply moved by the suffering of the workers who were systematically exploited by those who controlled capital. The workers were dehumanized. His goal was their liberation and humanization. He developed theories about how capital increased and became concentrated and what happened to workers in the process that could be, and were, separated from his deepest motivations. The relations could be objectified in terms of controlling power, and the goal could be the shift of such power from capital to labor, both conceived quite objectively. The actual experience of individual workers, so important to the young Marx, disappears from the theory and to a large extent from the practice of those who claimed to follow him. The world is confronted with a choice between a dehumanized capitalism and a dehumanized communism. It is hard to judge which has caused more suffering.

It is rarely emphasized that the standard teaching of the value-free research universities is that whatever subjectivity humans experience is irrelevant to what transpires in the world. It has no causal efficacy. It is epiphenomenal, that is, it is caused by what took place objectively, and it has no effect on that. In other words, what happens subjectively does not matter.

In my account of what happened to Adam Smith's thought, I did not go quite that far. Self-interest normally indicates the there is a subject who seeks benefits. Words like satisfaction are used. This seems to have a subjective character. Once that much is granted, economists can build their systems. This bases economics on final causes, which are not acceptable to "science."

This need for final causes in the social sciences is my reason for entitling the essay "the denigration of the subject" rather than "the elimination of the subject." However, among the purest university thinkers, this is a halfway house made use of by social scientists. They may need for the present to posit a final cause, the simpler and more elementary the better. The rarely discussed assumption is that the subjective state of "satisfaction" is the epiphenomenon accompanying the brain's particular ordering of neurons. The brain is determined by efficient causes to act in ways that produce this ordering of neurons. That this is accompanied by the subjective feeling of satisfaction plays no real role. When science advances sufficiently, scientific orthodoxy assures us that we will be able to explain economic behavior without reference to the subjective state of satisfaction.

As long as the occurrence of these subjective feelings is acknowledged, however, it is not quite true that the orthodox university teaching is that we are zombies. But it comes quite close. Since what distinguishes us from zombies is something that has no effect in the world, it seems to have no importance. In fact issues of importance, or any other value, do not arise.

Many years ago I saw the movie, *The Stepford Wives.* It presented a group of men who had a quite idyllic life, at least at home. Their wives did everything to please them, accepting in return whatever treatment they received. The viewer gradually realizes that the real human wives have been replaced by machines. I felt physically sick.

I encounter from time to time serious questions about our relation to the wonderful creatures we are now learning to create. They can already outthink us in many ways. Our remaining mental advantages are being identified and then rapidly eliminated or at least reduced. It seems that our creations may excel us in every form of mental activity. People seriously ask whether these highly intelligent beings are not, then, our superiors, so that we should cede the world to them. It is not evident that the lack of the epiphenomenon, subjectivity, is much of a counterargument.

In the seventeenth century philosophers argued that animals are machines. There are reports that animals were then tortured with the assurance that their cries meant no more than the squeaking of a door. The philosophers of that time assumed that we humans had souls that radically distinguished us from the animals.

Now we know that we are also animals. We are to be studied in the same reductionistic way as all the other animals. Everything about us that matters is material. No one is publicly asserting that we should be treated as zombies, but in fact those who envision and control the human future tend to define us as laborers and consumers or managers and capitalists. It is our objective functioning that is considered, not our subjective life. Much of this functioning can be better done by machines.

Our value in terms of objective functioning is exclusively instrumental. The very idea of intrinsic value disappears with the elimination of subjectivity. The intrinsic value of human lives seems to play no role when distributions of international wealth and power are calculated and changed by war. Politicians score points by claiming that opponents are responsible for the death of "our boys," but they rarely comment on the slaughter of those we fight against.

I have indicated that the denigration of the subject is inherently dehumanizing. There have, of course, been waves of resistance to the steady advance of this dehumanization. I indicated that when humans came to be known as part of nature, a number of major thinkers proposed the re-subjectifying of nature. Before them the Romantic Movement had made a similar proposal. More recently the existentialists focused attention on human existence as something that could not be objectified. The shift of philosophy to the study of language has kept the door ajar toward the subjective. But overall, one would have to say that these protesting proposals have been marginalized in the research university.

Protests have more traction in the professional schools. Teachers cannot ignore the question of interest and attention on the part of students. Lawyers are interested in motivation and the mental state of those who commit crimes. Some professors of management recognize that good human interaction is of central importance to the smooth functioning of organizations. Doctors know that physical health is affected by emotions. Some psychiatrists deal seriously with patients as subjects. Theologians can hardly avoid emphasis on beliefs, motivations, and feelings.

But even in these professional schools there is often a sense that progress consists in giving priority to the objective. In teaching, the emphasis is now on tests of how much information and how many skills have been acquired. Lawyers may chiefly look for precedents favorable to their client. In management, "objectives" are often emphasized as the basis of evaluation. Doctors favor chemical cures and physical operations. Even psychiatrists depend heavily on chemistry. Theologians may focus on behavior as what is most important.

I fear that as long as the basic philosophy is unchallenged, the process of objectifying everything will continue. Of course, there will always be resistance. No matter what the educational system teaches them to think, people do not really believe that their feelings are unreal or unimportant. Their actions are in fact affected by their feelings and their purposes. They know that. Even if they are socialized at some level to believe that this is not true, they cannot altogether eradicate their experience.

Philosophy should be grounded in experience. Typical of the formation of the dominant vision was beginning with one type of experience, sensory experience, especially vision. Vision seems to present us a world of objects. So philosophers turned their attention away from the act of seeing to the objects of seeing. This led to more careful examination of what is seen, and the science built out of the sense of the objective world initiated in this way has been brilliantly successful. At the same time, careful attention has shown that the objects of sight are phenomena rather than the independent objects first posited and still assumed. The late modern worldview is confused and fragile.

Scientists have in fact never given up the assumption that vision leads them to a world of objects. Immanuel Kant supported them by declaring that there is no other way to think about the world. He justified their continuing to suppose that events are causally connected even though there is no visual experience of causation. For the most part philosophers have given up on these puzzles and redefined philosophy so as to take no responsibility for them.

There is, however, a more sensible move. It was proposed by William James. Instead of beginning with the objects of vision, we should begin with the act of seeing and indeed the act of experience in its totality. If we focus on the act of experiencing, we will find that seeing is not its most fundamental character. Blind people still experience a physical and social environment. The relationship to the objects of sight is not the most fundamental relation.

Much more basic than the role of the objects of vision in experience is the role of the antecedent act of experiencing. In one moment the preceding moment is largely reenacted. This is a causal relationship, just what could not be found among the objects of vision. Each occasion plays a role as efficient cause in the successor.

If this relationship gives us a key insight into the nature of reality, then it is clear that what is given is radically subjective, but that its content consists primarily of what is given it by a previous subject that is no longer subjective. That is, only what is happening in this moment is subjective. This subject becomes the object of the next moment. Objects are past subjects.

Of course, this relationship of one occasion of my experience to the preceding occasion of my experience by no means exhausts what is happening in this moment. Presumably my current experience is also experiencing neuronal events. Now a very fundamental question arises. Are these neuronal events entirely "objective" in a different sense from my past occasion of experience? Do we experience two kinds of past events, one of past subjects and the other of past objects?

This dualistic idea must be taken seriously. We have long been accustomed to think that reality is made up of objects that have never been subjects. We know that we experience other people who are also subjectively experiencing the world, but we also experience chairs and tables that we assume never had any subjective experience at all. We suppose that they are material. When we think of the neurons composing our brain we are likely to think of how they appear in some vastly magnified photograph. They seem to belong to the world of tables and chairs, not that of other people.

This is a complex and difficult topic. The common sense of people with vision tends to distinguish things that are visible from those that are not. As we discover that the things that are visible are composed of things that are not visible to the naked eye, we are grateful for the possibility of magnification which shows that they still belong to the same world as visible things. But we cannot imagine that our own experience can be rendered visible. So "common sense" typically yields a dualism of the objects of experience.

This common sense has come to recognize that there are physical fields that do not directly participate in visibility. Fortunately, they can sometimes become indirectly visible through such things as electronic microscopes and X-rays. Gravitation is sometimes understood as a field phenomenon although it has not been made visible even indirectly. This common sense is open to the physical reality of many things that are now only indirectly experienced, but it imagines that they are somehow like the objects of vision.

Once the priority of vision is removed, there is little difficulty in positing a field of subjects. Some believe that Kirlian photography is affected by that field. I do not know. More think that auras make visible something of a person's character. But the issue of the reality of a field is clearly different from that of its relation to visibility. And the way some things reflect light does not give them a different metaphysical reality from those that exercise influence on others in different ways. Science can help us to overcome dualism. I judge that the way that neurons affect us is at the deepest level similar to the way that antecedent experience affects us. It is what happened neuronally that affects our experience, not its appearance mediated by light waves. It is better to think of our experience being affected by neuronal experiences than by what appears visually.

My point in all this is to argue that before assuming a dualism of experiential events and nonexperiential ones, we should see whether we can understand all unitary events as experiential. The biggest obstacle to attributing experience to things like neurons, I think, is that people too quickly limit experience to conscious experience. I share incredulity if the claim is made that neuronal events are conscious.

But we should have learned from depth psychologists that most human experience is not conscious. We can get some sense of what nonconscious human experience is by observing how physical feelings (of discomfort, for example) are sometimes conscious but often not. Also the boundary is vague. Even when they are not conscious they have an effect on the conscious aspect of the experience, emotionally, for example. To attribute unconscious emotion to the neurons seems to me reasonable.

To support such a hypothesis, we can examine the effect of human emotion on simple organisms. There have been thousands of experiments of cursing and blessing plants that show that these human emotions do affect them. Experiments with water seem to show that the arrangement of atoms in water molecules can be affected by human emotions. Much more decisively, neuroscientists have discovered that meditation can affect the brain quite dramatically. My hypothesis is that neuronal emotions affect human ones and are affected by them.

All of this is to argue for the hypothesis that the causal effect of the antecedent human experience on the present experience provides an example of the way that events in general affect successor events. That means not just in the human case but in all cases, what is currently happening is subjective. The past that is largely shaping the new subjects consists of former subjects now become data or objects for the present subjects.

I have spoken of human experience and of neuronal experience. I have urged that we consider the relation of one experience to its successor a paradigm case of a causal relation. Fundamentally, a neuronal experience will relate to a successor neuronal experience in a similar way. Also a neuronal experience will relate to a human experience in that way.

A very important question is: Where are such experiences to be found? Is there a rosebush experience, or a rock experience? Do molecules have experiences? Do beehives have experiences? To all these questions I would have answered negatively until recently. I thought the most primitive entities had to be subjects, but others could be societies of entities without a separate experience of their own. I thought that cells gave evidence of the sort of unity reflected in a unified experience, but that plants did not. I thought that multicell organisms had the requisite unity only when they had a central nervous system. I still see no reason to attribute subjective experience to a stone, but as I read more about plants I am forced to consider whether the responses plants generate to some stimuli do not require subjective unity. Perhaps also when bees swarm they generate a unified experience through which they become aware of a collective decision. Perhaps something like that can happen with human societies as well.

The late modern worldview is collapsing. Just as a new theory generated to support and apply the dominant dualistic worldview, namely evolution, undercut the worldview that nurtured it, so now at both ends of the spectrum, the dominant materialistic worldview is being eroded. The quantum world cannot be understood as material. And neuroscience provides evidence of the effect of meditation on the brain.

In a culture in which subjects are taken seriously and not limited to human experiences, the study of what our culture calls "parapsychological" is a natural and important part of science. This becomes possible when the philosophical understanding that fits the results of science best is articulated and accepted. I believe that Alfred North Whitehead has provided the best available formulation.

Whitehead recognized that many aspects of nature are explicable in deterministic ways and can be modeled on machines. Even though he opposed his organic model of the world to the dominant mechanistic one, he wanted to explain the mechanical aspects of nature as well. He wanted to show that human experience itself has its mechanistic characteristics.

In my account above I have featured the relationship between an occasion of human experience and the antecedent occasion of a person's life. He calls this relationship a physical feeling. Some physical feelings are of the physical feelings of antecedent occasion. A very important part of all occasions of experience is constituted by these physical feelings. He identifies these as "causal feelings" to honor the tendency of modernity to identify "cause" with "efficient cause." But in his view no occasion is simply the result of these efficient causes. As I have already indicated there are physical feelings of other things, especially the neurons involved in a human experience.

If there were nothing else, the mechanistic model would be accurate. But there are also hybrid feelings, and conceptual feelings, and reverted feelings, and propositional feelings, and physical purposes, and intellectual feelings, and strain feelings. And all of these have subjective forms in addition to objective data. And then there are decisions. The omission of all this in the late modern worldview condemns its science to a simplification that cannot fully explain anything.

This essay also will be guilty of a great simplification. This is not the place to summarize Whitehead's description of how an actual occasion of human experience actualizes itself. This book focuses on experiences that are outside the range of what the modern worldview considers natural and normal. These experiences clearly involve the agency of subjects, and thus already constitute a challenge to the late modern worldview. But in addition, they typically involve "action at a distance," a phenomenon that does not fit with the mechanical model. Thus far in my discussion I have not dealt with this.

The feeling that is most important in explaining this dimension of experience is called "hybrid feeling." This is one form of physical feeling. But up until this point I explained only "pure physical feeling." That is, I talked about physical feelings of physical feelings. These are responsible for the predictability of so much of the world, the predictability that is so important to science.

But every occasion also has "conceptual feelings." In a human being this may involve a new idea that occurs to one. In simpler entities, what is conceptually felt may simply be the forms of what is physically felt. The feeling of the already actualized form as also a potential available for renewed actualization is the sort of conceptual feeling that is universal.

When one occasion feels an antecedent occasion, this may be only its physical feeling, and then we have a pure physical feeling of the sort so important to modern scientific orthodoxy. But an occasion may also feel the conceptual feelings of antecedent occasions. The physical feeling of an antecedent conceptual feeling is a hybrid physical feeling. If the new idea that came to me a moment ago persists into the present, the current feeling of that idea is a hybrid feeling.

In discussing pure physical feelings, Whitehead accepts the consensus of physicists that these require spatiotemporal contiguity. There is no "action at a distance" in the sense of one occasion affecting the pure physical feelings of a distant occasion. There is no "action at a distance" when only the physical dimension is considered. But this limitation need not apply to the feeling of past conceptual feelings. The past occasions whose conceptual feelings are felt need not be spatially adjacent. Hybrid feelings are not limited in the same way as pure physical feelings. This opens the door to accepting the apparent reality of many experiences. For example, it has often been remarked that dogs seem to be aware that their masters are coming home before any sensory cue is possible.

Rupert Sheldrake wrote a book about this. He has also written extensively about morphic resonance. Sheldrake cites evidence that members of a particular species can learn from the experience of other members of the species even when they are separated by great distances. This has earned him excommunication from the scientific guild, but there has been no empirical refutation of his theories. If scientists would make the distinction between pure physical feelings and hybrid physical feelings, they could examine the evidence with open minds without abandoning the standard doctrine within its sphere of application, that is, to pure physical feelings.

This distinction of hybrid physical feelings also opens the door to theories of memory that differ from the hypotheses that are currently acceptable to most scientists. A memory of a past experience seems to be the effect of that past experience in the present one. Consider, for example, that a current scent leads to a vivid memory of a childhood event. That past event may be felt with remarkable specificity and detail. The modern theory requires that we assume that the neurons in the brain have preserved that past experience in detail and require only the right stimulus to reenact it. Whitehead allows us to skip all that. No doubt there are neuronal correlates to all experience, but in his view what is felt may be conceptual feelings of the past experience as such.

The relation to another's experience now is similar. As long as we are dealing with purely physical relationships, my relation is mediated by events that are physically immediate. Light rays affected by events in the area occupied by the other person reach my eye and affect events in the occipital lobe of my brain. Sounds also require mediation. Then the neurons in my brain integrate and interpret what is heard and seen.

Whitehead affirms that this occurs. At the purely physical level this is the only way in which acts at a distance affect me. But in his view feelings of the conceptual feelings of the other person, even if they are transpiring at a distance, may be felt immediately. I may have hybrid feelings of the other person as well as pure physical ones. Telepathic communication occurs in this way. There is increasing evidence that this kind of relatedness is found at many levels. What is called "quantum entanglement" appears to involve immediate connections at a distance. Physicists prefer to call this "entanglement" because this word obscures the "action at a distance" that is involved. But it in fact does not evade the reality.

Once we take the agency of subjects seriously, understand that objects are past subjects rather than lumps of matter, and recognize the possibility of "action at a distance, the "paranormal" becomes part of the "normal." Science can stop resisting the evidence. And human beings can take their own humanness seriously.

Among the major thinkers of the late nineteenth and early twentieth centuries who made the choice to include the subjective in their understanding of nature, several took great interest in parapsychological phenomena. Henri Bergson and William James are the most important examples. Those interested in this topic will do well to study them. Whitehead spent very little time on this topic. What he contributed was a clear account of how these phenomena are possible and how they relate to the world to which modern science continues to limit itself. A Whiteheadian holds with Whitehead that the working out of beliefs about these phenomena is to be done with the same care as any scientific work. What happens and what does not happen is a factual matter. It is a tragedy that so little attention is given to these extremely important questions. We have all the more reason to be grateful to that small group of people who persist in expanding our knowledge of the world of subjects. We are all the more grateful because we know they pay a high price for their openness and honesty.

CHAPTER TWO

# Parapsychology and Whiteheadian Panexperientialism

*David Ray Griffin*

ABSTRACT: *While the evidence from parapsychological research supporting the existence of telepathy and psychokinesis is very strong, the field is nonetheless regarded with suspicion and disregarded by most scientists and philosophers. Many of the underlying reasons for doubting the very possibility of such phenomena can be found in certain metaphysical and methodological choices made in modern science's formative period. These choices arose primarily out of political and religious motivations, and the ramifications of these decisions have badly skewed and limited science's understanding of the basic workings of nature and reality for most of the modern era. This chapter argues that a Whiteheadian panexperientialism provides a postmodern perspective that is congruent with the findings of contemporary science, yet allows for an open-minded approach to parapsychological phenomena, while also better addressing many of the other issues that remain insoluble through the categories of modern philosophy. However, precognition, in the sense of knowing the future in advance—except with respects to certain abstract features of the future that are already determined—is ruled out as impossible on logical as well as metaphysical grounds.*

ONE OF THE VIRTUES of the philosophy of Alfred North Whitehead is that it allows scientists and philosophers to look open-mindedly at apparent instances of parapsychological influence. The term "parapsychology" is now widely used in place of "psychical research," which became a distinct branch of science in the late nineteenth century.

The Society for Psychical Research was founded in 1882. According to its charter, it was founded

> to investigate that large body of debatable phenomena desig-
> nated by such terms as mesmeric, psychical and spiritual-
> istic . . . in the same spirit of exact and unimpassioned enquiry
> which has enabled Science to solve so many problems.[1]

The term "parapsychology" was originally applied only to those phenomena of psychical research that could be studied experimentally in the laboratory. But the two terms are now widely used interchangeably.[2]

Parapsychological phenomena are usually divided into three types: *extrasensory perception*, meaning the reception of information by a mind without the use of any of the physical senses; *psychokinesis,* meaning influence exerted by a mind without employing its body; and evidence for *life after death*, meaning the existence of the continuation of a mind after the death of its physical body. The present chapter focuses only on extrasensory perception.

## EXTRASENSORY PERCEPTION AND THE
## MODERN WORLDVIEW

The reality of extrasensory perception is controversial, but not primarily because of the absence of good evidence for it. Rather, it is controversial because it is in strong tension with the modern worldview, of which there have been two versions.

### *The first version of the modern worldview*

The first version was created in the seventeenth-century by thinkers such as Marin Mersenne, René Descartes, Robert Boyle, and Isaac Newton. This worldview had a mechanistic doctrine of nature, a dualistic view of the human being (with a material body and a nonphysical soul), and a supernaturalistic view of the universe.

A supernatural deity, besides being required to explain how the physical body and the nonphysical soul could interact, was also needed to explain how the biblical miracles could have occurred. This feature of the worldview was culturally very important, because the miracles were taken to prove Christianity as the One True Religion, and this feature is still central to conservative Christian churches today.

These miracles include the reported "mental miracles" of Jesus, such as when he knew the thoughts of scribes (Matthew 9:4), when he "saw" Nathanael when the latter was under a fig tree before Philip had called him (John 1: 46–49), and when he knew that Judas was going to betray him (John 13:27). This mind-reading power of Jesus has been taken as evidence of his deity, or at least that a supernatural deity was working through him. But why should such conclusions follow from Jesus's mind-reading ability?

The reason is the modern worldview, with its mechanistic orientation. According to historian Richard Westfall, "the fundamental tenet of Descartes' mechanical philosophy of nature [was] that one body can act on another only by direct contact."[3] Taking this idea seriously meant that there could be no causal influence between noncontinuous things, whether this be called "action at a distance" or "attraction at a distance." The mechanical philosophy, said Westfall, banished "attractions of any kind." He wrote:

> From one end of the century to another, the idea of attractions, the action of one body upon another with which it is not in contact, was anathema to the dominant school of natural philosophy.[4]

From this perspective, even Newton was regarded with suspicion, given the fact that his major discovery was the law of gravitation. Christiaan Huygens, who was the major Cartesian scientist after the death of Descartes himself, said in a letter about Newton: "I don't care that he's not a Cartesian as long as he doesn't serve us up conjectures such as attractions."[5] To protect himself from the charge of scientific heresy, Newton said that by using the terms "gravity" and "attraction," he was not giving a causal explanation, but merely describing the phenomenon.

Strictly speaking, to be sure, the rejection of influence at a distance between physical things should not rule out extrasensory perception of one mind by another. But the strong rejection of action at a distance in physics tended to lead to the rejection of this idea in relation to mind-mind relations as well. This rejection, moreover, was reinforced by the acceptance of the *sensationist* doctrine of perception, according to which we can perceive things beyond our own minds only by means of our physical senses.

Our sensory perceptions involve long causal chains connecting the perception with the perceived. For example, we see the sun by means of trillions of photons connecting the sun to our eyes. Accordingly, if all perception is by means of our senses, then there can be no influence at a distance. That is, it cannot happen *naturally*. One could perceive other minds without a long chain of physical relations only with supernatural assistance.

By contrast, parapsychology portrays extrasensory perception as a wholly natural, if in some respects extraordinary, phenomenon. From this perspective, therefore, Jesus's ability to know the thoughts of other people provides no evidence for his divinity, or even for the idea that a supernatural deity was working through him.

The first version of the modern worldview is still the view of conservative Christian churches, who continue to use the so-called mental miracles of Jesus to prove the unique truth and saving power of Christian faith. Accordingly, parapsychology, with its position that extrasensory perception is a fully natural capacity, is threatening to this type of Christianity.

But even without this religious motive, scientists and philosophers who have internalized the modern worldview have regarded extrasensory perception as impossible, absurd, anti-scientific, superstitious.

## *The second version of the modern worldview*

The scientific community did not long remain with the first version of the modern worldview. Finding the need to refer to a supernatural agent to explain natural phenomena distasteful, and coming to consider ridiculous the idea that such an agent could interrupt natural laws, the scientific community created a new version of the modern worldview.

In this new version, the mechanistic view of nature was retained. But mind-body dualism was replaced by epiphenomenalism (according to which the mind cannot affect the brain). This was in turn replaced by materialism, according to which the mind and the brain are in some sense identical. And supernaturalism was replaced by deism, according to which God did not influence the world after creating it, which was eventually replaced by atheism. This mechanistic, materialistic, atheistic worldview has been accepted as the scientific view since the late nine-teenth century.

This new scientific worldview required the epistemology known as "sensate empiricism." Empiricism as such is the sensible doctrine that no entities should be affirmed except those that can be experienced—an epistemology that should obviously be the basis for making scientific statements. But the adjective "sensate" adds the insistence discussed above as "sensationism"—the doctrine that we can have no experience of anything beyond our own minds except by means of our physical senses. Although John Locke and David Hume are often simply called "empiricists," what they initiated was *sensate* empiricism.

This doctrine rules out the position of the parapsychological community, according to which the form of nonsensory perception called "extrasensory" is fully natural. Therefore, the ability to "read minds" must be considered either supernatural, as conservative theists generally hold, or simply impossible, as the scientific community generally holds. In either case, parapsychology is dismissed as a pseudo-science. For example:

- In a book entitled *Parapsychology: Science or Magic?*, psychologist James Alcock said: "Parapsychology is indistinguishable from pseudo-science."[6]

- Physicist John Wheeler, upset that the Parapsychological Association was a member of the American Association for the Advancement of Science, distributed a paper at the 1979 meeting, "Drive the Pseudos Out of the Workshop of Science," which was then published in the *New York Review of Books.*[7]

- Philosopher Antony Flew, also calling parapsychology a pseudo-science, argued that the Parapsychological Association should be "politely disaffiliated."[8]

## RADICAL EMPIRICISM AND PANEXPERIENTIALISM

One scientist who did not agree was William James, who was a well-known psychologist at Harvard before turning to philosophy. James rejected sensate empiricism in favor of "a thicker and more radical empiricism," which included, in his words, "the phenomena of psychic research so-called."[9]

We need a scientific worldview, James argued, that would allow these phenomena to be regarded as fully natural, albeit exceptional, occurrences. He said, for example: "Science, so far as science denies such exceptional occurrences, lies prostrate in the dust for me; and the most urgent intellectual need which I feel at present is that science be built up again in a form in which such things may have a positive place."[10]

Although James himself went part of the way to articulating such a position, the philosopher who most fully developed such a position was Alfred North Whitehead, who was positively influenced by James more than by any other philosopher. Besides expanding James's radical empiricism, with its acceptance of nonsensory perception, Whitehead also developed an ontology that explains the possibility of not only extrasensory perception, but also psychokinesis and evidence for life after death. In the present chapter, however, only extrasensory perception is discussed.

Whitehead's ontology is best described as panexperientialism, which is closely related to his version of radical empiricism.

## Whitehead's panexperientialism

The first relevant point about panexperientialism is the very fact that it describes the basic units of the world as *experiences*. Part and parcel of the seventeenth-century claim that influence at a distance is inconceivable was the view that the ultimate units of nature were bits of matter, with no inside in which hidden powers, such as the power to exert or receive influence at a distance, could be residing. As Mary Hesse's study of the concept of action at a distance shows, this idea lost repute in physics after the introduction of the idea of matter as devoid of any inside. Given such an account of the ultimate units of nature, it seemed self-evident that causation could only be exerted by contact.[11]

According to panexperientialism, by contrast, every basic unit is an "occasion of experience." Within this ontology, it is not self-evident that causal influence can occur only between contiguous things. It seems at least thinkable that one experience could receive influence from another distant experience, and that this experience could in turn exert causal influence upon the other.

Each occasion of experience is a subject for itself before it becomes an object for others. Every actual entity, in other words, has an "inside"

before it has an "outside"—before it is an object for others, thereby exerting causal influence on them. Every occasion of experience thereby has powers to exert influence that are hidden from any human observer.

As to how an occasion of experience receives influences from others, it begins its subjective process by *prehending* previous occasions of influence. Whitehead uses the term "prehension" to indicate this act of grasping: a grasping that may be conscious or—what is the usual case—unconscious. Whitehead also referred to prehensions of other things as *feelings* of them.

How do we get from the idea of exerting and receiving influence to the idea of action at a distance? The salient point is that the previous occasions of experience that are prehended need not be contiguous, whether spatially or temporally, with the prehending occasion. The prehending occasion, insofar as it is constituted out of its prehensions of past occasions, is likely to be constituted primarily out of its prehensions of contiguous ones. But it will also be partially constituted out of its prehensions of occasions that were not contiguous.

With regard to *exerting* influence at a distance, the hidden power involves the distinction between the two "poles" of an occasion: the physical pole and the mental pole. In the dualistic worldview, to call something "physical" indicates that it is devoid of experience, whereas to call it "mental" indicates that it does have experience. But in panexperientialism, that cannot be the meaning.

Rather, the physical pole of an actual occasion is the occasion insofar as it is constituted out of its prehensions of prior occasions. Its physical pole is the occasion as subject to *efficient* causation. The mental pole, by contrast, is the occasion's self-determination in light of its prehension of possibilities, out of which the occasion can exert self-determination, otherwise called *final* causation.

This distinction between the physical and mental poles provides the basis for a distinction between two ways in which an occasion can be prehended by subsequent occasions: If it is prehended in terms of its *physical* pole, we have a *pure* physical prehension. If it is prehended in terms of its *mental* pole, the transaction is called a *hybrid* physical prehension. (A hybrid prehension is still *physical,* because its object is still another actual entity, not a mere ideal or possibility.)

It is in these hybrid physical prehensions that Whitehead sees influence at a distance as most likely. He said, "provided that physical science maintains its denial of 'action at a distance,' the safer guess is that [pure physical prehension] is practically negligible except for contiguous occasions." He saw no reason to suppose, however, that *hybrid* physical prehensions should be limited to contiguous occasions. In fact, he said, the denial of this limitation would be the more natural supposition. Instances of telepathy, added Whitehead, provide some empirical evidence in support of this suggestion.[12]

Given the fact that causation is simply the reverse side of physical prehension,[13] the point of the prior paragraph can be translated from the language of "prehension" into that of "causation." Insofar as the occasion exerts influence in terms of data from its physical pole, we can speak of *pure physical causation.* Insofar as it exerts causation in terms of data from its mental pole, we can speak of *hybrid physical causation.* An occasion of experience's capacity to exert hybrid physical causation on subsequent events is its "hidden" power to exert causal influence at a distance.

## Whitehead's radical empiricism

Like James, Whitehead affirmed the reality of nonsensory perception, and he did so by discussing much more fully James's definition of radical empiricism. "The relations between things," said James, "are just as much matters of direct particular experience, neither more so nor less so, than the things themselves." Put otherwise, "The parts of experience hold together from next to next by relations that are themselves parts of experience."[14]

In speaking of relations, James included, perhaps primarily, *causal* relations. Whitehead referred to the experience of causal relations as the most fundamental type of perception. He called it, in fact, "perception in the mode of causal efficacy." Far from being derivate from sensory perception, sensory perception is derivative from it.

In their radical empiricism, James and Whitehead were taking issue with Hume's empiricism, according to which we perceive only sensory data, so we have no empirical basis for talking about causation, in the sense of the influence of one thing on another. By contrast, Whitehead said that the type of perception on which Hume focused should be called "perception in the mode of presentational immediacy," because it gives us only data that are immediately present to us through our conscious experience, such as bright lights, but no information about where those data came from. In Hume's own words, "the mind [cannot] go beyond what is immediately present to the senses, either to discover the real existence or the [causal] relations of objects."[15]

Perception in the mode of presentational immediacy, which provides the kind of "clear and distinct" impressions that Hume considered fundamental, gives us sensory data. When this mode of perception is taken as fundamental, nonsensory data will seem impossible.

In Whitehead's philosophy, however, rather than being fundamental, sensory perception is derivate from perception in the mode of causal efficacy, which is pre-sensory. Accordingly, the kinds of nonsensory perceptions focused on by parapsychologists are more fundamental than sensory perceptions, since they both precede sensory perception during the formation of experience and provide the data upon which conscious sensory experience is based.

## PARAPSYCHOLOGICAL EVIDE-NCE FOR EXTRASENSORY PERCEPTION

Besides being philosophically possible, nonsensory perception of the type normally called "extrasensory" is also *actual*. Parapsychology has provided abundant evidence for this claim, with the evidence dealing primarily with telepathy and clairvoyance.

### Telepathy

The term "telepathy," which literally means "feeling at a distance," usually refers to the experience by one mind of the contents of another person's mind.

### Spontaneous Cases

One type of parapsychological research consists of investigations of putative spontaneous cases of telepathy. In 1970, psychiatrist Ian Stevenson published a book entitled *Telepathic Impressions,* which contains 195 cases. Cases were included only if they fulfilled three criteria:

- The percipient had an accurate feeling about a distant person while having had no normal way of knowing about that person's situation.

- The percipient then told someone else about it or took appropriate action.

- This response was independently corroborated.

A case in 1949 involved a young woman named Joicey Acker Hurth. Three months after she was married, she and her husband were staying with his parents in Cedarburg, Wisconsin, which is about a thousand miles from her home in Anderson, South Carolina. Although she had been completely happy, one night she woke up sometime after midnight feeling very sad and crying. When her husband awakened and asked why she was crying, she said she felt that something was wrong. Not having slept the rest of the night, her appearance the next morning led her parents-in-law to ask if there had been a "lover's quarrel."

Then, while fixing breakfast, Joicey suddenly exclaimed, "It's my father! Something is terribly wrong with my father!" Because her father had been very healthy and a letter from him only a few days earlier had mentioned no problems, she had—the others reminded her—no reason for her concern. A few minutes later, however, a telephone call from her aunt informed her that her father was in a coma, due to a drug he had taken for a backache, but without proper instructions. Joicey got to the hospital just before he died.

This was not a once-in-a-lifetime experience for Joicey Hurth, incidentally: She reports having had six such experiences, four of which were sufficiently verified to be included in Stevenson's book.[16]

Laboratory Experiments

Not resting content with the thousands of verified reports of this nature, however, parapsychologists have engaged in experiments in which the possibility of acquiring the information through sensory means can be more completely ruled out.

Working on the assumption that people are probably more receptive to extrasensory influences while they are asleep, when there is less competition from sensory percepts, the "dream laboratory" at the Maimonides Medical Center in New York ran a series of experiments. After the subject had gone to sleep and begun to dream (as indicated by brain waves and rapid eye movements), a person in another room would seek to "send" images from a randomly selected picture. The subject would then be awakened and asked to describe his or her dream. Outside judges, not knowing which of several pictures was the actual target, would then, by studying the transcription of the description, decide whether it was a "hit."

In one case, the target picture was *Zapatistas,* a painting by Carlos Orozco Romero depicting Zapata's Mexican-Indian followers, who traced their ancestry to the Mayans and Aztecs. The painting shows armed horsemen and marching men, with mountains and dark clouds in the background. The subject, a psychiatrist named William Erwin, said this in describing his dream:

> A storm. Rainstorm. It reminds me of traveling—a trip— traveling one time in Oklahoma, approaching a rainstorm, thundercloud...I got a feeling of memory, now, of New Mexico, when I lived there. There are a lot of mountains around New Mexico, Indians, Pueblos.

The next morning, when asked if anything more came to mind, he said:

> Here it gets into this epic type of thing...a DeMille super-type colossal production. I would carry along with it such ideas as the Pueblo going down to the Mayan-Aztec type of civilization.

The judges had no problem in agreeing that this was a clear "hit."[17]

*Clairvoyance*

The other main type of extrasensory perception is clairvoyance, where the person derives the information not from another mind but directly from a physical state of affairs. Although the literature of psychical research contains numerous reports of spontaneous clairvoyance, many of them investigated and verified, I here turn directly to the experimental evidence.

In the early days of the Duke parapsychology laboratory, there were many card-naming tests for clairvoyance in which the subject, shielded from all sensory clues, tried to name the card that was on the top of the deck. Recently, however, card-naming tests were superseded by many new kinds of experiments.

Remote Viewing

One type involves "remote viewing," which can be considered clairvoyance or a combination of it and telepathy. One test involved Marilyn Schlitz, an anthropologist, and Elmar Gruber, a German parapsychologist. Gruber, while in Rome, was to go to randomly selected places, while Schlitz, back in Michigan, was to try, at the prearranged time, to "see" where Gruber was. On one of the ten trials, he was sent to a hill close to the airport, from which he could see the terminal and the planes taking off. The hill had many holes, dug by people looking for coins. Schlitz wrote:

> Flight path? Red lights…A hole in the ground, a candle-shaped thing…Something shooting upward…The impressions that I had were of outdoors and Elmar was at some type of—I don't know if institution is the right word—but…a public facility. He was standing away from the main structure, although he could see it…I want to say an airport but that just seems too specific. There was activity and people but no one real close to Elmar.[18]

According to the five judges who evaluated the 10 trials, Schlitz made a direct hit on 6 of them, including this one.[19]

## Ganzfeld Experiments

Another type of experiment, called the *ganzfeld*, can also be considered a combination of telepathy and clairvoyance. The subject's sensory input is minimized by various means, such as placing halved ping-pong balls over the eyes and playing white noise through headphones while the subject is sitting in a reclining chair. After the subject is thoroughly relaxed, the "sender" in another room seeks to impress images from a picture—which was randomly selected by a computer program—on the subject's mind. The subject then describes the images he or she is having, after which judges are asked to say to which of four pictures— one of which was the target picture—the description best corresponds.

In one case, the other three pictures were of a flower, a Chinese nobleman, and a parking lot with rows of snowbound automobiles, while the target picture had a pickup truck traveling down a curving country road. The subject said:

> There was a road…a hard-packed pebble road…And, there was a very fleeting image of being inside of a car and I could see just the rearview mirror…A feeling of going very rapidly…Also,

at one point, the feeling of being out in the country and wide open spaces...I had the feeling of driving out in the country.[20]

After the session, upon seeing the target picture the subject said, "That's it—that's what I've been seeing."[21] Not all sessions produced such clear hits. But after a long series of experiments, it was determined that 45 percent of them showed significant results, compared with the 25 percent that would be expected from chance alone.[22]

The *ganzfeld* experiments, which have been examined extremely closely by critics, led to the inclusion of a section on "Psi Phenomena" in the 10th edition of the standard *Introduction to Psychology* (long known as "Hilgard and Atkinson").[23] Taking a purely empirical approach, the authors criticize those who reject parapsychological phenomena on the grounds of impossibility, saying that "such a priori judgments are out of place in science; the real question is whether the empirical evidence is acceptable by scientific standards."[24]

## THE PSEUDOSCIENCE CHARGE

However, it seems to be widely felt that "scientific standards" are not applicable in relation to evidence for extrasensory perception, on the grounds that parapsychology is not a true science, but merely a pseudo-science. What possible response could be made to this charge?

One possible response involves the attempt to formulate criteria for establishing a "line of demarcation" between science and pseudo-science—a line that would show all generally recognized sciences to be in the former category and all the disliked fields to be in the latter. Scholars in sociology and the philosophy of science have concluded that this attempt has proved to be a failure.[25]

One reason for this failure is that the argument is often circular. For example, psychologist Ray Hyman, who had his own reasons for rejecting parapsychological beliefs, criticized the criteria used by James Alcock, writing, "the categories of both science and pseudoscience are fuzzy...It looks very much like the criteria themselves were chosen in order to exclude parapsychology."[26]

Nevertheless, the conviction that parapsychology cannot possibly be considered one of the sciences remains, mainly because of the conviction that parapsychology's alleged phenomena conflict with science.

- Alcock said that genuine parapsychological occurrences would imply a "relationship between consciousness and the physical world radically different from that held to be possible by contemporary science."[27]

- In an essay asking "Is Parapsychology a Science?" philosopher Paul Kurtz said that its findings "contradict the general conceptual framework of scientific knowledge."[28]

- In an essay entitled "Science and the Supernatural," George Price relegated the phenomena of parapsychology to the category of the "supernatural"—by which he meant the nonexistent—on the grounds that "parapsychology and modern science are incompatible."[29]

*Science as mechanistic*

According to this argument, parapsychology cannot possibly be a science, because it conflicts with some of the fundamental principles of science. In what way does it allegedly conflict with science? The main ground for this claim is that science is necessarily mechanistic.

- Making his well-known claim—"The essence of science is mechanism. The essence of magic is animism"—Price argued that a scientific claim about some phenomenon requires the possibility of "a detailed mechanistic explanation."

- Antony Flew (quoted earlier) stated that the decisive objection to parapsychology's alleged phenomena is the lack of a "conceivable mechanism."

- Psychologist Donald Hebb, saying that parapsychologists have "offered enough evidence to have convinced us on almost any other issue," admitted that his reason for rejecting it "is—in a literal sense—prejudice," adding that he could have found the evidence convincing if he had "some guess as to the mechanics of the disputed process.[30]

*Basic limiting principles*

This frame of mind has also been illustrated in a response of philosopher Jane Duran to C. D. Broad, a highly respected British philosopher. Broad had developed a list of "basic limiting principles," meaning ones that have been widely accepted as limiting what is credible. One of these principles, Broad pointed out, is this one: "Any event that is said to cause another event (the second event being referred to as an 'effect') must be related to the effect through some causal chain."[31]

Having studied psychical research, Broad argued that the evidence for telepathy was strong enough to reject this principle. Duran, however, said:

> The absence of a specifiable and recognizably causal chain seems to constitute a difficult, if not insurmountable, objection to our giving a coherent account of what it means to make such a claim [and hence] for concluding that telepathy [is] not possible.[32]

Duran's argument simply begs the question. It could be summarized thus:

- *Limiting Principle:* All causation between noncontiguous events is transmitted by a chain of contiguous events.

- *Broad's Response:* Parapsychology shows that sometimes an event is affected by a noncontiguous event directly, without being mediated by a chain of contiguous events.

- *Duran's Counter-response:* We know that Broad's claim is false, because all causation between noncontiguous events is transmitted by a chain of contiguous events.

As illustrated by the statements of Price, Flew, Hebb, and Duran, the main reason to consider parapsychological data impossible is the belief that science is necessarily and completely mechanistic, so that there could be no influence at a distance. But Whitehead, who understood the nature of modern science as well as anyone, explained why, although causation is largely mediated through chains of continuous causation, there could also be influence at a distance.

APPARENT PRECOGNITION

However, there is one type of putative extrasensory perception about which an *a priori* denial is appropriate. Such denial is appropriate in relation to claims about self-contradictory entities. For example, no amount of physical evidence could show the existence of a round square, because a "round square" is self-contradictory.

Precognition means noninferential knowledge of an event before it occurs. This alleged knowledge is usually taken to be based on perception, which would require the prehension of an event prior to its existence. Such a prehension would imply "backward causation"—the influence of the future event back upon the present. But many parapsychologists have accepted this view, according to which the precognized event caused the precognition of it, so that the "effect" existed before its "cause."[33]

However, "the past" by definition is settled, so nothing in the present could affect it. By the same token, the present cannot be affected by something in the future, because by the time a future event has occurred, that which is now present would be in the past.

Whitehead has explained more fully why there can be no prehension of future events. A future occasion of experience cannot be prehended because "no future individual occasion is in existence."[34] Moreover, they cannot be "known" before they exist, because their existence will involve an element of self-determination in the moment, which is in principle not knowable in advance. In the words of Charles Hartshorne, the leading process philosopher behind Whitehead himself, "future events, events that have not yet happened, are not there to be known."[35]

To put the point in terms of causation, there can be no backward causation (called "retrocausation") from the future on the present, because in the present the future occasions do not yet exist: They cannot exert causation until they have passed from the subjective to the objective mode of existence, and future events have not even begun the subjective mode of existence.

In still other terms: These events will exert causation on the basis of what they will *be;* what they will be will be determined by what they *become;* and this process of becoming involves partial *self-determination in the moment.* The idea that they could exert causal influence before they have decided just what they are to be is nonsense. True precognition, accordingly, is impossible.

*Impossibility*

Some advocates of parapsychology, however, do not think we should be deterred by the apparent impossibility of precognition. Such was the position, for example, of J. B. Rhine, the founder of experimental parapsychology. On the one hand, recognizing that perception and causation are two sides of the same process, Rhine agreed that the idea of precognition, which implies retrocausation, is problematic: "It is hard to understand how the act of perception, which is the result, could occur before the cause." Rhine even admitted that, "If there were ever an occasion in science on which it would be proper to use the word impossible," this would be the idea of precognition.

However, quoting the statement that "science knows no impossibles," he said that "theory must conform to experience." Therefore, contending that tests had empirically demonstrated ESP of future events, Rhine said that he had to change his worldview to allow literal perception of future events.[36] Many advocates of parapsychology have followed Rhine on this matter, saying that any *a priori* rejection of precognition is just as wrongheaded as *a priori* rejections of extrasensory perception and psychokinesis.

## Self-contradiction

But Rhine was mistaken to say that scientists should not exclude anything *a priori*. He was certainly correct that no empirical data should be ignored. But it is also correct to rule out any proposed interpretation of the data that is self-contradictory. And whereas there is nothing self-contradictory about extrasensory perception and psychokinesis, the same is not true of precognition.

Antony Flew made this point clearly. While rejecting extrasensory perception and psychokinesis as well as precognition, he pointed out that precognition is different in kind from the others. Whereas extrasensory perception and psychokinesis are only *contingently impossible*, he said, precognition is *logically* impossible.[37]

Scientists have in the past declared various things to be impossible that later turned out to be actual. The earlier view of these things as contingently impossible was based on generalizations from experience. Hence the view of them as contingently impossible could be reversed. But precognition is a *logical* impossibility:

> Because causes necessarily ... bring about their effects, it must
> be irredeemably self-contradictory to suggest that the (later)
> fulfillments might be caused by the (earlier) anticipations. By

the time the fulfillments are occurring the anticipations already
have occurred.[38]

As Flew illustrates, one need not accept Whitehead's philosophy to
conclude that precognition is impossible.

### Not mirror of ordinary causation

There are, in addition, other reasons to reject precognition and hence
retrocausation, while accepting extrasensory perception. One reason has
been given by philosopher Stephen Braude: The term "retrocausation"
suggests a type of causation that mirrors ordinary causation, except for
going in the opposite direction. But in ordinary causation, every effect
becomes in turn a cause, with effects spreading out into the indefinite
future. But the presumed effects of alleged retrocausation are not
presented as having effects expanding into the indefinite past.[39] Few if
any people would suggest that a dream about Jesus experienced in 2015
had an effect upon events in first-century Palestine.[40]

### Contrary to freedom

Still another problem with literal precognition is that it conflicts with
our assumption that we have a degree of freedom, so that our actions
are not totally determined. This assumption presupposes that, while
the past is settled, the future is partly open. Taken literally, *precognition*
means that one *knows* in advance exactly what will happen in the future.
To call a belief about the future *knowledge* entails that the belief cannot
be wrong, and this belief would entail that the future is already settled.

### Alternative interpretations

Accordingly, there are various good reasons to maintain that precognition
is impossible. Saying this, however, does not mean that the kinds of
experiences typically called "precognitive" are to be rejected *a priori*.
It only means that they must be interpreted other than as literal
precognition. Fortunately, there are many alternative explanations, some
of which may obtain in some cases, whereas other interpretations may
obtain in other cases.

For example, a person has a dream that a friend is going to die
suddenly. The person then finds out that the friend committed suicide

the following day. The person concludes that the dream was a case of precognition. However, a more likely interpretation is that the dream was based on learning unconsciously about the friend's intention to commit suicide. Accordingly, the experience could be accepted without any notion of the future event causing the dream. I suggest elsewhere, moreover, that there are several more possible alternative interpretations of apparent precognition.[41]

With regard to Rhine's claim that precognition must be accepted because it has been demonstrated experimentally, Robert Morris, in a survey entitled "Assessing Experimental Support for True Precognition," said that "alternative, on-line interpretations do exist for all studies that offer evidence for retroactive influence."[42]

RECONCILING PARAPSYCHOLOGY
WITH THE REST OF SCIENCE

The claim of true precognition, and hence retrocausation, is the main contention that makes parapsychology seem completely contrary to science. Psychoanalyst Jule Eisenbud, who has been called parapsychology's "premier theoretician,"[43] said, "the radical assumptions about time that have been suggested to account for "precognitive" phenomena are irreconcilable on all fronts with all other correspondences known to science."[44]

Eisenbud supported some of the alternative explanations of apparent precognition mentioned above.

If the parapsychological community, recognizing that true precognition is logically impossible, would remove it from the list of parapsychological phenomena, this removal would overcome the main reason for considering parapsychology unscientific because irrational. If this were to happen, it would likely become somewhat easier to carry out the recommendation made by the 10th edition of *Introduction to Psychology:* that evidence for parapsychological connections be judged strictly in terms of scientific standards.

CONCLUSION

William James, as discussed above, said "the most urgent intellectual need [that he felt] is that science be built up again in a form in which [the phenomena of psychic research] may have a positive place."[45] Although this was not the main motive behind Whitehead's creation of his philosophy, he did—building on James's own suggestions— create a science-based philosophy that did just that. Whitehead's panexperientialism, with its radical empiricism, showed not only the possibility of extrasensory perception, which was discussed here, but also the other two types of parapsychological phenomena—psychokinesis and evidence suggestive of life after death—which have been discussed elsewhere.[46]

This assessment of Whitehead's importance for parapsychology has recently been supported by an outstanding and potentially paradigm-changing book on psychology called *Irreducible Mind: Toward a Psychology for the 21st Century.*[47] This multi-author book was written primarily by professors of psychiatric medicine, including the lead author, Edward F. Kelly. In the final chapter, Kelly said that James' unfinished program was "taken up and integrated with emerging developments in physics by the Anglo-American mathematician, philosopher of science, and metaphysician Alfred North Whitehead." Kelly continued:

> [Whitehead's] work in fact represents the most systematic effort to date to elaborate a comprehensive metaphysical system specif-ically intended to be compatible with *both* the new basic science *and* with all available facts of human experience.[48]

Kelly's stress on "all available facts of human experience" was central to his appreciation of Whitehead. He, in fact, began the chapter by quoting this statement by Whitehead: "The rejection of any source of evidence is always a treason to the ultimate rationalism which urges forward science and philosophy alike."[49]

Just as Whitehead said that "philosophy can exclude nothing," so that it should start with *assemblage*,[50] Kelly and his colleagues apply this method with regard to psychology.

*Irreducible Mind* is largely an 800-page rejection of physicalist theories of mind-body relations, according to which the mind can be reduced to the brain. The authors support this rejection by "assembling in one place large amounts of credible evidence for a wide variety of empirical phenomena that appear difficult or impossible to explain in conventional physicalist terms"[51]—phenomena that had been explored by William James and especially James's friend and colleague Frederick Myers, who was the primary intellect behind the founding in London of the Society for Psychical Research.

As with many issues, not incidentally, James lay behind Kelly's agreement with Whitehead about assemblage. In a passage noted by Kelly, Whitehead said that James was one of the "four great thinkers"—along with Plato, Aristotle, and Leibniz—"whose service to civilized thought rests largely upon their achievements in philosophical assemblage."[52]

CHAPTER THREE

# Parapsychology

## *John Palmer*

ABSTRACT: *This chapter presents an overview of parapsychology with an emphasis on the theory and empirical findings most relevant to Whitehead's ontology in general and the mind-body problem in particular. Parapsychologists study what we call "psi," which includes apparent paranormal acquisition of information ("extrasensory perception") and apparent paranormal effects on physical processes ("psychokinesis"). The case for psi nowadays rests primarily on meta-analyses of data from four methodological paradigms that are briefly described. A philosophical argument is presented that these findings confirm a Kuhnian anomaly rather than a paranormal principle of nature. Two different approaches to demonstrating postmortem survival are discussed: evidence of psi in survival-related contexts (exemplified by mediumship) and mental activity from an essentially non-functioning brain (exemplified by near-death experiences). Quantum-mechanical theories of psi and relevant empirical evidence are described, primarily because they include attempts to explain consciousness through quantum processes in the brain. Would their confirmation be good or bad news for non-materialists?*

THE PURPOSE OF THIS CHAPTER is to present an overview of research and theory in parapsychology, emphasizing its relevance to the mind-body problem, which is central to Whitehead's ontology. Parapsychology is an academic discipline dedicated to applying the scientific method to an understanding of mental phenomena (parapsy-chologists love this word) labeled by the Greek letter psi. Psi is defined as interactions between living organisms and their environment not attrib-utable to known physical processes. We use the adjective "paranormal" to describe these psychic processes. Psi has two subcategories. The first is extrasensory perception (ESP): paranormal acquisition of information from the environment. The second is psychokinesis (PK): paranormal effects upon the environment. Note that psi is defined negatively: its reality is established by ruling out known physical processes.

## ATTEMPTS TO ESTABLISH THE REALITY OF PSI

The traditional way to prove psi has been to provide a "conclusive" labo-ratory experiment with airtight controls that rule out all conventional explanations, however unlikely. The allowable alternatives include fraud, not only by the participant but also by the experimenter. The latter, not required of other scientists, is impossible to completely rule out, rendering the approach unfalsifiable. It is identified with a prominent critic of the day, C. E. M. Hansel,[1] who was taken to task by an equally prominent critic, Ray Hyman, who noted that Hansel's insinuations of experimenter fraud with no evidence were unfalsifiable.[2]

## META-ANALYSIS

More recently, the criterion has shifted to meta-analysis, a statistical technique also used in mainstream science, whereby a scientific finding cannot be explained as a "chance" occurrence—and thus not worth further consideration—if a conglomerate analysis of (ideally) all relevant published experiments purported to demonstrate the effect is statistically significant. Sometimes such an outcome is claimed to demonstrate that the effect is replicable—meaning the effect has been significantly demonstrated in multiple experiments, preferably by different investigators—which is what most scientists are really looking for. In parapsychology, however, a significant meta-analysis demonstrates only that somewhere in the database there is evidence for psi. This means that the proportion of significant studies must be greater than the proportion expected by chance. Unfortunately, the specific statistical test used in a parapsychology study is much less powerful than the one used in meta-analysis. Thus, it is easy to get a significant meta-analysis but a nonsignificant replication analysis, which is what I found in a review of experiments on non-intentional or implicit psi.[3] In meta-analysis, alternative explanations other than chance (e.g., sensory cues in an ESP test) are ruled out by demonstrating lack of a significant relationship between, say, the ESP scores and quality codes assigned to the methodologies of individual experiments by raters who are not shown the results of the studies to eliminate bias. A significant negative relationship means that the significant results can be attributed to bad methodology.

Meta-analyses have provided significant evidence for psi from four major methodological paradigms, although not all the meta-analyses applied quality codes. The first two paradigms are free-response ESP tests in which participants are asked to free-associate to the target, in contrast to, say, a card-guessing test in which they must answer with one of the four playing card suits. Judges are then shown four or five potential targets (without being told which is the real target) and asked to pick which one best reflects the participant's mentation. The two free-response paradigms are *ganzfeld* (e.g., Storm, Tressoldi and Di Risio 2010) and *remote viewing* (RV; e.g., Utts 1996),[4] and they are distinguished in four ways.

1.  Ganzfeld participants tend to be just anyone, whereas RV participants tend to be selected, usually on the basis of previous success in informal tests of RV.

2.  In the ganzfeld, the task is preceded by the induction of an *altered state of consciousness* (ASC) that eliminates patterned stimulation from the environment by having participants look into a (usually) red light through halved ping-pong balls while listening to pink noise (a pleasant variation of white noise) through headphones. There is no ASC induction in RV, although some successful participants are known to self-induce one.

3.  Ganzfeld targets tend to be emotional (e.g., dramatic scenes from a movie), whereas RV targets are not (e.g., buildings).

4.  In ganzfeld studies, the participant serves as the judge, whereas inRV studies the role is fulfilled by one or more "outside" judges given a transcript of the participant's mentation.

The third paradigm is PK applied to the output of *random number generators* (RNGs; e.g., Radin and Nelson 1989).[5] With most RNGs, participants must influence electronic noise converted to an initially random sequence of 1 and 0s depending, say, on whether the noise is above or below baseline at the moment of sampling.

The fourth paradigm is *distant mental interactions in living systems* (DMILS; e.g., Schmidt et al. 2004).[6] The definition encompasses psychic healing, but most DMILS research involves someone trying to influence someone else's normal physiological activity, usually responses of the autonomic nervous system such as skin conductance. It is unclear whether the agent directly affects the percipient's physiology (PK) or the participant's physiology responds to ESP knowledge of the agent's effort.

## RECONCEPTUALIZING THE PSI CONTROVERSY

The way the debate about the reality of psi has been framed has made the controversy less productive and more combative than it needs to be. I propose that the root of the problem is that the term "psi" is used both descriptively and theoretically.[7] As a descriptive term, it labels experiences and events that appear to be psychic on the surface. As a theoretical term, it labels the paranormal process that makes them psychic. Thus one can say, absurdly, but without fear of contradiction, that "psi explains psi." Appreciation of this distinction led me to conclude that the question we should be asking is not the traditional "Does [theoretical] psi exist?" but "How can [descriptive] psi be explained?" The latter question has several advantages. First, it belies critics' frequent assertion that parapsychology lacks a subject matter; the subject matter consists of the experiences and events that comprise descriptive psi. Second, it encourages process-oriented, theory-based research, which is the only way we will ever understand what really is going on. Third, it means that the burden of proof is shared by psi proponents and their critics; with the traditional question, it falls exclusively on proponents.

This third point needs elaboration. Answering the new question requires both proponents and critics to demonstrate that their explanations of the results of successful psi experiments, both individually and collectively, meet the same standards of evidence that apply in the rest of science. However, in the new scheme, psi proponents must abandon the traditional principle that paranormality can be claimed if all conventional alternatives have been ruled out. The problem is that you can never be sure you have thought of all the possibilities. Indeed, there are examples of published evidence of psi later being called into question by newly uncovered conventional explanations.[8] These possibilities are sometimes labeled by the catchy phrase "[E]rror [S]ome [P]lace." Proponents must instead confirm a particular paranormal theory or explanation of the event, just as critics must confirm a particular conventional explanation of the event. While proponents must also still rule out known conventional explanations of the event, what proponents gain by meeting this new criterion is that Error Some Place is no longer a valid argument.

Finally, the traditional question, at least as both sides in the debate have applied it, has only two possible answers: yes and no. If the psi interpretation of the event is not confirmed, it is concluded that the conventional explanation has been established. This, of course, is illogical, but the nature of the traditional question tends to obscure that. In my scheme, the new question, "How can psi be explained?" has three possible answers. If a paranormal process is confirmed, the answer is "paranormal." If a conventional process is confirmed, it is "conventional." If neither process is confirmed, it is "anomalous," in the Kuhnian sense.[9] Largely because no paranormal theory of psi has yet been confirmed, my answer to the question is "anomalous."

## IMPLICIT PSI

It is increasingly common in parapsychology for researchers to test for psi in experiments where the participant is not asked to use psi. This para-doxical objective is most often achieved by having participants engage in a non-psi task with psi targets secretly embedded in them. For example, in one of a prominent series of successful experiments, Daryl Bem turned a test commonly used in parapsychology into an ESP test by, for example, asking participants which of two pictures they like best. Unbeknownst to them, on each trial one of the pictures was randomly selected as an ESP target, and the responses were scored accordingly.

## DECISION AUGMENTATION THEORY

Implicit psi is central to Decision Augmentation Theory (DAT),[10] which is purported to explain ostensible PK in Random Number Generator experiments, as, actually, experiments in precognition (ESP of the future). One can think of the output of an RNG as a moving sequence of the

digits "1" and "0." Even if the sequence is random (no PK), there will be
blocks that have a significant excess of, say, 1s, like a really good poker
hand. The idea is that the participant uses precognition to determine
exactly when to initiate the test (e.g., by a mouse click) so as to capture
one of these "biased" sequences. There has been a vigorous debate about
whether DAT accounts for RNG results.

## EXPERIMENTER PSI

The most important implication of implicit psi in my view is that
recognition of its existence has required parapsychologists to take
seriously the possibility that experimenters psychically influence the
results of their own experiments, usually without intending to do so.[11]
It had previously been taken for granted that demonstration of psi in
the lab required an intention to use it, and only the participant had that
intention. Implicit psi is non-intentional by definition, which implies
that the experimenter now has to be considered a possible psi source as
well. If one makes the reasonable secondary assumption that success in
using psi depends partly on one's motivation to see a successful outcome,
the experimenter becomes the more likely psi source, at least if the
participants are unselected. There is little direct experimental evidence
for experimenter psi, but there is no question that parapsychologists differ
widely in their success in obtaining significant results, and several of
the successful ones have demonstrated psi ability serving as participants.
In reality, I think that in most successful psi experiments there is input
from both participant(s) and the experimenter (or principle investigator).

## GLOBAL CONSCIOUSNESS PROJECT

One reason to bring up experimenter psi in this chapter is its relevance to the research project in parapsychology that comes closest to
testing the transpersonal worldview: the Global Consciousness Project.
A noteworthy feature of RNGs is that they can continuously collect data
unattended for long periods of time. Roger Nelson, originator of the
project, and his collaborators keep a battery of RNGs running at multiple
locations throughout the world.[12] Nelson predicted and has found that
these RNGs collectively produce non-random output during events on
which large numbers of people are focusing attention, such as the final

game in a World Cup soccer tournament. Nelson interprets his results as demonstrating the operation of a consciousness field. Though not exactly a collective consciousness, the consciousness field is still transpersonal in the sense of implying that the consciousness goes beyond each individual witness of the event. The alternative interpretation, of course, is experimenter psi. This alternative is especially inviting if one assumes that motivation to demonstrate psi is important. Those watching the soccer game have no such motivation and are not even aware of being participants in a parapsychology experiment.

SURVIVAL RESEARCH

*Mental Mediumship*

Of all the areas of parapsychology mentioned thus far, that which most directly addresses the ontological issues raised by Whitehead is research on postmortem survival. Parapsychologists have adopted two approaches to obtain evidence for survival. The first is to demonstrate that a discarnate spirit is the source of information obtained by ESP. The prototype for this approach is mental mediumship research,[13] where the question is whether the information received by a medium comes from a discarnate spirit, the mind of a living person (especially the person receiving the reading), or some objective record (e.g., a newspaper obituary).[14]

The traditional approach to confirming the survival hypothesis through mediumship studies is to demonstrate that the quality of the data obtained from the medium (the volume and specificity of accurate information for which the medium had no normal access) is better than that obtained in ESP research in non-survival contexts such as those described earlier in this chapter.

This criterion is problematic for several reasons. First, the quality of information often obtained in modern free-response ESP tests is just as good as that found in the best mediumship cases. The second problem has not been recognized because the debate has been incorrectly characterized as between "survival" and "super-psi." The latter is a pejorative term coined by survival advocates to make the point that psi must be stronger than it has been shown to be in standard ESP experiments to provide a valid alternative to the survival hypothesis. What users of the false survival/

super-psi dichotomy fail to recognize is that the process of information transfer is by definition psi in both mediumship and standard ESP studies. Recognition of this fact leads one to ask the following question: If it is the same process in both, why, from a pro-survival perspective, would one expect ESP to be of better quality in mediumship cases? I can't think of a good answer to this question. On the other hand, from an anti-survival perspective, one can plausibly predict better performance in mediumship research because a medium would be more motivated to use ESP than the typical participant in a standard ESP experiment given that the task is more important or meaningful to the medium.

In my opinion, a better approach is to look for *types* of paranormal effects that are limited to survival contexts, such as the demonstration of skills. An example is one of Ian Stevenson's cases in which a child with apparent memories of a previous life also demonstrated at a very early age an ability to play drums, a skill also possessed by the person who the boy claimed to be the reincarnation of.[15] I am aware of no credible cases of such precocious skills outside of a survival context, but I have not done a systematic search. If I am correct, such a survey should be a priority for survival researchers.

Most serious mental mediumship studies were conducted by members of the British and American Societies for Psychical Research in the late nineteenth and early twentieth centuries. Elaborate steps were often taken to minimize the possibility that mediums had access by sensory means to the information contained in their readings, but nothing was done to assess the likelihood that the successful matches of the medium's statements and verified external events were due to chance, i.e., lucky guesses. Some modern mediumship research has solved this problem by applying proper statistical analysis to the results, and one of these studies achieved publication in a mainstream medical journal.[16] However, none of the few mediumship studies that provide valid statistical evidence of ESP make a convincing case for a discarnate spirit as the information source, for the reasons outlined above.

*Near Death Experiences (NDEs)*

The second approach to testing the survival hypothesis is to say that the brain is incapable by itself of producing certain kinds of mental events. The phenomena in question need not occur in survival-related contexts to be considered psychic. This is amply illustrated in the book *Irreducible Mind*, an 800-page tour de force that outlines in exhaustive detail the case for survival based on this kind of evidence.[17] Psi is just one of many anomalous phenomena considered. Another example is savants, people who, for example, can perform extremely complex mathematical calculations almost instantaneously with no props.

In survival research, the prototype for this second approach is the near death experience. Briefly and simplistically, in a fully developed NDE, persons facing imminent demise typically have the experience of the soul leaving the body, traveling to heaven or some equivalent place, meeting deceased relatives and/or religious figures, and then being told that it is "not your time" and instructed to return to the body. At some point during the process there is often a "past-life review," in which NDErs seem to re-experience all the events in their life in rapid sequence. NDE imagery is described as vivid and realistic, more like perception than imagination. Partly for this reason, NDEers typically are convinced they actually experienced the afterlife and lose their fear of death.

Proponents of the survival hypothesis seek to establish that the NDEers conviction has a basis in reality, that their mind or soul really did leave the body and get a glimpse of the afterlife. In keeping with the second approach, they argue that the brain, particularly in the incapacitated state it is in when one is on the verge of death, is incapable of producing what NDEers experience with respect to such attributes as vividness. Critics turn this argument on its head, maintaining that the physiological processes associated with being near death (e.g., temporal lobe seizures, anoxia, release of endorphins) could easily produce NDE imagery. The debate rages on, unresolved.

Of course, if the impairment of the brain is severe enough, the critic's argument breaks down. Thus, the strongest evidence for survival from NDEs comes from two cases in which imagery was produced when the brain was essentially shut down.

## Pam Reynolds case

Reynolds' experiences occurred during surgery. In order to remove an aneurism in her basal artery, the surgeons felt it necessary to induce hypothermic cardiac arrest.[18] In layman terms, they froze her brain. During part of the procedure, Reynolds stopped breathing, her heart stopped beating, and her EEG was flat. Afterwards, she reported having had an

NDE during the part of the procedure when she was "brain dead." She also correctly described the saw used to cut though her scalp and what it sounded like in operation. Finally, she correctly described a conversation the surgical staff had among themselves during the procedure.

The main problem with the case from an evidential standpoint is that the claim that the experiences occurred during the part of the procedure when Reynolds was brain dead is based not on her real-time experience (she obviously was in no position to give a blow-by-blow account during the operation!) but her subsequent *memory* of that experience. The probability that these memories were distorted, particularly in respects such as timing, is quite high. What is more, she would presumably like to believe that the imagery occurred when she was "dead," and such expectations and preferences are known to color how we perceive and remember events. She could have seen the saw on the operating table before she lost consciousness, and made an unconscious "lucky guess" as to what it sounded like, which informed her "memory" of the sound. Even if it could be established that the sawing and the conversation occurred when she was effectively brain dead, she could have gotten the information beforehand by precognition. She was probably in a kind of altered state of consciousness that parapsychologists consider psi conducive shortly before losing full consciousness. I am referring here to when the information entered her brain. It is possible that she never consciously experienced the conversation until she "recalled" it after the operation. The same could be true of the NDE itself (i.e., a false memory). If there is ever a circumstance when we would expect the mind to play tricks on us, this is it.

## Eben Alexander case

Eben Alexander was a neurosurgeon steeped in the culture of materialistic science when his worldview was turned upside down by a powerful series of NDEs described in his first book on the subject.[19] The occasion was his contraction of a rare bacterial meningitis that is almost always fatal and that left him in a coma for seven days. As in the Reynolds case, the evidentiality of the NDEs rests on the premise that Alexander's brain was in no shape to create such experiences at the times they occurred.

The case is weaker than the Reynolds case, because there was no EEG or other measure of brain activity during the times that his NDEs presumably occurred. The conclusion about his brain state rests primarily on inferences from previous cases where such measures presumably were available. Although Alexander was obviously in very bad shape, the fact that he survived suggests that the disease was not quite as severe as in the previous cases, in which it seems the disease was fatal.

The second problem is the same as the main problem in the Reynolds case, namely that we must rely on Alexander's memory of the experiences to determine when they occurred. Even if we assume that his brain was nonfunctional during the entirety of his coma, the NDEs may have occurred during the possibly extended period when the brain damage was not severe enough to induce a coma. The subsequent accessibility of vivid memories of the NDEs could be after-effects of the disease if inhibitory neurons were damaged more than excitatory neurons. I wish this possibility would be explored by NDE investigators on both sides of the debate. It could explain why NDEs in general are so vivid as well as the puzzling phenomenon of terminal lucidity.

### Assessing the Brain Dysfunction Argument

There is a fundamental problem with the brain incapacity argument as presented in *Irreducible Mind* that makes it unlikely that it could ever overcome the materialist objection by itself. Even if Kelly and his co-authors were able to convince materialistic scientists that the processes they document cannot be explained by known brain functions, the fallback of the latter would be to simply say that "Brains can do things that we didn't realize they could do," thereby maintaining their physicalism. The only way to counter this maddening, but effective, retort is to do what I suggested earlier in this chapter: confirm a paranormal theory of psi (or consciousness) that explains NDEs and the other relevant anomalies.

### PHYSICAL THEORIES OF PSI

There are two classes of theory in parapsychology, which can best be expressed in terms of ESP. The first class addresses the question of how information gets from the source to the receiver. The second addresses the question of how the information is processed by the brain or mind of the receiver, leading either to it becoming conscious or being blocked. This second class of theories falls primarily in the domain of psychology, whereas the first falls in the domain of physics. It is the latter—theories of psi grounded in physics—that is most relevant to this chapter. As we will see momentarily, these theories don't necessarily require a materialist ontology.

Until the 1960s, these explanations of psi tended to appeal to Newtonian physics, the most prominent hypothesis being that the information was transmitted via extremely low frequency electromagnetic waves. Although these waves can travel over long distances without attenuating and are difficult to block, they can't easily account for the full range of demonstrated psi effects and have fallen out of favor. A post-Newtonian approach that has received less attention than perhaps it should is represented by multidimensional space theories (e.g., Rauscher and Targ 2001).[20] The main idea, to put it very crudely, is that in some higher space/time dimension than the standard four, the spatial and temporal distance between the source and receiver in an ESP experiment translates to zero in the four-dimensional world. A helpful metaphor is that of "flatlanders" who live in a world that they perceive as having only two-dimensions (length and width) but in fact has height as well. If an object were dropped from above, they would see it suddenly and miraculously appear out of "nowhere," what parapsychologists call an *apport*.

### Quantum Mechanics

By far the most attention has been paid to the universally accepted theory of quantum mechanics (QM). I will focus my attention there ecause of its relevance to the mind-body problem. This relevance stems from the fact that some of its interpretations evoke the amorphous construct of *consciousness*. However, I must first identify two more basic (and well defined) concepts in QM that are relevant to psi: observation and nonlocality.

*Observation:* This term comes to the fore in what is called the measurement problem in QM. Briefly, a quantum process or event exists initially in a superposition of probable states expressed mathematically as the wave function. Then one of these probable states is selected to become actualized. The selection process is called collapse of the wave function and the process that collapses it is called observation. Where this becomes relevant to us is that physicists differ in how they define observation. According to the majority Copenhagen interpretation, observation is the physical process of measurement. The minority view, pioneered by Von Neumann, defines observation as most of us would, as a person looking at the process. However, the term Von Neumann used for the collapse process was not "perception," but rather "consciousness," and its metaphysical connotations came along for the ride.

*Nonlocality:* The source for this term in QM is identified variously with the Einstein-Podolsky-Rosen (EPR) paradox and with Bell's Theorem. Both make reference to a "thought experiment" that was later conducted with results supporting QM. The experiment also serves to define nonlocality. Send two previously connected ("entangled") particles (A & B) off in different directions. How you then measure a characteristic of A (e.g., spin) is correlated with how the characteristic manifests in B at exactly the same time, in such a way that no model that assumes information is sent from A to B via a physical signal propagating at less than or equal to the speed of light, can reproduce the observed correlation. This looks a lot like psi, and at first some parapsychologists thought that is was, but physicists quickly pointed out that one cannot construe the correlation of states as communication of information. Yet it is nonetheless something parapsychologists can see as a cause for optimism. I like the way Dean Radin puts it (loosely paraphrased): nonlocality does not prove or explain psi, but the fact that it happens in nature makes psi much more plausible and likely.[21]

## QUANTUM MECHANICS AND PARAPSYCHOLOGY

### *The Observational Theories*

Quantum mechanics has inspired several attempts to explain psi, the most prominent being the Observational Theories (OTs).[22] The key assumption of the OTs is retrocausality. In a psi experiment, the psychic act occurs not when participants attempt to exert psi but when they observe the results of the effort, the feedback. Most attempts to test the OTs have involved PK on an RNG. The experiment begins by someone having the RNG generate a sequence of (random) numbers without attempting to exert psi influence. The sequence is recorded as sounds on a tape, say a high pitch sound for each 1 (the target) and a low pitch sound for each 0. The participant then listens to the tape. The theory says that this "observation" of the sequence acts backward in time to determine the sequence that the RNG originally "generated." If the participant is manifesting positive psi in this example, the original sequence will have a significant excess of 1s.

Several such experiments have yielded significant results, supporting the OTs (e.g., Schmidt and Stapp 1993).[23] The problem is that, to my knowledge, no published experiment has ruled out the more straightforward alternative explanation that whoever generated the RNG sequence used implicit psi *at that time* to bias the RNG output. Such an experiment would require a control condition identical to the experimental condition except that no one ever listens to the tape. If there were significantly more 1s in the experimental than in the control condition, the OT hypothesis would be confirmed—with one caveat. There has been no agreement among OT theorists as to what level of feedback is needed for psi to occur. The experiment I just described is only successful if the feedback is for each trial. If all one needs to observe is, say, the statistical significance of the results, the test fails because someone must observe this to know if the result confirms the OTs.

*The Double-Slit Experiment*

A more impressive demonstration of psi as a quantum process was an adaptation of one of the classic experiments in QM.[24] The principle this experiment put to the test is that the behavior of subatomic particles is determined by how they are measured. Photons are shot into a barrier with two slits and then measured when they hit a photographic plate on the other side. As predicted by QM, the photons form a single interference pattern on the plate; they behave like waves. However, if detectors are located at the slits, each photon is recorded as passing through only one of the slits, creating a diffraction pattern; the photons behave like particles. Can psi influence this process? Radin had volunteer participants either focus their attention on the apparatus (no slit detectors) with the intention of influencing the beam psychically or to simply relax. They found that the ratio of the spectral power of the interference and diffraction patterns on the plate was significantly smaller on attention trials. It appears that psi influenced a QM process.

*The Bigger Picture*

Because the physical measurement process was the same in Radin's experiment whether the participants were "observing" the slits or not, his results imply that consciousness, as distinct from physical measurement, can at least contribute to state vector collapse. This brings us back to the central issue of QM and consciousness, with all the implications of the latter for the mind-body problem.

*QM and the Brain*

In my opinion, the most important QM question for those of us interested in the mind-body problem is whether consciousness (and psi) can be explained as or by QM processes in the brain. For such a theory to be credible, the process hypothesized must meet the conditions of QM, especially that they be truly microscopic. There are currently two main candidates. The first is by Henry Stapp, who identifies the QM process with the firmly established process of exocytosis, the release of neurotransmitters into the synaptic cleft.[25] The other author, Stuart Hameroff, builds his theory around an entity rather than a process: Consciousness is created in the brain by microtubules, polymers that are involved in human cellular function.[26] I don't understand either QM or neurochemistry well enough to evaluate these theories, but parapsychologists I know who are better equipped than I in this regard prefer Stapp's theory.

Note that these theories are based on the assumption that the brain creates or at least sustains consciousness. The confirmation of any such theory would create a serious problem for advocates of the survival hypothesis, because even if consciousness is immaterial, its dependence on the brain for its existence or at least its functionality means that when the body dies, consciousness for all practical purpose dies with it. There might be a way around this by appealing to some form of panpsychic ontology such as Whitehead's, but it would require the awkward assumption that the brain could continue to function post-mortem with its structural integrity destroyed.

The big bang: Looking even more broadly, we might ask how far we can extend the domains of nonlocality and entanglement. A speculation that caught my eye is that everything in the universe was entangled at the big bang and will remain entangled forever.[27] If we apply this principle to individual minds, we end up with the transpersonal worldview, the other major theme of this volume.

## CHAPTER FOUR

# Parapsychology Needs a Theory— and It Has One

*James Carpenter*

ABSTRACT: *Parapsychological phenomena (extrasensory perception, psychokinesis, precognition) appear to be real capacities, as attested by 100 years of careful research. Yet our knowledge of them is still sketchy, and they seem to be generally unruly and rare. To make genuine scientific advance, and for scientists in general to be interested, the phenomena must be made more predictable and understandable by theory. First Sight Theory offers significant promise in this regard. It places the phenomena into the context of contemporary work in cognitive and neuropsychology, and it shows how they function normally in an unconscious way in every moment of human life. It also spells out how we can predict when the expression of parapsychological information (called psi "prehension," after Whitehead) will be strong and when it will be weak, and when it will be direct versus when it will lead in a contrary direction. Viewed through the lens of this theory, these capacities can be seen to function in the same way other unconscious cognitive processes do, and be understood as normal and predictable, not anomalous and mysterious.*

MOST PEOPLE WHO TRY to make sense of the renegade science of parapsychology come to believe this: parapsychology needs a theory. If one looks closely and open-mindedly at the scientific work accumulated for over one hundred years, the findings seem fascinating.

When they are compiled into careful meta-analyses, they seem to be quite real. Yet they are also at odds with how we are used to understanding the world works, and they seem to conflict with our everyday experience of reality.

What people most often mean by the need for a theory is some accommodation of physics to these findings, such that the "laws of nature" will permit them to exist at all. There have been several interesting and thoughtful forays into this effort, as one sees in a recent and imposing two-volume work.[1] Several experts in quantum mechanics have argued that parapsychological findings have not actually been incompatible with theoretical physics for a long time.

As interesting as these issues are, they are not my primary concern, and I believe that an accommodation with physics is not the biggest reason we need parapsychological theory. Leave laboratory findings for a moment and consider the raw experiences that led people to think of the need for scientific parapsychology at all. Suppose you had a dream of death and burning buildings shortly before the attacks of September 11, 2001. Perhaps the coincidence seemed eerie and meaningful. You might wonder if you experienced a premonition or, as the parapsychologists would say, an instance of precognition.

Imagine that you have an aunt who claims to generally know who is calling whenever her phone rings (she has no caller ID). Imagine further that you test her out by having a handful of different friends and relatives call her, and you find that she is uncannily accurate. Is she demonstrating a telepathic connection before the ordinary electronic one?

Let's say you are coaxed into going along when a friend wants to consult a medium. During the session, the medium announces that a spirit named Charles is present who wants to say something to his child. Your father's name was Charles, and you become intrigued. Then the medium says he is calling you by a silly nick name that, in fact, he called you when you were young—a name that no living person but you knows about. Has a human soul survived death and dropped in to tell about it? Or has the medium been able to reach into your past and pull out a unique and important detail?

Now imagine that a friend of yours recently got a verdict of imminent death from his physicians. Members of his church banded together to secure his healing with concerted prayer. Then his physician is amazed because an MRI reveals that his tumor has vanished without a trace. Has prayer healed a deadly disease? Or, as the more secular parapsychologist might say, has a psychokinetic effect transpired?

Knowing things before they happen (precognition), knowing things happening beyond the range of the senses (clairvoyance), affecting physical events with nothing but thought (psychokinesis), mentally connecting to others (telepathy): These are the things that parapsychologists have tried to shape into a science. When such things seem to occur, should we consider them real, or are they coincidences inflated by self-deception? If we should decide that they are probably real, what can be made of them? They are so aberrant, so infrequent, so unpredictable.

There is always a minority of people who treasure magic and surprise and are happy to make these things the bedrock of their days. They are buoyed by a sense that the whole world is mysterious. These people enjoy parapsychological findings because they fit in with a magical worldview. Most people, however, are more practical and want to live in a world that is predictable and understandable. More practical people may be card-carrying scientists or they may belong to innumerable other walks of life. If something surprising turns up, they want to work on it until they make it reasonable and somehow fit it into an orderly world. Or they want to forget about it.

When some practically minded scientists turned to the "paranormal" phenomena of telepathy and so on, they invented the science of parapsychology.

The first, and sometimes the favorite, hypothesis for these scientists has always been the one of error and misunderstanding. First, see if instances of apparent telepathy are really merely apparent. Perhaps we can explain them, or explain them away, by some of the common tendencies that humans have of misunderstanding things. People can be terrible judges of probability, particularly when something is especially recent or important or dangerous. Memory is much more malleable and subjective and creative than we generally appreciate. An idea that we like is apt to feel truer than one we don't. Our minds are constantly creating meanings, but logic and probability and objectivity are not the most powerful forces at work when we do this. How can we protect ourselves against our own self-deception?

Like Ulysses, who wished to not throw himself overboard should he become enchanted by the Sirens, we make a pact against ourselves. We lash ourselves to the mast of scientific protocol. This means first that we must move beyond anecdotes, those anomalous stories that are delicious for some and disturbing for others. We will gather many observations systematically, measure them carefully, report them all, and evaluate them mathematically.

Movement in this scientific direction began in the latter part of the nineteenth century, when a few scientists wished to move beyond the unruly, naturalistic observations drawn from mediums and séance rooms toward the orderly observations permitted in the laboratory.

The French Nobel laureate physiologist Charles Richet first introduced the use of statistical evaluation of results to parapsychological studies when he applied them to card-guessing tests he carried out with a woman who had experiences that suggested telepathic ability.[2]

This new approach gathered steam in the first decades of the twentieth century. In Holland, H. I. F. W. Brugmans and his colleagues tested a young student of physics named Van Dam who had reputed telepathic abilities. Van Dam was blindfolded inside a curtained booth and asked to reach through a curtain and point with his finger to one square on a 6 x 8 checkerboard placed on a table in front of him. Brugmans was in an overhead room and watched through a soundproofed window in the floor and selected the numbers identifying the target squares. Van Dam was right in his placements with an odds against chance of 121 trillion to one.

In Britain, Ina Jephson asked 240 persons to shuffle a deck of playing cards, pull one out at random, and guess it without looking at it, then reshuffle and repeat the procedure, for 5 guesses at a sitting. She collected 6,000 such guesses and evaluated the results with the help of Sir Roland Fisher, one of the fathers of the science of statistics. Her results were also very highly significant. In the United States, George Estabrooks, a Harvard graduate student, carried out telepathy tests between pairs of persons, sometimes separated into different rooms. His results were also highly significant, with odds against chance of millions to one.[3] All of these reports showed statistically significant evidence for extrasensory perception.

However, problems also quickly became apparent with these brand new methods. Brugmans' targets were not truly random (so statistical evaluation was difficult); Jephson's participants were allowed to test themselves and report their own results (so their honesty had to be assumed); both Richet and Brugmans focused on individuals previously thought to be especially gifted (permitting no generalization to people at large); and several showed unstable results, which declined to chance under certain conditions.

By the time William McDougall and J. B. Rhine set up their new laboratory at Duke University in 1927, some important considerations had come to light: methods for testing should be standardized and easily repeated; targets should be truly random; statistical evaluation should be state of the art; any sensory contact at all between the participant and the target had to be excluded by design; a wide range of persons should be tested; and the stability or instability of results had to be systematically studied. Following all of these principles, Rhine and his staff went through a period of exploration, testing Duke students and each other with specially designed cards carrying simple geometric figures. They found out what procedures seemed to work best, and they found several participants who performed especially well. Then they used their best methods and formally tested their best guessers. Rhine reported the first forays of work at Duke in 1934.[4]

Even this early, Rhine felt confident in concluding that his laboratory had found solid evidence for extrasensory perception involving an agent (which might be thought of as telepathy). He found similar evidence for ESP without any agent (pure clairvoyance), even under double-blind conditions with 100 yards and several buildings between target and subject. He also found instances in which scoring dipped significantly *below chance* in apparently meaningful ways—sometimes when participants were trying to miss, and sometimes when they were sick or dosed with alcohol or otherwise felt indisposed to take the test. By 1938, he had accumulated sufficient evidence to declare that his laboratory had also established an ability of persons to guess targets before they were determined (guessing cards first, shuffling them later). He called this precognition. In 1943, his laboratory released a long series of studies that provided evidence for an ability to influence the fall of dice thrown mechanically: psychokinesis. The four of these together—clairvoyance, telepathy, precognition and psychokinesis—came to be referred to together as different expressions of one underlying process, called *psi*. In recent years, some have replaced this arbitrary name with the term EM (extended mind) phenomena, which does seem to capture the essence of what we are trying to study.

Work on these problems using the methods developed by Rhine spread to other universities and laboratories. Many reported corroborating findings; some others did not. In the middle and later decades of the twentieth century, much parapsychological work studied the effect of psychological variables on the direction of scoring. For example, persons who believed that ESP is possible under the conditions of the study tended to produce scoring that was above chance. People who rejected this possibility tended to score below chance, missing the targets more frequently than would be statistically expected.[5] A similar over- vs. below-chance split was observed in regard to the subject's anxiety level: emotionally secure people tended to score above chance, more anxious people averaged below.

Techniques of testing developed and became more sophisticated. For example, for testing psychokinesis, dice were replaced with electronic random number generators, sometimes driven by radioactive decay. Asking people to produce evidence of psi by consciously guessing or willing has often given way to measurements of the implicit expression of extrasensory information, as, for example, unconscious psychophysiological responses (such as subtle changes in skin conductance, indicating increased arousal, when disturbing stimuli were shown to a distant partner.) Methods were also developed for bridging the gap between laboratory procedures and more naturalistic expressions of psi, including anomalous events of haunted houses, the information given by mediums, access to information in states of revery and inward-focus, and—in a large scale, formerly secret, but well-funded government program—the application of clairvoyant impressions in the service of spying for national security.[6]

By the dawning of this century, one could say that parapsychology had made many significant advances in the quest to bring its unruly phenomena into some semblance of scientific order. Since the mid-twentieth century, parapsychological problems have been taken up by many researchers in many countries, and these serious workers have produced many careful findings. Several of these findings have been found to be at least as replicable as those in other areas of the behavioral and neurosciences. Meta-analyses combining many studies on several general areas of work have increased our confidence that the phenomena, whatever exactly they might represent, are real and not spurious. A particularly well-done and heavily scrutinized example is the work by Daryl Bem and his colleagues on "feeling the future," which showed that participants do in fact respond in behaviorally implicit ways to events that have not yet transpired, under easily repeated experimental conditions.[7] Thus the complaint that the phenomena are not replicable can now be made only by critics who are ignorant of the scientific literature.

Of course, there are important problems. Although some effects are replicable in general terms, no one has consistent, powerful, utterly reliable control over EM abilities. If someone claims otherwise, you might suspect flim-flam or psychosis. Decline effects,[8] particularly of well-scoring individuals, continue to be the rule more than the exception. A few cases of fraud have occurred and been exposed—although not more than in any other branch of science, and I would wager that cheating is probably much less frequent than in many mainstream areas in which financial and career incentives make scientific fraud rewarding.

In spite of its progress, and the innate interest of its problems, research in this field is still barred from most universities and journals and professional conferences. Sources of potential research funding almost always firmly shut their doors against it. Parapsychologists who seek exposure and discussion of their hard-earned findings run into what has been called the "woo woo taboo." Academic scientists who seek jobs and tenure almost always find that any history of involvement in the subject is a kiss of death.

Nowhere else is this aversion as great as in my own profession of psychology. Some of it is honest skepticism, and well-warranted. Psychologists know more than anyone else about how irrational people can be and how badly we can mislead ourselves. However, some of the aversion goes beyond that and seems much more emotional than rational, even though the rationalizations that can be given to justify it are legion. Whatever the deeper reasons may be, they seem to be unconscious, out of sight even to the critics themselves.

I think part of the deeper reason is actually shared by everyone. It is due to the fact that we all share a human mind that has evolved an automatic tendency to construct a world of experience out of the information given to our senses, and to reject any idea that appears to contradict this constructed, shared world. This is eminently practical and has permitted our survival and dominance of the planet. We are all pragmatists, reflexively; we work with what works for us, and regard with suspicion or even disgust anything that seems to depart from that consensual fabric. We may find anomalies interesting, but at an emotional level, where most of our thinking really goes on, we dislike them. In this way, our kind has avoided countless foolish errors and dead ends. But sometimes this tendency is a liability.

## AN ANALOGY: THE SCIENCE OF OPTICS

When developments in optics permitted the invention of a telescope and a microscope, many intelligent and sensible people firmly rejected the idea that the world was actually much larger and much smaller than everyday perception allowed. And when the entities discovered in these expanded worlds—the planets and galaxies and microbes and molecules—began to force new ways of understanding the universe upon us, many violently rebelled. This rebellion seems quaint and odd now, because we have all accomodated our thinking to these extentions of reality. But in their day, these negative reactions were often vicious, even murderous.

It seems obvious that as long as the extended realities seen in magnifying and reducing lenses were presented as curious anomalies, people might be fascinated for a moment and then return to their practical affairs and their familiar sensory world with its manifold concerns. What was necessary for a cultural—and scientific—accomodation to a genuine extention of reality was the hard work of people who tried to understand the things found in the realms of the extra large and extra small and their hard work in communicating these interpretations, defending them, correcting them, and then returning to them to learn more and more.

It was necessary that some people constructed some theories and then went on with the sometimes onerous and dangerous task of teaching these theories to the others. Thus what was not sensible in a sensory way could eventually become sensible in a conceptual way. This led to the construction of the edifice of modern science.

Parapsychology is in a situation analogous to the very early development of the science of optics. We have created some methods that let us produce some anomalies with some regularity. They are things that our everyday sensory world would not lead us to expect. They are fascinating anomalies. But scientific method and some degree of reproducibility of a phenomenon do not raise us to the level of scientific understanding—or even pre-scientific understanding.

Accomodating these anomalies to our current theories of physics is not our primary need. It is no more basic than the need people once felt to accommodate the reality of distant galaxies with biblical doctrine—even though that seemed to be a very pressing, political need at one time. The primary need we have now with parapsychological anomalies is some way to think about them, understand them, anticipate them. We need interpretations of our anomalies that have some predictive value. Without some way of interpreting these anomalies, we cannot expect serious people to dwell for long on them. Without some framework for understanding, we cannot expect science to consider them worth exploring. Without some conceptual scaffold upon which to build our research, we cannot expect to make much progress in constructing real understanding. With such a scaffold, we can anticipate psi phenomena rather than be surprised by them. As our anticipations bear out sometimes, and sometimes not, we can refine and improve our next anticipations.

In short, we need theory.

## FIRST SIGHT THEORY

I developed First Sight Theory (FST) in an attempt to help fill this gap. Since all the more stable regularities that have been reported to date with parapsychological phenomena involve psychological variables, I wanted a psychological theory. For a fuller explication of this theory and an assessment of its empirical utility, please see the text *First Sight: ESP and Parapsychology in Everyday Life*.[9]

I set out to build my theory in the spirit of Sigmund Freud: not in trying to explain mental disorders, but in trying to plot a course into understanding unconscious mental life. Freud did not use telescopes or microscopes to move beyond our immediate sensory understanding of things; he used a bevy of apparently random and meaningless things that people experience and do (starting with anomalous physical symptoms and dreams) as vehicles into an unconscious stratum of the mind that he proposed to exist. Instead of the sensible world of physical objects that could be imagined in vistas too distant or small to see, he took the human world of thoughts and feelings and wishes and intentions and imagined that something like them also existed out of sight *within each person*. A kind of thinking can go on unconsciously, he reasoned, and a kind of wishing can exist outside of our knowledge, but still drive our behavior and experience. He and his colleagues and subsequent workers

developed a handful of techniques—dream interpretation, word association, projective tests, analysis of jokes and errors, analogy of symptom to
early trauma, and the like—and used them to draw lines of connection
between hypothesized unconscious mental events and our conscious
behavior and experience.

Although some areas of psychiatry and clinical psychology still use
latter-day developments of Freud's work, First Sight is more directly
connected to other work on unconscious mental life that cognitive
psychologists have been developing in recent decades (many of whom
would be embarrassed at any association with Freud's name)!

## SUBLIMINAL PERCEPTION

Can a perception be unconscious? Our everyday experience would lead
us to think not. What we experience is what we experience. But this
shows how trapped everyday consciousness is within itself. We must
reach beyond this to even ask the question.

Anomalous observations suggesting that perception could be unconscious have been around for a long time, but for decades the topic
remained neglected, almost as taboo as psi. For example, individuals
with damage in their visual cortex could be shown a common object
and report honestly that they had no idea what it was. Then, if asked to
match that object with the one among a set of 5 or 6 that was the same,
and do it by feeling with their hands, they could do so well above chance.
There are many variations on this kind of thing, which has been given
the provocative name of "blindsight."

*Subliminal perception* or *Perception Without Awareness* (PWA) are
more general terms for phenomena that show that conscious perception
is not necessary for the demonstrable acquisition of information. If
a picture or a word is flashed on a screen too faintly or briefly to be
consciously perceived, it may still show reliable effects on experience
or behavior a short time later. For example, in a typical study, one
group of experimental participants might be flashed the word *tools* too
quickly to grasp, while another group is flashed the word *food*. These
flashes, surprisingly, may be so brief that not even a flicker of light can
be discerned. Then all participants are shown, one at a time, a string of
words that are either tools or foods, and asked to signal the moment they
can identify what the word is. Those who were unconsciously exposed

to the word *tools* will tend to identify words such as *hammer* or *saw* a bit more quickly than words such as *bread* or *potato* that signify foods, and the other group will do the opposite. The unconscious exposure of the initial word has acted as a *prime* that has facilitated the perception of words in its class but not the words in the other class.

Currently, the study of subliminal primes has become common in experimental psychology. We now know that they can show effects on thinking, feeling, decision-making, psychophysiological response, and spontaneous behavior. In fact, they seem to be a preparatory phase of every single bit of experience and behavior, although I have not found this obvious extrapolation to be explicitly ventured—except in First Sight. But more on that in a moment.

Subliminal primes were not always so frequently and cheerfully studied by psychologists. In fact, only a few decades ago, anomalies like blindsight and subliminal effects received sporadic interest, but they were hotly debated, and much research and polemic was devoted to trying to explain them away as errors of experimental design or statistical evaluation. For example, one saw many snarky references to psychologists who might be silly enough to assume the existence of the *homunculus,* a little man inside the head who saw everything unconsciously in order to decide whether or not it should be admitted to consciousness. Clearly rational scientists were above recourse to such inner spirits. It is not clear that the debate over the reality of subliminal perception was ever conclusively resolved, although improvements in method did come from the controversy. What apparently happened instead is that some change in our culture permitted an implicit sense that the phenomena were more acceptable.

One big difference between the 1950s, when this debate raged most fiercely, and today is that the use of computers is now ubiquitous. Everyone accepts the fact that most of the "thinking" that a computer does never appears on the screen. Daryl Bem has proposed that this fact accounts for the current sense that unconscious cognitive processes are plausible. Trying to understand human thought by analogy to the "thinking" of computers is popular nowadays in experimental psychology. We metaphorically say that computers think, and then unconsciously apply a computer's ways of thinking back to ourselves.

Bem's explanation sounds reasonable to me. There are many "cybernetic" models of the mind that are now guiding research. One never hears snide remarks about the "homunculus" anymore, and new research using subliminal primes is reported in mainstream journals and conferences on an almost daily basis.

## UNCONSCIOUSLY EXPRESSIVE BEHAVIOR

Just as *experience* may reflect the influence of unconscious sensory information (subliminal perceptions), our *behaviors* may also reflect the action of unconscious mental processes and information. As Freud found, behavioral patterns such as neurotic symptoms may be unconsciously expressive of early traumas and unconscious conflicts.

Subliminal perception and unconscious expression of meaning are connected. In fact, we would have no way of knowing about subliminal perception unless the participant in an experiment gave a verbal report of some experience, or did something else that otherwise unwittingly implied the action of the subliminal information. In our subliminal interface with the world, there are two intertwined but discriminable aspects—a receptive side (subliminal perception) and an expressive side (unconsciously expressive behavior.)

Consider this psychological experiment. A group of participants is divided into two subgroups. One is exposed subliminally to words suggesting cooperation and group accomplishments. The other is exposed to words that have nothing to do with that. Then the participants are all placed into group discussions. Their behavior is rated according to how cooperative, friendly, and constructive it is. The subjects who have been primed with the words that implied the value of group cooperation are found to act more friendly and cooperatively. They are never consciously aware of the words that flickered as mere bits of light before their eyes. Yet their behavior is influenced by the meanings of the words. Their behavior unconsciously expresses the subliminal content. Are their perceptions also influenced? Presumably so, although in this particular study this is not measured. One would guess that they are quicker to see the friendly aspects of the persons around them, more alert to the possibilities of cheerful cooperation that the situation presents. And they act accordingly.

Unconsciously expressive behavior was of special interest to Sigmund Freud, and to the later generations of psychotherapists influenced by the psychoanalytic school of thought. In a day's work, a typical therapist might see a deep depression that proves to be expressing an old sense of guilt at taking someone's life in war, or deal with a child's attention problems that started after she was forced to "love" a stepfather and reject a father, or sympathize with the exaggerated symptoms of PMS that worsened in a woman after she discovered her husband's wish to have an affair. When the veteran is feeling too heavy to leave his bed he is not thinking of the act of killing, and while the child is too scattered to complete a homework assignment she is not remembering her betrayal of her father, and when the young wife is trying to cope with her swinging moods, she is not consciously in touch with the destruction of trust. Yet when these dots are connected in the therapy, the symptoms get better, demonstrating the expressive power of the unconscious experience.

We do not need to look to the especially painful situations of psycho-therapy to see unconsciously expressive behavior at work. In a real sense, every bit of behavior is unconsciously expressive. As I drive down the freeway, I continually adjust my speed as the situation develops, change lanes, lengthen or shorten the distance to the next car. Am I consciously deciding to do all these things? In a sense, I must be: no one is driving my car but me. But these are hardly conscious, deliberative decisions. If I reflect on my experience a bit after the fact, it is more that I change lanes, and then understand that I decided to do so. We say, "it was automatic." Decisions were somehow involved, but they were not the kind of conscious reflections that we might use in trying to evaluate an argument or plan a vacation or solve an equation. They are really more unconscious than conscious, and they are taking into account a flood of information that barely enters my reflective awareness.

Judging from the wealth of unconscious priming studies that appear in the psychological literature, subliminal perception must be going on all the time, although the studies never seem to present it that way. Scientific reporting rules require that one limit one's discussion to the situation being studied. As a theorist, I do not need to be so constrained.

## TWO ANALOGIES AT THE BASIS OF FIRST SIGHT THEORY

First Sight Theory assumes that extrasensory perception (ESP) is analogous to subliminal perception, and psychokinesis (PK) is analogous to unconsciously expressive behavior. In fact, it assumes that they are pretty much the same things and work in largely the same ways, except that the sensory constraints that are assumed with subliminal perception and unconsciously expressive behavior are removed. The interactions with the world that we call psi (EM interactions) take place beyond the sensory ken.

Removing these constraints places the organism into a very extended world in a primary way. It implies that the mind is unconsciously in touch with reality before it can ever impinge upon our sensory sphere. This is why the model is called *first sight*.

Psi has often been called *second sight*, implying that it is a mysterious and occasionally supplementary add-on to our normal sensory capacities. To say that psi is *first sight* is to say that it is primary, something that precedes our every thought and action. It always comes first.

## BASIC PREMISES

Two basic assumptions are required before this model of the mind can seem sensible. These premises may not be testable in themselves, but they may be very useful in providing a framework for other assertions that are testable.

1. *Organisms are psychologically unbounded. They transact with reality in an unconscious way beyond their sensory boundaries.* We refer to these transactions collectively as *psi*. We refer to the receptive aspect of these transactions as extrasensory perception (ESP), and the expressive side of the transactions as psychokinesis (PK). If the receptive transaction is associated with some event yet to occur in the future, we call it precognition.

2. *All experiences and all behaviors are constituted out of unconscious psychological processes carried out purposefully on multiple sources of information, including psi (EM) information, as mediated by unconscious intention and contextual appraisal. Some of these processes are preparatory for others. Psi processes initiate the preparatory chain.*

The first premise seems straightforward enough, however much one might think it true. The second premise must be unpacked and elaborated some to make more sense. It is about how the mind pre-consciously constructs every bit of experience and behavior.

- These unconscious construction processes are automatic in the sense that they are not volitionally conscious—we are not aware of choosing to do them. However, they are not impersonal or mechanical. They are not simply electrochemical neurological processes that mindlessly generate experience and behavior the way a chemical combination of hydrogen and oxygen can generate water. They are psychological processes. Insofar as it can think at all, an organism thinks unconsciously as well as consciously.

- It is important to emphasize that the automatic processes are not impersonally mechanical. They are personal and purposive. They are guided by the goals and values of the individual. Hence even in the same situation, their actions will never be quite the same for any two people. For example, when I was driving my car "unconsciously" as described above, many implicit decisions were made quickly without reflective deliberation. At the same time, these decisions were all purposive in that they acted toward fulfilling my goals of avoiding an accident and arriving at a specific location at a certain time.

- Unconscious thought considers multiple sources of information constantly, including psi information, as well as sensation, memory, imagination, goals, and values. Consideration of these various sources occurs rapidly, holistically, and efficiently.

- When it is forming a conscious perception, the mind unconsciously assesses with the goal of bringing to consciousness the most useful possible awareness at the moment, and prompting the most useful possible bit of behavior.

- This assessment is always in context. What matters most in a given moment is contingent upon the particular situation and its demands and objectives. This contextual assigning of importance may shift quickly as situations develop, and as internal considerations arise and compete for ascendance.

- Elements of meaningful information engaged beyond the sensory limits of the organism cannot properly be called perceptions, since they are by nature unconscious. First Sight

Theory calls them *prehensions,* a term borrowed from Alfred North Whitehead. The term means literally *to grasp,* and both the receptive and the active connotations of that are useful here. ESP grasps in the sense of taking something in as the meaning that it is, PK grasps something in the sense of seizing it and acting upon it.

- Since the constructing processes are unconscious, they are never directly available to introspection. Hence, there is no such thing as an "ESP experience," just as there is no "subliminal experience." Similarly, there is no "PK action" in the sense of something deliberately done. By the same token, there is no such thing as the deliberate expression of an unconscious prime or repressed motive.

- We can discern the action of unconscious processes of construction by virtue of their *inadvertent expressions.* I will have more to say about this later.

- Every bit of experience and behavior has a very rapid, preconscious history. For example, every perception is preceded by a host of subliminal prehensions of sensory information that are unconsciously assessed and holistically combined. Subliminal prehension is itself preceded by unconscious consultation of extrasensory prehensions that are also assessed and holistically merged. Subliminal prehensions guide and orient the development of conscious experience. Similarly, extrasensory prehensions orient the appraisal and use of subliminal sensory prehensions. All of these prehensions are assessed within the context of the particular and general objectives of the person whose mind is doing this constructing. Extrasensory prehensions initiate the constructive engagement with reality. They come first, hence they are our "first sight."

- This continuous, implicit guidance is the basic, every-moment, function of psi. It is what "psi is for." The occasional, sporadic incidents that we think of as "psi experiences" only represent the rare moments in which we can glimpse a continually ongoing unconscious process in action.

## IF PSI IS GOING ON ALL THE TIME, WHERE IS IT HIDING?

Common sense reminds us that we cannot see around corners, or predict tomorrow's news events, or make things happen just by wishing. If psi is real, and all this ongoing activity is actually happening, we should be able to see it somehow, shouldn't we? Where is psi hiding?

It is in the most obvious possible place. More commonly experienced than family or friends or work or play.

### *Psi is hiding in every thought*

Psi is implicitly present in every thought because it has acted as an initiating part of the processes that unconsciously crafted the thought. It is hiding because it is an intrinsically unconscious process. We can see it only by implication. Parapsychological experiments can be thought of as the ways we have developed to see something about this process at work. Explicitly construing psi this way can help us develop better experiments that allow us to see these things more clearly.

### An example

Let me illustrate these ideas with a vivid experience that an acquaintance had recently. He injured his knee. How? By running away, as hard as he could, from an angry swarm of bees that he had stirred up while walking in the woods. They chased him fiercely for at least 30 yards, stinging him on the wrist and face, and leaving several stingers in his jacket.

His experience, and his story, begins with the bees and the need to escape. However, we know from much psychological research that there is a preamble to the story that he does not know about. We know that each experience has an unconscious prehistory. Before he understood that a swarm of bees was after him, there was a part of a second in which he knew that small moving things were in the air; he did not yet know what to make of them, but sensed that they were important and needed to be understood. A split second before that, tiny flickers of movement registered in his preconscious mind subliminally, and he was unconsciously alerted to attend to a certain area because something important was about to develop. And even before that, according to First Sight Theory, he became alerted extrasensorily to danger in a certain direction. This pre-sensory warning sharpened his subliminal attention in a certain place and toward a certain class of meaning and helped him understand as quickly as possible the need to run from bees!

This, assuming it happened as I say, is ESP at work. There is no ESP "experience," no precognitive dream, no telepathic message uncertainly deciphered. There is a preconscious process going on that involves reality beyond the bounds of the senses, which helps guide the development of each bit of experience and behavior. This is ESP as we use it constantly.

Why do we need to assume that there is a subliminal sensory orienting of attention and emotion in the direction of the bees shortly before anything is consciously experienced? Because it is easy enough for psychologists in experiments to contrive situations that let them catch evidence of such pre-experiential orientation. Just expose something too briefly to see consciously and then ask the right questions. Why should we assume that an extrasensory quickening of attention begins even before that? Because parapsychologists in their experiments also catch evidence of such preconscious responses when sensory access to the information is entirely blocked. We know that these things happen. We know that even our crude experiments can show it. It seems absurd to stretch the principle of parsimony to the point that we assume these things only occur in certain moments in laboratories. They must go on all the time. And our minds must have inherited these capacities because they were so useful in our evolutionary development.

## TWO NEGATIVE FACTS

Even by the late 1930s, when J. B. Rhine's *Extrasensory Perception* was published, a couple of negative conclusions about psi were evident, and all of the subsequent research has reinforced them.

1. Obvious psi experiences, such as significant deviations in card tests, or dramatically precognitive dreams, do not go on all the time. They are more often absent from our experience than present.

2. When psi is measured in an experiment, the direction of the deviation is not always positive. It is often negative, below chance expectation. This is something that probably would never have come to light in naturalistic observation of everyday experience. We would not keep such careful track of dreams

that do not come true to notice that they lead away from the actual future more than they should by simple chance. Yet this is what the research shows to happen sometimes.

The innocent skeptic in each of us recoils at these facts and needs to be reassured that this is not a wild goose chase. As I said above, what tells us that psi in fact goes on at least some times is the powerful results of many well-conducted studies, and the powerful statistics that we find when good studies are combined into meta-analyses. Yet clearly it is a messy picture.

Of course, it could not be otherwise. If obvious expressions of psi were not sporadic and sometimes misleading, they would never have seemed like mysteries. Like hearing and vision, we would use them comfortably and unthinkingly from the moment of birth. Obviously, if they are in fact genuine engagements with reality, they are not simple senses that by some miracle no one had noticed before. They are something else.

## TWO BASIC GOALS OF A SCIENCE OF PSI

While there are many things we might hope to learn about psi, two of them are bedrock.

1. We need to be able to understand and predict when expressions of psi will be strong enough to be visible in experiments and in everyday life.

2. We need to be able to understand and predict whether the expressions of psi will be truth-telling (positive, above-chance expectation) or lie-telling (negative, below-chance expectation).

This is why we need a theory that helps us understand how psi works and guides us to make these predictions. The rest of this chapter spells out how First Sight Theory attempts to address these goals.

## A FEW TERMS

You can understand the basics of First Sight Theory (FST) without learning a ponderous new vocabulary. However, a few terms are new, or are used in unusual ways, so they bear mentioning at the outset. You have already been introduced to a few of them.

- *Prehension:* This is a basic act of engagement with some aspect of a meaningful reality. In the context of FST, prehensions are understood to sometimes be unconscious and active beyond the bounds of the sensory sphere.

- *Personal Unconscious Psychological Processes* (PUPPS): These are processes of engagement (classes of prehensions) that the mind employs unconsciously toward the end of constructing behavior and experience. These include long-term memory, creative gestations, implicit goals and values, subliminal sensation, and psi.

- *Expressive Psi:* A psi prehension may be expressed either within one's own body, or outside of it, in the extended physical world. If the expression is within the body, it is the homely and constant process of doing what we unconsciously intend. It is common behavior, understood as a product of unconscious mental processes. If the expression of a psi prehension is beyond the body, in the behavior of objects, or in such things as the disease processes of other people, we speak of the expression as psychokinesis (PK), including mental healing. Parapsychologists usually think of such healing as one especially important kind of Distant Mental Influence on Living Systems (DMILS).

- *Receptive psi:* This includes extrasensory perception (ESP), clairvoyance, telepathy, remote viewing, and precognition.

- Unconscious Intention: FST assumes that everyone has intentions that are unconscious as well as conscious, and that these unconscious intentions are especially important in determining the expression of unconscious prehensions.

- *Direction:* Whether the expression of psi is positive or negative. A positive direction of expression leads to an increased likelihood that the meaning represented by a prehension will be expressed in some way. A negative direction of expression leads to a decreased likelihood of such expression.

- *Extremity:* The expression of a psi prehension may be either strong or weak. If it is strong, it may be noticed as an anomalous "psychic experience," or seen in a statistically significant departure from chance expectation in an experiment (a result extremely discrepant from chance expectation). If extremity is weak, no expression of psi will be discernable inside the lab or outside it.

- *Inadvertencies:* These are consciously non-meaningful experiences and behaviors that implicitly express unconscious prehensions. When specifically involving psi information, they are called *Psi Inadvertencies.*

*Direction* and *Extremity* are particularly important concerns in FST. They are assumed to be unconsciously "chosen" as a function of unconscious intention. *Direction* is determined by the valuation made in light of unconscious intention. *Extremity* depends upon the consistency of unconscious intention.

## SOME GENERAL FEATURES OF FIRST SIGHT THEORY

First Sight is a general theory. It is not limited to the understanding and prediction of psi phenomena, although its main point of application is that. It is intended to be a general framework for understanding how the mind unconsciously apprehends and makes use of reality in forming experience and behavior. It is a model of how we employ Personal Unconscious Psychological Processes (PUPPS). This includes how we make use of unconscious long-term memories, how we employ implicit goals and values, how we deal with subliminal sensory information, how we generate creative solutions to problems, how we intuitively grasp complex problems and form responses to them, how we transact with others nonverbally and intuitively. It also includes psi. In fact, it is an important working hypothesis of First Sight Theory (FST) that all of these processes of unconscious transaction tend to follow similar working patterns. This is an important idea in FST, called the *Hypothesis of Functional Similarity.* Because of this generality, FST is unabashedly cannibalistic. It takes in findings from these fields (memory, creativity, intuition, nonverbal communication, etc.) and does its best to assimilate the hard work that many bright people have done. This mainstream work has absorbed person-hours and funding undreamed of in parapsychology, and it is a rich source for general theory-building and cross-disciplinary collaboration.

First Sight is an existential but still scientific theory. As you read, you may notice an unusual tone to FST, which I try to keep constant. Consider these two statements:

1. "The subliminal stimulus aroused an implicit behavioral response."

2. "John's unconscious mind apprehended the subliminal information and used it to implicitly guide the construction of his next bit of behavior."

If you read scientific journals, the first statement feels familiar and comfortable, the second seems peculiar and unjustified. This is because we all work within a meta-theoretical framework that holds that a scientific statement must be reductionistic. The process "just happens" without any reference to intention. It must contribute some bit toward building that ultimately inclusive and completely impersonal account of everything toward which science strives. In many ways, this stance has been a good thing. It once wrested science free from the grip of the medieval church. It still protects science from unwarranted assumptions that might lead to countless dead-ends. But in regard to parapsychology, it is problematic. Extended Mind phenomena seem to imply the unconscious but purposive action of personal minds. First Sight Theory keeps this personal, purposive aspect front and center. It does not understand instances of psi as things that *happen to people*. It assumes that they are things that *people purposefully (but unconsciously) do*. Remember, an action may be purposive without being considered and deliberative. It only has to be modified or directed by an individual's goal and intention. Analogous phenomena happen continuously at an unconscious physiological level. For example, we know that the secretion of glucose (an unconscious process) begins to ramp up in the brain the instant strong muscular exertion is *about to be consciously decided upon*. The extra glucose is needed in light of the individual's purpose, to fuel the muscular work, but it is not consciously directed. At the same time, First Sight is intended to be a scientific theory in the sense that it should help build a predictive, "lawful" understanding of this strange class of events. Personally, I think that science in general will ultimately have to accommodate the primary reality of personal meaning. I am heartened that some theoretical physicists are also lately saying things that move in a similar direction.[10] Some psychologists have added their voices too, such as Joseph Rychlak.[11]

*If First Sight is on the right track, psi is different than we have thought*

- Psi is not rare or unusual. It is continuously active, although unconscious.

- Psi is not anomalous. It is normal, and follows familiar patterns found with many well-studied psychological processes.

- Psi does not belong only to a few gifted people. It is universal and used by everyone all the time.

- Psi is not inherently unpredictable. It is utterly reliable in its implicit use, and its predictability is something our scientific work needs to build.

- Psi is not a magical and arbitrary "bolt from the blue" carried out by mysterious and alien forces. It is something people do in the context of their purposes, just as with everything else they do.

- Psi is not disturbing or dangerous. Its expression is not aberrant or psychologically unhealthy. It is ordinary and beautifully useful.

## TWO BASIC CHARACTERISTICS OF PSI

*Psi is unconscious.* It is intrinsically unavailable to direct experience. We cannot feel it going on, or "read" its contents. It is like many other biological and psychological processes that we cannot directly experience, such as the secretion of enzymes for digestion, or the "blinding" of extraneous features in the formation of visual gestalts. There are no psychic experiences or psychokinetic actions, in the conscious, deliberate way we normally speak of experience and action.

*Psi is bidirectional.* A psi prehension may direct us toward an expression of a meaning in experience and action, or it may point us in the other direction, away from such expression. This is more than it first appears. Pointing toward the thing is obvious enough. Like a subliminal prime, it may lead us to feel the suggested feeling, or be quicker to perceive the class of meanings. However, it may do the opposite. This does not represent a simple failure to include the meaning. It means that the meaning is kept out of expression to a greater degree than it would be simply by chance.

A similar process has been observed in research on subliminal perception (another PUPP). If a prime is associated with something that a participant in the experiment has been encouraged to avoid, that same information tends to be less easily perceived than it would be simply by chance. This has been called *negative priming*. In parapsychology the analogous phenomenon is called *psi-missing*.

Negative memory has also been studied to some extent. I expect that many of you, like me, have had the embarrassing experience of telling some interesting story about something that happened to you long in the past only to find out that it had actually happened to someone else! This is why we understand that memory cannot always be trusted. It can reverse in important ways. All PUPPS are bidirectional, and can work negatively as well as positively.

*Since psi (like all PUPPS) is an unconscious process, its action can only be seen implicitly*

All PUPPS are basically orienting processes that contribute to an optimal apprehension of situations and an optimal response to them. These processes are unconscious by their nature. But being orienting processes, it is possible to discern traces of the resulting orientations in experience and behavior. It is usually easier to see this in other people than in ourselves.

Consider one prominent PUPP, subliminal perception. We know that subliminal apprehensions can act as primes, evoking feelings or making different classes of meaning more accessible to awareness, etc. For example, subliminal primes suggesting love and security have been shown to evoke happier ratings on mood scales and lower physiological distress when arousal is measured by appropriate instruments. In such studies, the mood ratings and the psychophysiological measures are *implicit measures* in regard to the primes. The participant producing these behaviors does not understand the relationship between the prime and the behavior. She produced the behavior inadvertently from her point of view. It is only the researcher who is privileged to see the connection.

If we ask the participant, "Are you calmer because of the flicker of light that you just saw?" or "Can you tell me what words were just flashed on the screen?" these would be *explicit measures*. And the responses would not be very accurate. They probably would not be reliably different from chance. In assessing the action of PUPPS, implicit measures work much better than explicit measures.

Here is the nub of it. The mind uses psi prehensions to orient its unconscious, preconscious processes. This orientation is toward certain meanings, or away from them, depending upon the direction unconsciously chosen. The orientation guides the development of optimal acts of behavior and physiological response and conscious experience. Before consciousness can be achieved, the preconscious orientations can be glimpsed at work by attention to the inadvertent implications of behavior, physiological response, and unfocused bits of conscious experience.

There are three main classes of inadvertent events that may implicitly express psi prehensions:

1. Implicit experiences. One may experience a visual image, or a dream, or feel a shift of mood that proves to bear an implicit reference to a psi prehension.

2. Implicit behaviors. One may make a choice that turns out later to be propitious, as if it referred to that future event; or generate subtle levels of physiological arousal that are found to be correlated with stressful stimuli that will soon be experienced.

3. Implicitly meaningful actions of some physical process beyond the physical boundaries of the individual. At the moment of a beloved man's death in another state, a book that had been a gift from him might anomalously fall from its shelf onto the floor. While wishing for certain deflections on a computer monitor, a random event generator wired into the system may mysteriously cooperate by generating enough numbers of a certain kind to produce the deflection. We speak of such things as PK.

In each of these cases, the expression of psi is always implicit and inadvertent, from the point of view of the one producing the behavior.

You might object, "What about psychic experiences? Aren't they what started parapsychology to begin with? Are you saying they are not real?

No, not at all. But a little reflection lets us see that they all can be understood as implicit expressions of an unconscious process. It is just that they are instances in which the inadvertent connection can be seen by the person experiencing it. Let me revisit the handful of experiences that I used earlier to represent puzzling psychic events. In one case, you had a dream of burning buildings right before 9/11. In another your aunt can predict who is calling on the phone. In the third, a medium gives you a nickname known only by you and your dead father. In the last, a friend is healed of a deadly cancer after prayer. None of these represent explicit knowledge or action.

You no more controlled the content of your dream than you can control any dream. When you woke from it you did not know that an attack was coming. You see the connection only in retrospect. Your aunt does not know what person is calling in the way she explicitly knows whether or not it is raining by looking outside the window. When the phone rings, a certain face or name pops into her mind unbidden. She has learned that this popped-up picture often tells the truth, so she expresses it. Similarly, the medium is "hearing" a dissociated "voice" who gives him surprising bits of material, again uncontrolled and largely unbidden. He trusts this voice enough to tell you about it. Your friend's church members do not explicitly act upon his cancer the way a surgeon or a radiation oncologist does. They neither cut, nor burn, nor see their action explicitly performed. They appeal to a gracious God, and hope and perhaps expect some good results. When they learn of the cure, its occurrence is mysterious (implicit), and they are at least partly surprised.

In any case, such dramatic, visible expressions of psi at work are rare. If FST is correct, subtler expressions are ongoing all the time, and we can see these too, given proper procedures.

Are there such people as "psychics," from the point of view of First Sight? Yes. They are people who have come to be unusually good at interpreting implicit contingencies in their own inadvertent experience and behavior.

Are there such people as "physical mediums" or "healers" or "poltergeist agents?" Yes. They are people who are unusually prone to express psi prehensions in the behavior of physical systems *beyond* their own bodies, rather than in the implicit behavior *of* their own bodies. Like the person demonstrating physiological arousal to a distant stimulus, or the one who inadvertently chooses some alternative with a good outcome rather than one with a bad outcome, these people express psi prehensions implicitly. In their case, however, it is the behavior of physical systems beyond their physical reach that implicitly express their prehension.

*Assuming that psi is unconscious and bidirectional*
*leads us to think of research on psi differently*

- Studies should rely less on asking participants to produce deliberate expressions of psi information in hopes that the right conditions will somehow evoke it and catch it. Instead of trying to capture an instance of a rare ability, we should try to find evidence of an implicit, ongoing process in action. We will not try to capture psi, as much as reveal it.

- In framing our hypotheses about how psi should be implicitly expressed, we should borrow liberally from our numerous and better-funded colleagues in mainstream science who also study PUPPS, acting in the spirit of the Hypothesis of Functional Similarity. We will get many good leads. At the same time, we will contribute to mainstream science by exploring processes that most scientists do not know about but that nevertheless impinge in countless ways upon things they study.

- We should try to construct hypotheses about factors that predict the direction of the expression of psi (assimilation or exclusion) and factors that affect the extremity or strength of the expression (heavily or lightly weighted) separately, and test them independently. This has rarely been done in parapsychological research in the past.

SUMMING UP

In trying to understand and predict psi (EM) occurrences, we need to look at two aspects of them: whether they will be positive expressions (assimilation) or negative expressions (avoided rejections), and we need to know whether these expressions will be strong or weak. We will look to the hypothesized unconscious intentions of the person involved to try to determine this. We will want to know if those intentions should lead the person to assimilate or reject the information, and we will want to know how consistently and strongly those directional intentions will be maintained. Since such hypothetical unconscious intentions are not directly observable, to try to predict their direction and consistency, we will look at some other things that can be observed and measured, which we expect to predict direction and consistency in different ways. We will look at various aspects of the information itself in the context of the situation at the moment and the needs of the particular person. And we will look at various momentary and more habitual states and attitudes of the person. And we will assess certain qualities of the situation. In each of these areas, FST generates testable hypotheses. A fair amount of evidence supporting some of them has already accumulated, although almost all of it has accumulated willy-nilly, without benefit of theoretical guidance.

Does all of this seem complex? Well, yes it is, to some extent, but it is really no more complex than trying to predict any meaningful human behavior. It makes this effort seem less complex to remember that we are using the very same sorts of considerations that psychologists have found useful in predicting "normal" sensory behavior.

From a First Sight perspective, certain kinds of research questions spring to mind more readily than others. We will not tend to be especially interested in knowing the chemical constitution of a PK target, for instance, or whether or not a participant is shielded from ambient electromagnetic radiation. We will be more inclined to ask questions like the following:

- What most arrests a person's attention?

- What is most interesting and important to a particular person, or group of persons?

- How do we access any implicit meanings differently depending upon different situations or states of mind?

- What needs are most salient for different people or groups of people?

- What factors are known to influence unconscious psychological processes other than psi, such as subliminal perception or memory? What kinds of influence are observed?

- What kinds of goals are most likely to be pursued at a persistent pitch?

- What sorts of people are most able to sustain an intention over time? (These last two are presumed to relate to the strength of an effect, independent of its direction.)

*In a Nutshell*

Parapsychology needs a theory, and in First Sight, parapsychology has a theory—a psychological theory. Does it tell us the truth? So far, it seems to, at least to some extent. However, almost all of the good research that we need to do to really test it and improve it has not been done yet. Such is the fledgling state of this borderline field. All that we have to do is very exciting. It is no less than an extremely important, but almost completely unmapped, new world of engagement with reality that we have yet to learn about.

More important than whether or not First Sight is telling us the truth is whether or not it will be a useful scaffold upon which to build meaningful research that will lead us to truth, brick by brick. I do believe that it can be useful in that way.

If we are on the right track, even in very general terms, we must change our ideas about what psi is and how we should study it.

To reiterate, psi is not rare, it is constantly active and present.

It is not unpredictable and unruly, it is potentially quite lawful and understandable.

Psi is not something that belongs only to a few rare people and special circumstances. It is something that everybody uses all the time unconsciously.

Psi is not tricky and unreliable. It is extremely useful.

It is not inscrutable and hopelessly mysterious. It can be studied with normal methods of inquiry.

In the briefest nutshell, I close with the words of the eminent psychologist Daryl Bem, from a review he wrote of *First Sight:* Psi is not a psychological anomaly.

## CHAPTER FIVE

# First Sight:
# A Whiteheadian Perspective

*John H. Buchanan*

ABSTRACT: *This chapter explores the close similarities, as well as some differences, between James Carpenter's First Sight Theory and Alfred North Whitehead's process philosophy. Their close affinity arises from a number of shared commitments, but it is reflected most closely in Carpenter's use of Whitehead's term prehension, a direct intuitive grasping of past experience, to describe the basic functioning of extrasensory perception. It is argued that Whitehead's metaphysics can answer Carpenter's call for a metapsychology capable of providing a fundamental experiential framework for parapsychology: one that unifies it with the general field of psychology and science at large. Whitehead's philosophy is able to serve such a function for a number of reasons, including its sophisticated theory of the psyche, its coherent account of mind-body interaction, a theory of perception that includes the possibility of direct intuitions of external realities, as well as a panexperiential understanding of the nature of reality.*

PART ONE: WHITEHEAD AND TRANSPERSONAL ANOMALIES

SEVERAL JOURNEYS with psychedelic substances in my late teens first brought to my attention, in a most vivid fashion, the inadequacy of the modern worldview not only for interpreting these extraordinary experiences, but also for understanding human experience in general. After searching long and hard for the best way to make sense of these troubling issues—namely, the meaning of transpersonal and parapsychological phenomena and the nature of reality—I was fortunate enough to be pointed towards "process thought," in particular, Alfred North Whitehead's philosophy of organism. Whitehead's highly original analysis of the nature of reality and the cosmos brings together, in one coherent system, the findings of contemporary science, and our moral and religious intuitions, with the ultimate aim of taking into account the entire range of human experience.

I have found Whitehead's metaphysics to be a powerful tool for explicating many "anomalies" in the fields of parapsychology and transpersonal psychology. Not coincidentally, these same anomalies are particularly useful for revealing where our current philosophical and scientific thinking is in most need of revision.

After reviewing why process thought is so valuable in this regard, I turn a Whiteheadian eye to James Carpenter's extraordinary parapsychological theory, "First Sight." His book, of the same name, presents an original integrative theory that demonstrates a comprehensive and robust command of the parapsychological field. And, as it turns out, First Sight shares much of Whitehead's vision.

## WHY WHITEHEAD?

Transpersonal psychology, including the field of parapsychology, is an ideal subject to interface with Whitehead's philosophy—for a number of reasons. First, Whitehead provides a unique theory of "mind." Unlike most contemporary theories, the human psyche is not seen as an epiphenomenon of the brain, as a dual aspect of brain activity, or as solely dependent on neuronal functioning. Rather, the human psyche is envisioned as a series of momentary *occasions of experience*. These occasions arise out of the *direct reception* of data from past events, which are then synthesized into a unified experiential "feeling." Almost all of this integrative activity takes place at an unconscious level; consciousness is the occasional "crown of experience."

Second, Whitehead's theory of mind is also a more general theory of *experience* as the fundamental mode of reality. The universe is an "ocean of feeling," an interflowing, interconnected matrix of momentary events. These events (occasions of experience) interact to produce the more complex entities and organic communities that populate our universe. (Whitehead, however, is not suggesting that "everything is consciousness," or that rocks and cars have a guiding center of awareness. Rather, many of our world's macroscopic objects are composites or *aggregates* of the truly subjective events that occupy our universe, such as those belonging to electrons, atoms, molecules, cells, and animals.)

Third, Whitehead provides a workable model of mind/brain interaction. Neurons, too, are made up of subjective events and are in constant interaction with the momentary events that make up the human psyche. Thus both the human psyche and the body's neurons are understood to be series of momentary events composed of integrative, subjective activity; the crucial difference between psychic and neural events being one of complexity, not kind. Presumably, the experiential activity of neuronal occasions always occurs at an *unconscious* level, while human psychical occasions, of course, often entail conscious awareness. Let me clarify that I am describing two different levels of the "unconscious" here, both of which are factors in human experience. First are the unconscious feelings and activity of the brain's neurons; these feelings enter directly into the foundation of every moment of the human psyche. Second, there are the unconscious psychological processes that occur *within* the occasions of experience constituting the flow of the human psyche.

The neural event matrix of the brain is in constant, direct interaction with the succession of experiential events that constitute the human psyche. Causal influence flows between *all* events: thus this system exhibits both the bottom-up *and* top-down causation characteristic of Whitehead's model. While in conflict with strict materialistic interpretations, this notion of causality is in accord with our everyday experience of mind/body interaction, with the body's feelings flowing into our awareness and our psyche's conscious intention directly influencing the body's actions.

Fourth, Whitehead also provides a novel theory of perception that makes comprehensible (admittedly, in a rather complex manner) our interactions with the world and our knowledge about it. Three modes are theorized: the primary perceptual mode of *causal efficacy*, which involves the direct flow of data from past events into the newly forming event; *presentational immediacy*, which represents our sheer conscious sensory awareness; and *symbolic reference*, the final phase of our normal perception whereby the other two modes are synthesized to create our everyday world filled with meaningful objects.

Fifth, this theory of perception offers a primary mode of interacting with the world that precedes and surpasses normal sensory perception by providing the psyche *direct experiential contact* with past reality. Through this primary perceptual mode, Whitehead argues that telepathy is *possible,* though not necessarily real. Its actual existence is a subject for empirical investigation and verification.

Sixth, for our purposes here, two critical consequences follow from this novel theory of perception. First, this primary mode of perception (causal efficacy) means that nonordinary experiences—experiences beyond the normal range of everday life—are capable of conveying *real information and knowledge* about the nature of the universe and reality. Second, the entire universe is *intrinsically permeable and accessible* to this nonsensuous kind of perception hypothesized by Whitehead and Carpenter (as we will see.)

Furthermore, Whitehead's theory is open to the possibility of purely spiritual beings, and posits the existence of a central unifying entity that is in interaction with all of reality. Thus a wide variety of authentic mystical experiences are at least possible, if not likely, via enhanced perception in the "mode of causal efficacy."

Finally, Whitehead's metaphysics is congruent with current scientific theory and could thus provide not only a metatheory unifying transpersonal psychology with the rest of the field of psychology, it could also unite psychology with the other scientific fields, all within a paradigm based on the philosophy of organism: the universe understood as complex social organizations of self-actualizing quantum events.

## WHITEHEAD'S METAPHYSICS 101

While we will not be able to go into Whitehead's metaphysical ideas in any depth here, I do want to mention a few key notions that may prove helpful for exploring Carpenter's theory of First Sight.

*Actual occasions* are conceived as unified pulses (or moments) of synthesized feelings of past events. To arrive at this fundamental notion of reality, Whitehead's theory generalizes quantum events, and then combines them with William James's "drops" or pulses of experience, as a way of characterizing all basic entities in the universe.[1] Moreover, Whitehead also generalizes the insights of cell theory to describe the universe in terms of *societies of organisms*. By introducing momentary events as the fundamental underlying organic unit, Whitehead is able to coherently account for the real independence of individual events *and* for the direct interconnections between enduring individuals, such as molecules, cells, and human psyches.

Whitehead accomplishes this metaphysical breakthrough with his revolutionary notion of *prehension:* a direct grasping of the activity of past events, or to use his terminology, "occasions of experience." Primitive perceptions or "feelings" of past events enter directly into the subjective constitution of newly forming events. Thus events are internally related: that is, *experientially* interconnected and interflowing. This is the same fundamental process whereby quantum events create themselves out of their probability density matrices, that is, the influences from their field of past events. In sum, the universe is composed of socially connected fields of interacting bursts of feeling, which are intrinsically permeable to human intuition.

## A COMPLEX AMPLIFIER

Whitehead suggests that the human body can be thought of in terms of a *complex amplifier*.[2] The human organism acts as a magnifier of vibrations (pulses of feeling) from the universe, employing especially the sensory and nervous systems as antennas, transmitters, and amplifiers. The vague data that reaches our body is amplified into the more highly refined information that underlies our clear and distinct conscious sensory experience. Aside from this entire system being understood in terms of experiential events, this part of Whitehead's thought closely follows current neurophysiological theory.

What *is* quite different from the conventional scientific understanding of perception is that the *human psyche* functions in its own right as a receiver, an amplifier, and a transmitter. According to Whitehead's theory, the events of the psyche receive and provide additional amplification and transformation of the body and brain's previous processing of sensory data. And what is *really* different, and of utmost importance for the possibility of parapsychological and transpersonal phenomena, is that the psyche's events *also* receive and amplify the vague data flowing in directly from the *universe at large*. The completed psychic event, in turn, *radiates out* waves of intentional feeling that influence all future events. When the psyche acts as a receiver and amplifier of data/feelings coming directly from other human psyches, we call this intuition or telepathy. When the psyche is employed in the mode of projecting directed "waves of feeling," intention or psychokinesis may be the result.

## NONORDINARY STATES

One of our most experienced researchers into nonordinary states of consciousness, Stanislav Grof, offers a suggestive definition of psychedelics: nonspecific amplifiers of unconscious processes; or, in one of his earliest formulations, they are said to act as "a powerful unspecific amplifier or catalyst of biochemical and physiological processes in the brain . . . that facilitates the emergence of unconscious material."[3] Whitehead's analysis suggests two fundamental methods of generating this amplification of unconscious processes: first, through *intensification* of unconscious feeling using psychedelics, experiential therapy, dance and drumming rituals, or active meditations; second, through the *relaxation* of repression via insight meditation, relaxation methods, or sensory deprivation. By *repression,* I am pointing to a Whiteheadian reading of the standard psychoanalytic use of the term: a habitual patterning of experience that canalizes memory, emotion, and thought into familiar and safe modes of feeling. Both of these methods heighten access to normally unconscious intuitions and information: the first by overwhelming the repression barrier with intensified feeling, the second by "softening" this barrier and thereby facilitating the flow of unconscious material entering into conscious awareness.

Grof has described an incredibly rich array of transpersonal experiences that appear spontaneously and cross-culturally when normally unconscious feeling and information are allowed to emerge more fully into conscious awareness. Parapsychological phenomena constitute one small dimension of this wide range of extraordinary experiences that Grof has categorized phenomenologically in his transpersonal cartography (see, e.g., *Beyond the Brain*). However, because psychical phenomena are more amenable to experimental study, they are of special import for challenging the adequacy of the materialist paradigm, which is still often adopted, consciously or unconsciously, by modern—and postmodern—scientific and philosophic thought.

## PART TWO: FIRST SIGHT AND PROCESS VISION

### *Prehension versus Psi*

Reading through Carpenter's book, *First Sight,* I was fascinated by how well it meshes with Whiteheadian thought. Thus it was a surprise to discover that Carpenter did not have extensive knowledge of Whitehead's philosophy when he formulated his psi theory. Rather, Carpenter drew largely from his reading of McCurdy's ideas and use of prehension.[4] Whatever the origins of his theory may be, Carpenter's application of *prehension* for interpreting parapsychological phenomena fits extremely well with Whitehead's understanding of reality. Following closely in Whitehead's metaphysical footsteps, Carpenter writes: "*Prehension* should be understood to be a kind of grasping that can be both conscious and unconscious, and also both receptive and active."[5] In fact, the very name of his theory, First Sight, is evocative of Whitehead's belief that there exists a more *primary mode* of perception based on direct intuitions of past events. However, Carpenter does not "intend to imply all the connotations that Whitehead attached to the term."[6] Perhaps he is thinking here of Whitehead's complex and detailed analysis of the psyche's unconscious processes, as well as his elaboration of various subspecies of prehension. While one might also guess that Carpenter is putting in abeyance Whitehead's generalization of prehensive experience to *all* of reality, Carpenter does suggest that psi is an "ordinary and continuous part of the psychological functioning of all organisms."[7] Although Carpenter probably does not intend to make the full Whiteheadian turn of interpreting *all* of reality in terms of events, organisms, and societies thereof, as we shall see, this would have the benefit of making his psi theory of perception more coherent and would link it directly to a postmodern scientific understanding of reality that is congruent with contemporary physics.

## FORMATION OF EXPERIENCE

I have been assuming that the reader has already read Carpenter's essay on his theory of First Sight, which directly precedes this chapter. But just in case, let me give a partial introduction of sorts by comparing the *formation of experience* via Carpenter's special understanding of "psi" versus Whitehead's use of "prehension."

*Psi,* like Whitehead's notion of prehension, brings in data from the entire universe and constitutes the initial stage of all unconscious processing. For Carpenter, psi is not perception in the normal sense, nor an experience or ability.[8] Whitehead's theory is a bit more concrete on this point: prehension is perception in its most *basic* form: the direct experiential reception of past feeling—or, put another way, the direct feeling of past events.

Another thing to bear in mind is that Whitehead's analysis is based on how experience creates itself, in the form of a very brief event, as an "occasion of experience." For the human psyche, this duration is perhaps in the range of 1/10th to 1/20th of a second. My impression is that Carpenter's theorizing is operating in a more traditional framework, where multiple areas of human psychological and neurological activity overlap and interact to generate conscious awareness. Thus, when he says that psi guides and shapes intentional experience, but is not a form of perception, his model of the formation of experience is more loosely drawn than Whitehead's, which *would* say that "psi" (as *physical* prehensions) is a perceptual mode and that any feelings or data appearing in conscious experience *must* arise from prehensions occurring in the early unconscious phases. All in all, though, Whitehead's approach is very congenial with Carpenter's, who also says that psi is "the leading edge of the formation of all experience,"[9] as are physical prehensions in the philosophy of organism.

It may be helpful to examine more closely how both these theorists conceive of the phases or steps involved in the generation of human experience. We will quickly observe a close similarity between Whitehead's phases of concrescence and Carpenter's "Inner Roles."[10]

Whitehead describes all momentary events as being susceptible to "genetic analysis," that is, analyzable in terms of these phases of development. His first phase involves "grasping" (prehending) the feelings of past events: that is, the reception of data. The second phase heightens or lowers the importance of specific elements of the data by selecting certain possibilities for further processing. The third and fourth phases involve transmutation and more complex integrations to create a final synthesis—an occasion of experience.

Carpenter, independently, I believe, describes a similar process of experiential formation in terms of four "inner roles." Concerning his first phase, or step, Carpenter says that because "we are in touch with virtually everything," experience starts with a "narrowing process," which he names The Prophet. Carpenter associates this "initial step of selection and deselection" with "the basic psi process."[11] Thus, in effect, Carpenter is equating psi with what Whitehead calls "physical prehensions," direct causal connections of feeling flowing between past events and newly forming occasions. Carpenter's second phase is represented by The Artist, who sharpens attention to certain aspects of the selected data—just as latent potentials are highlighted during the second phase, according to Whitehead's analysis. The third phase ushers in The Scientist, who focuses attention more intensely, in a manner resembling the higher-level syntheses described by Whitehead, while The Person of Ordinary Consciousness *potentially* (not all human-level events include consciousness) emerges as the outcome of both theorists' final phase.[12]

The similarities seem obvious and reveal a deep theoretical sympathy. But there are some important additions that Whitehead can offer to better orient First Sight Theory both philosophically and scientifically, or at least to make clear certain points that might otherwise raise doubt or confusion.

For example, Carpenter suggests that we make our own experience.[13] However, even though each momentary event involves self-creation, that is, "makes itself," it is important to emphasize that past events also contribute greatly to our experience.[14] The trick is how to reconcile self-creation with the influence of past events: at one extreme lies idealism and even solipsism; at the other, strict determinism.

Whitehead's understanding of efficient and final causation is helpful for explicating how a human subject is involved with its world. Efficient or "physical" causation is understood simply as the effects of past events on newly forming moments of experience. How this differs from the materialist view is that this influence is an *internal* influence, the effect being directly absorbed into the new event's subjective activity. Final causation, or self-causation, is simply the occasion's own contributions to *how* it processes and synthesizes the data received from past events. As might be expected, simple events, such as atoms, tend merely to repeat what they receive; highly complex events like human psychic occasions are more prone to creative and original supplementations. In this way, the universe preserves order while also fostering novelty.

## CONSCIOUSNESS AND PSI

Moving on to the highest phase of experiential formation, we find conscious awareness. For both First Sight Theory and process philosophy, consciousness is the *crown* of mental processing, *not* its source. But how much of the feeling from the depths can reach the light of conscious experience? How much can *ever* be consciously revealed about the data buried within these unconscious depths?

Whitehead argues that the data from the early phases of unconscious activity cannot enter *directly* into consciousness, because all feelings from the primitive phases of experience must undergo extensive processing. "It seems as though in practice, for human beings at least, only transmuted feelings acquire consciousness, never simple physical feelings."[15] In other words, data from the earliest phases of experiential processing, what Carpenter calls psi, never enter unchanged into conscious awareness.

According to First Sight, too, psi data itself cannot be directly experienced consciously. Carpenter puts strict limits on this possibility: "The extrasensory exchange is intrinsically preconscious and not ever available to consciousness... It is not the case that we 'know' via psi and then somehow inhibit that 'knowing' in favor of conscious awareness." Carpenter does not want to explain this in terms of a barrier or filter that prevents this material from reaching consciousness. "A better metaphor than 'filter' would be to say that preconscious psi prehensions are not blocked from consciousness but rather serve as a bridge to it."[16]

One thing Carpenter is getting at here is that we should *expect* parapsychological phenomena to be vague and dimly perceived. Whitehead says the same about perception in the mode of causal efficacy; only presentational immediacy is dependably clear and distinct. An unfortunate consequence of this situation is that scientific and philosophic reasoning, which rely primarily on "clear and distinct" evidence, necessarily neglect fundamental and valuable aspects of reality.

However, awareness does sometimes open up much more clearly to those feelings from the earlier phases: in particular, in nonordinary experiences. But even during extraordinary states of consciousness, Grof finds little unambiguous evidence of parapsychological phenomena such as telepathy or psychokinesis. Why are these psi powers so elusive even during nonordinary states, which are often so effective for accessing data from the early phases of unconscious experience?

Perhaps this elusiveness is due in part to a phenomenon that Carpenter elucidates in *First Sight*. The more *focused* one's attention, the less accessible psi data becomes. Thus when we make an attempt to "capture" or hone in on a psi insight, consciously or unconsciously, this very action of focusing attention undermines the unconscious channels that have been open to psi data (see Carpenter's "switching corollary").[17] Other possible reasons for this "elusiveness" are discussed later in this chapter.

## PSYCHOKINESIS AND ESP

ESP, functioning via Carpenter's psi or through Whitehead's prehension, is founded on the psyche's immediate unconscious connection to the universe at large. In this way, data from past events enter directly into human experience, creating the potential for telepathic access to other entities. Thus the possibility of telepathy or ESP is a natural consequence of the very structure of human experience—and of reality. In the same way that the direct flow of past data into new occasions creates the possibility of ESP, so, too, the flow of data *out of* the completed event provides a mechanism for psychokinesis (PK). These paranormal faculties are two sides of the same causal process operative in all human experience.

This is why Carpenter views ESP and PK as *reciprocal* functions, depending on which side of the effect you consider. Or, as Carpenter puts it: "Psychokinesis is the *expression* of psi information. Extrasensory perception is the *impression* of psi information as it is reflected in the experience or behavior of a person or other organism."[18] This bears a remarkable resemblance to David Griffin's characterization of ESP as *receptive* psi and PK as *expressive* psi.

Both also see PK as arising out of an *unconscious intention*. Griffin recognizes the depth conscious as the region of experience with sufficient latent power to create PK effects. From his Whiteheadian perspective, Griffin envisions PK as an intention cascading through future events as a *persuasive attunement* arising out of hybrid physical prehensions reverberating and amplifying through a series of human occasions in order to generate the necessary intentional impact on another entity.

Whitehead's metaphysical interpretation of *all* actuality being composed of "organisms"—that is, of occasions of experience and their associated social groupings—helps explain how PK effects could be extended to physical objects, which are not usually thought of as having "minds" to influence. From a Whiteheadian perspective, though, the multilayered atomic events that aggregate into so-called physical objects are themselves simple "organisms" capable of receiving and responding to "persuasive attunements" radiating out from a human psyche. In this regard, it may be helpful to imagine such attunements in terms of inducing a change in the "vibrational" patterns of organization of the relevant object.

But PK has a more prosaic, and much more critical, function than influencing dice or the bending of spoons. Carpenter suggests that the primary function of PK is to bring intention to the processes of the nervous system; that is, PK is responsible for mind-brain interaction.[19]

This is similar to Whitehead's outlook, where neurons feel/prehend the intentions of the psyche. In fact, the momentary events of the human psyche are seen to be in especially intense and intimate interrelationship with the neural cellular events. This continuous interactive process is so central to human experience that it might be prudent to distinguish mind/body "psi" relations from those psi prehensions that access events *outside* the body/mind channels, which might be thought of as ESP and PK "proper."

## THE PROBLEM OF PRECOGNITION

Parapsychological evidence for precognition, if its implications are taken to confirm absolute knowledge of the future, presents a serious challenge to Whitehead's entire philosophical edifice. For *true* precognition implies *total determinism;* this is in direct conflict with the creativity that lies at the heart of process thought. This interpretation of precognition would also undermine Whitehead's understanding of causality and the nature of time, making Whitehead's metaphysical scheme untenable.

I do not think many theorists who advocate for the authenticity of precognitive experiences intend to imply a completely deterministic view of reality.[20] Nor do I believe they are endorsing a rejection of basic logical principles. For example: *logically,* for future events to be truly known in advance, they must already fully exist; but then they are not actually in the future, which, by definition, consists of those events that do not yet exist as accomplished facts.

Some of the more difficult precognitive studies to explain without recourse to "true" precognition are the *presentiment* experiments performed by Dean Radin, and others.[21] Some of these parapsychological experiments do seem to suggest that definite knowledge about the future is obtained. For example, a series of studies measuring "anticipatory" or "prestimulus" response found that subjects reacted to a disturbing—versus nondisturbing—stimulus shortly *before* it was displayed. This "preresponse" was in the form of small, but statistically significant, physiological reactions such as changes in electrodermal activity.[22] Significantly, these changes occurred *before* a random number generator selected which type of stimulus to display.

Carpenter does say that there is no evidence of conscious or clear knowledge of the future.[23] Indications of precognitive activity tend to be reflected only through inadvertent behaviors and unconscious physiological processes. Like other psi phenomena, precognitive psi activity tends to be vague and to occur at the margins of awareness, which might be taken to suggest that this information itself is "tentative," that is, not a direct perception of a future event. (Or, it could simply be the usual haziness that surrounds most psychic phenomena.)

But what to make of these studies that seem to show that subjects exhibit heightened physiological responses *before* viewing emotionally evocative stimuli, which have been selected by a random number generator? How might advance knowledge of a random future event be understood from a Whiteheadian perspective?

David Griffin has given this matter much thought. While he believes that evidence of precognition exists, he also argues that the explanation for this *cannot* be that future events have been directly perceived, that is, that retrocausation has taken place. Griffin offers a number of alternative *nondeterministic* explanations for precognitive phenomena, some of which are described in his excellent *Parapsychology, Philosophy, and Spirituality.*[24]

Griffin's four primary alternative explanations for precognitive phenomena are as follows.

1. They really only involve knowledge of a *probable* future, not a settled one.

2. They might arise from clairvoyance combined with unconscious inference.

3. They might be due to telepathy combined with unconscious inference.

4. They might result from psychokinesis influencing future events to conform them to one's "precognitive" intuitions.

(Griffin also suggests a number of other more remote possibilities, such as nonhuman spiritual entities influencing events.)

While these interpretations may well account for many cases of precognition, I do not see how any of Griffin's principal alternatives would be easily applicable to these "presentiment/prestimulus response" study results. Random number generators do not seem susceptible to telepathic or clairvoyant probing in a way that would reveal reliable information about their future activity, nor to relevant psychokinetic manipulation.

It appears to me that the issue of precognition is still an open one. Nevertheless, any theory of precognition that asserts the existence of apodictic perceptions of a settled future must be vigorously questioned by Whiteheadians, since this kind of literal precognition would seriously undermine process philosophy's metaphysical understanding of reality— and our everyday understanding of reality as well.

## A PROCESS METATHEORY

Carpenter wants parapsychology to become an integral part of the field of psychology.[25] Whitehead's philosophical scheme presents an effective route for making that a reality. A metaphysical approach of this kind would appear necessary to resolve the issues that have led parapsychology to be relegated to the outer fringes of the psychological community, since these problematic issues are themselves based on some old and deeply imbedded metaphysical hypotheses. While First Sight takes a phenomenological stance and assumes the experiential unity of mind and body,[26] Whitehead offers a detailed positive interpretation of this issue, one that has significant implications for all of psychology.

Whitehead's philosophy furnishes a direct link to neurophysiology by offering a unified framework for understanding the entities studied by psychology and neurology. We have already seen how "mind-body" interaction is coherently conceived within a Whiteheadian model. This same model should prove useful for studying the activity of neural cells all the way down to their molecular and sub-molecular components. This is especially the case as more and more scientific discoveries reveal a surprising amount of spontaneity, responsiveness, and decision-making present at these microscopic levels.

Furthermore, the philosophy of organism could bring the entire field of psychology into coordination with contemporary physics through a shared understanding of the fundamental nature of reality in terms of unitary, interacting events. This intimate relationship with contemporary physics is not coincidental: Whitehead's metaphysics was specifically designed to fully incorporate both quantum theory and relativity.

Carpenter writes that what scientists from other fields want from parapsychologists are replicable psi experiments and a mechanism for how the mind can interact with distant minds and matter.[27] Whitehead provides just such a mechanism: the human psyche as a complex amplifier of the direct intuitions it receives from past events. Whitehead also offers some novel reasons why experimental replicability has proven difficult.

If the human nervous system has evolved to collect the kind of information that is most central to our survival, then our psyches should be highly attuned to focus on those things revealed by conscious sensory perception—which, according to Whitehead, is largely dependent on the unconscious activity of "transmutation." *Transmutation,* which is similar to First Sight's holistic weighing and averaging,[28] is the process whereby many unconscious feelings or individual bits of data are unified into one general impression. For example, we perceive a rock as a grey mass, not as thousands of small grey dots. As an analogy, think of how a George Seurat painting looks at a distance (transmutation), versus close up. Which of these ways of seeing the world would work better for surviving in a dangerous environment? While such focusing of awareness on the highly refined product of conscious sense perception is helpful for many human activities, it also turns attention away from the much more subtle and vague intuitions related to psi phenomena.

A related factor that might impede psi reception, especially ESP, is that data from the early unconscious phases of experience appears only weakly in conscious experience, *especially* when derived from a single event, such as another human mind. "Owing to the vagueness of our conscious analysis . . . perhaps we never consciously discriminate one simple physical feeling in isolation."[29] Furthermore, *hybrid* physical prehensions, upon which telepathic communication would likely be based, may be even more difficult to distinguish than pure physical prehensions.

On another note, Whitehead's philosophy and First Sight appear to be on common ground regarding the moral implications of psi phenomena. Both would seem to be in agreement with the spiritual traditions that hold it is self-defeating to use psi powers for selfish ends, as we share a deep community with all things, but neither would see anything inherently harmful in psychic powers per se. Hopefully, these theories can help heal any remaining rift between parapsychology and transpersonal psychology, which have been divided at times over the significance of parapsychology—very unnecessarily, I think. Whitehead's philosophy places psi powers in the same general field of phenomena as other spiritual experiences, thus they should not be considered inherently problematic, but rather, as with most things, judged by *how* they are used. I believe this would be a welcome correction to the past tendency in some quarters to downplay the theoretical and applied importance of psi, apparently following in the footsteps of some Eastern spiritual schools that portray parapsychological phenomena as mere distractions along the way to enlightenment. While this may be true as far as it goes, it does not seem an adequate justification to disregard an entire range of human experience, especially when these phenomena may well play an important role in the evolution of human consciousness, along with yielding remarkable anomalies that could help guide us towards the reformulations necessary for realizing a new postmodern paradigm.

Finally, Carpenter writes evocatively that his theory suggests we are not "ultimately alone": we swim in an "unconscious sea."[30] The Whiteheadian idea of the universe as an "ocean of feeling" embodies a comprehensive cosmology that explains in exactly what sense these things are true. Carpenter's "unconscious sea" in which we swim, according to Whitehead, is a universe composed of mostly unconscious experiential events, some of which are occasionally crowned by consciousness. The Whiteheadian "ocean of feeling" bestows a pervasive flowing environment that embraces and connects us all, so that we are *not* ultimately alone. This cosmology also helps account for Carpenter's conviction that each person is epistemologically and ontologically extended into all of reality.[31] Such a conviction flows naturally out of Whitehead's vision of each new moment arising out of its feelings of the entire past, and then informing all future events. To paraphrase Whitehead's ultimate principle: The many become one, then the new one joins that many—in an everlastingly process.

## CONCLUSION

This essay has concentrated primarily on how Whitehead's ideas could be of benefit to parapsychology. Equally important is how parapsychology, in particular Carpenter's theory of First Sight, provides strong support for Whitehead's revolutionary understanding of the nature of reality. This is especially true for Whitehead's brilliantly novel, so naturally controversial, concept of prehension. For if Whitehead's metaphysical scheme can be shown to be the best interpretation of reality at the quantum level (as some physicists are now arguing) and at the most complex levels of human experience as well, then we will have come a long way towards demonstrating its far-reaching applicability. And if the extensive parapsychological research supporting the existence of ESP is finally endorsed by the scientific establishment, then the remnants of the materialistic, mechanistic paradigm still informing the modern scientific worldview will need to be supplanted by something much like a Whiteheadian understanding of reality.

CHAPTER SIX

# Revision and Re-enchantment of Psychology

*Stanislav Grof*

ABSTRACT: *Drawing on observations from more than fifty years of research into an important subgroup of non-ordinary states of consciousness, here referred to as "holotropic," this chapter suggests a revision of some basic assumptions of modern psychiatry and psychology. The proposed changes involve a novel understanding of the nature of consciousness and its relationship to matter, one that does not consider consciousness as a mere byproduct of brain activity. An experiential cartography is proposed that encompasses dimensions of the human psyche far beyond current psychological theory. In light of the new observations, spirituality appears to be an essential attribute of the human psyche and of existence in general.*

## MODERN CONSCIOUSNESS RESEARCH AND PSYCHOLOGY OF THE FUTURE

PSYCHEDELIC RESEARCH and the development of intensive experiential techniques of psychotherapy in the second half of the twentieth century moved the work with non-ordinary states of consciousness from the world of healers in preliterate cultures into modern psychiatry and psychotherapy. Therapists who were open to these approaches and used them in their practice were able to confirm the extraordinary healing

113

potential of holotropic states and discovered their value as goldmines of revolutionary new information about consciousness, human psyche, and the nature of reality. I became aware of the remarkable properties of holotropic states in 1956 when I volunteered as a beginning psychiatrist for an experiment with LSD-25. During this experiment, in which the pharmacological effect of LSD was combined with exposure to powerful stroboscopic light ("driving" or "entraining" of the brainwaves), I had an overwhelming experience of cosmic consciousness.[1]

This experience inspired in me a lifelong interest in holotropic states; research of these states has become my passion, profession, and vocation. Since that time, most of my clinical and research activities have consisted of systematic exploration of the therapeutic, transformative, heuristic, and evolutionary potential of these states. The five decades that I have dedicated to consciousness research have been for me an extraordinary adventure of discovery and self-discovery. I spent approximately half of this time conducting psychotherapy with psychedelic substances, first in Czechoslovakia in the Psychiatric Research Institute in Prague, and then in the United States, at the Maryland Psychiatric Research Center in Baltimore, where I participated in the last surviving American psychedelic research program. Since 1975, my wife Christina and I have worked with Holotropic Breathwork, a powerful method of therapy and self-exploration that we jointly developed at the Esalen Institute in Big Sur, California. Over the years, we have also supported many people undergoing spontaneous episodes of non-ordinary states of consciousness—psychospiritual crises or "spiritual emergencies," as Christina and I call them.[2]

In psychedelic therapy, holotropic states are brought about by the administration of mind-altering substances, such as LSD, psilocybin mescaline, and tryptamine or amphetamine derivatives. In holotropic breathwork, consciousness is changed by a combination of faster breathing, evocative music, and energy-releasing bodywork. In spiritual emergencies, holotropic states occur spontaneously, in the middle of everyday life, and their cause is usually unknown. If they are correctly understood and supported, these episodes have an extraordinary healing, transformative, and even evolutionary potential.

My initial encounter with holotropic states was very difficult and intellectually, as well as emotionally, challenging. In the early years of my laboratory and clinical research with psychedelics, I was bombarded daily with experiences and observations, for which my medical and psychiatric training had not prepared me. As a matter of fact, I was experiencing and seeing things that—in the context of the scientific worldview I obtained during my medical training—were considered impossible and were not supposed to happen. Yet, those obviously impossible things were happening all the time.

In the history of science, individuals who suggested far-reaching changes in the dominant paradigm have not enjoyed very enthusiastic reception; their ideas were initially dismissed as products of ignorance, poor judgment, bad science, fraud, or even insanity. I am now in the ninth decade of my life; this is the time when researchers often try to review their professional career and outline the conclusions at which they have arrived. More than half a century of research of holotropic states—my own, as well as that of many of my transpersonally oriented colleagues—has amassed much supportive evidence for a radically new understanding of consciousness and of the human psyche. The fact that it challenges the most fundamental metaphysical assumptions of materialistic science should not be a sufficient reason for rejecting it. Whether it will be refuted or accepted should be determined by unbiased future research of holotropic states.

## HOLOTROPIC STATES OF CONSCIOUSNESS

In this chapter, I will summarize the conclusions from more than half a century of research of an important subgroup of non-ordinary states for which I coined the name "holotropic." Before I address this topic, I would like to explain this term that I will be using from now on. All these years, my primary interest has been to explore the healing, transformative, and evolutionary potential of non-ordinary states of consciousness and their great value as a source of new revolutionary data about consciousness, the human psyche, and the nature of reality.

From this perspective, the term "altered states of consciousness" commonly used by mainstream clinicians and theoreticians is not appropriate, because of its one-sided emphasis on the distortion or impairment of the "correct way" of experiencing oneself and the world. (In colloquial English and in veterinary jargon, the term "alter" is used to signify castration of family dogs and cats.) Even the somewhat better term "non-ordinary states of consciousness" is too general, since it includes a wide range of conditions that are not relevant from the point of view of the focus of this article, such as trivial deliria caused by infectious diseases, abuse of alcohol, or circulatory and degenerative diseases of the brain. These alterations of consciousness are associated with disorientation, impairment of intellectual functions, and subsequent amnesia; they are clinically important, but lack therapeutic and heuristic potential.

The term "holotropic" refers to a large subgroup of non-ordinary states of consciousness that are of great theoretical and practical importance. These are the states that novice shamans experience during their initiatory crises and later induce in their clients for therapeutic purposes. Ancient and native cultures have used these states in rites of passage and in their healing ceremonies. They were described by mystics of all ages and initiates in the ancient mysteries of death and rebirth. Procedures inducing these states were also developed and used in the context of the great religions of the world—Hinduism, Buddhism, Jainism, Taoism, Zoroastrianism, Islam, Judaism, and Christianity.

The importance of holotropic states of consciousness for ancient and aboriginal cultures is reflected in the amount of time and energy that the members of these human groups dedicated to the development of "technologies of the sacred," various procedures capable of inducing them for ritual and spiritual purposes. These methods combine in various ways drumming and other forms of percussion, instrumental music, chanting, rhythmic dancing, changes of breathing, and cultivation of special forms of awareness. Extended social and sensory isolation, such as stays in a cave, in a desert, on arctic ice, or in high mountains, also play an important role as means of inducing this category of non-ordinary states. Extreme physiological interventions used for this purpose include fasting, sleep deprivation, dehydration, use of powerful laxatives and purgatives, and even infliction of severe pain, body mutilation, and massive bloodletting. By far the most effective tool for inducing healing and transformative non-ordinary states has been ritual use of psychedelic plants.

When I recognized the unique nature of this category of non-ordinary states of consciousness, I found it difficult to believe that contemporary psychiatry does not have a specific category and term for these theoretically and practically important experiences. Because I felt strongly that they deserve to be distinguished from "altered states of consciousness" and not be seen as manifestations of serious mental diseases, I started referring to them as holotropic. This composite word means literally "oriented toward wholeness" or "moving toward wholeness" (from the Greek *holos* = whole and *trepo/trepein* = moving toward or in the direction of something). The word holotropic is a neologism, but it is related to a commonly used term heliotropism—the property of plants to always move in the direction of the sun.

## HOLOTROPIC STATES AND THE SPIRITUAL
## HISTORY OF HUMANITY

The name holotropic suggests something that might come as a surprise to an average Westerner, that in our everyday state of consciousness we identify with only a small fraction of who we really are and do not experience the full extent and experiential potential of our being. Holotropic states of consciousness have the potential to help us recognize that we are not "skin-encapsulated egos"—as British philosopher and writer Alan Watts called it—and that, in the last analysis, we are commensurate with the cosmic creative principle itself. Or that—using the statement attributed to Pierre Teilhard de Chardin, French paleontologist and philosopher—"we are not human beings having spiritual experiences, we are spiritual beings having the experiences of being human."

This astonishing idea is not new. In the ancient Indian Upanishads, the answer to the question: "Who am I?" is *"Tat tvam asi."* This succinct Sanskrit sentence means literally: "Thou art That," or "You are Godhead." It suggests that we are not *"namarupa"*—name and form (body/ego), but that our deepest identity is with a divine spark in our innermost being (Atman), which is ultimately identical with the supreme universal principle that creates the universe (Brahman). Hinduism is not the only religion that has made this discovery. The revelation concerning the identity of the individual with the divine is the ultimate secret that lies at the mystical core of all great spiritual traditions. The name for this principle could thus be the Tao, Buddha, Shiva (of Kashmir Shaivism), Cosmic Christ, Pleroma, Allah, and many others. Holotropic experiences have the potential to help us discover our true identity and our cosmic status.[3] Sometimes this happens in small increments, other times in the form of major breakthroughs.

THE NATURE OF CONSCIOUSNESS AND
ITS RELATIONSHIP TO MATTER

According to the current scientific worldview, consciousness is an epiphenomenon of material processes; it allegedly emerges out of the
complexity of the neurophysiological processes in the brain. This thesis
is presented with great authority as an obvious fact that has been proven
beyond any reasonable doubt. However, if we subject it to closer scrutiny,
we discover that it is a basic metaphysical assumption that is not supported
by facts and actually contradicts the findings of modern consciousness
research. We have ample clinical and experimental evidence showing
deep correlations between the anatomy, physiology, and biochemistry
of the brain, on the one hand, and states of consciousness, on the other.
However, none of these findings proves unequivocally that consciousness
is actually generated by the brain. Even sophisticated theories based on
advanced research of the brain, such as Stuart Hameroff's suggestion
that the solution of the problem of consciousness might lie in understanding the quantum processes in the microtubules of brain cells on
the molecular and supramolecular level,[4] fall painfully short of bridging
the formidable gap between matter and consciousness and illuminating
how material processes could generate consciousness.

The origin of consciousness from matter is simply assumed as an
obvious and self-evident fact based on the metaphysical assumption of
the primacy of matter in the universe. In the entire history of science,
nobody has ever offered a plausible explanation as to how consciousness
could be generated by material processes, or even suggested a viable
approach to the problem. We can use here as illustration the book by
Francis Crick (1994) *The Astonishing Hypothesis: The Scientific Search for
the Soul.* Its jacket carried a very exciting promise: "Nobel Prize-winning
Scientist Explains Consciousness."[5]

Crick's "astonishing hypothesis" was succinctly stated at the
beginning of his book: "You, your joys and your sorrows, your memories
and your ambitions, your sense of personal identity and free will, are
in fact no more than the behavior of a vast assembly of nerve cells and
their associated molecules. [Who you are is] nothing but a pack of
neurons."[6] At the beginning of his book, "to simplify the problem of
consciousness," Crick narrows it to the problem of optical perception.
He presents impressive experimental evidence showing that our visual

perception is associated with distinct physiological, biochemical, and electrical processes in the optical system from the retina to the suboccipital cortex. There the discussion ends as if the problem of consciousness was satisfactorily solved.

In reality, this is where the problem begins. What is it that is capable of transforming chemical and electric processes in the brain into a conscious experience of a reasonable facsimile of the object we are observing, in full color, and project it into three-dimensional space? The formidable problem of the relationship between phenomena (things as we perceive them) and noumena (things as they truly are in themselves—*Dinge an sich*) was clearly articulated by Immanuel Kant.[7] Scientists focus their efforts on the aspect of the problem where they can find answers—the material processes in the brain. The much more mysterious problem—how physical processes in the brain generate consciousness—does not receive any attention, because it is incomprehensible and cannot be solved.

The attitude that Western science has adopted in regard to this issue resembles the famous Sufi story of Mullah Nasruddin. On a dark night, Mullah Nasruddin, a satirical Sufi figure, is crawling on his knees under a street lamp. His neighbor sees him and asks: "What are you doing? Are you looking for something?" Nasruddin answers that he is searching for a lost key and his neighbor offers to help. After some time of unsuccessful joint effort, the helper is confused and feels the need for clarification. "I don't see anything! Are you sure you lost it here?" he asks. Nasruddin shakes his head; he points his finger to a dark area outside of the circle illuminated by the lamp and replies: "Not here, over there!" The helper is puzzled and inquires further: "So why are we looking for it here and not over there?" "Because it is light here and we can see. Over there, it is dark; we would not have a chance!"

In a similar way, materialistic scientists have systematically avoided the problem of the origin of consciousness, because this riddle cannot be solved within the context of their conceptual framework. The idea that consciousness is a product of the brain, of course, is not completely arbitrary. Its proponents usually refer to a vast body of very specific clinical observations from neurology, neurosurgery, and psychiatry to support their position. The evidence for close correlations between the anatomy, neurophysiology, and biochemistry of the brain and consciousness is unquestionable and overwhelming. What is problematic is not the nature of the presented evidence, but the conclusions that are drawn from these observations. In formal logic, this type of fallacy is called non sequitur—an argument in which its conclusion does not follow from its premises. While these experiments clearly show that consciousness is closely connected with the neurophysiological and biochemical processes in the brain, they have very little bearing on the nature and origin of consciousness.

The fallacy of attributing the cause of consciousness solely to material and biological processes can be illustrated by looking at the relationship between the TV set and the television program. The situation here is much clearer, since it involves a system that is human-made and its operation well known. The final reception of the television program, the quality of the picture and of the sound, depends in a very critical way on proper functioning of the TV set and on the integrity of its components. Malfunctioning of its various parts results in very distinct and specific changes of the quality of the program. Some of them lead to distortions of form, color, or sound, others to interference between the channels, etc. Like the neurologist who uses changes in consciousness as a diagnostic tool, a television mechanic can infer from the nature of these anomalies which parts of the set and which specific components are malfunctioning. When the problem is identified, repairing or replacing these elements will correct the distortions.

Since we know the basic principles of the television technology, it is clear to us that the set simply mediates the program and that it does not generate it. We would laugh at somebody who would try to examine and scrutinize all the transistors, relays, and circuits of the TV set and analyze all its wires in an attempt to figure out how it creates the programs. Even if we carry this misguided effort to the molecular, atomic, or subatomic level, we will have absolutely no clue why, at a particular time, a Mickey Mouse cartoon, a Star Trek sequence, or a Hollywood classic appear on the screen. The fact that there is such a close correlation between the functioning of the TV set and the quality of the program does not necessarily mean that the entire secret of the program is in the set itself. Yet this is exactly the kind of conclusion that traditional materialistic science drew from comparable data about the brain and its relation to consciousness.

There actually exists ample evidence suggesting exactly the opposite, namely that consciousness can under certain circumstances operate independently of its material substrate and can perform functions that reach far beyond the capacities of the brain. This is most clearly illustrated by the existence of out-of-body experiences (OBEs). These can occur spontaneously, or in a variety of facilitating situations that include shamanic trance, psychedelic sessions, hypnosis, experiential psychotherapy, and particularly near-death experiences (NDEs). In all these situations consciousness can separate from the body and maintain its sensory capacity, while moving freely to various close and remote locations. Of particular interest are "veridical OBEs," where independent verification proves the accuracy of perception of the environment under these circumstances. In near-death situations, veridical OBEs can occur even in people who are, for organic reasons, congenitally blind.[8] There are many other types of transpersonal phenomena that can mediate accurate information about various aspects of the universe that had not been previously received and recorded in the brain.[9]

Materialistic science has not been able to produce any convincing evidence that consciousness is a product of the neurophysiological processes in the brain. It has been able to maintain its present position only by ignoring, misinterpreting, and even ridiculing a vast body of observations indicating that consciousness can exist and function independently of the body and of the physical senses. This evidence comes from parapsychology, anthropology, LSD research, experiential psychotherapy, thanatology, and the study of spontaneously occurring holotropic states of consciousness. All these disciplines have amassed impressive data demonstrating clearly that human consciousness is capable of doing many things that the brain (as understood by mainstream science) could not possibly do and that it is a primary and further irreducible aspect of existence.

CARTOGRAPHY OF THE HUMAN PSYCHE

Traditional academic psychiatry and psychology use a model of the human psyche that is limited to postnatal biography and to the individual unconscious as described by Sigmund Freud. According to Freud, our psychological history begins after we are born; the newborn is a tabula rasa, a clean slate. Our psychological functioning is determined by an interplay between biological instincts and influences that have shaped our life since we came into this world—the quality of nursing, the nature of toilet training, various psychosexual traumas, development of the superego, our reaction to the Oedipal triangle, interpersonal dynamics in the nuclear family, and conflicts and traumatic events in later life. Who we become and how we psychologically function is determined by our postnatal personal and interpersonal history.

The Freudian individual unconscious is also essentially a derivative of our postnatal history; it is a repository of what we have forgotten, rejected as unacceptable, and repressed. This underworld of the psyche, or the id as Freud called it, is a realm dominated by primitive instinctual forces. Freud described the relationship between the conscious psyche and the unconscious using his famous image of the submerged iceberg. What we thought to be the totality of the psyche is just a small part of it, like the section of the iceberg showing above the surface. Psychoanalysis discovered that a much larger part of the psyche, comparable to the submerged part of the iceberg, is unconscious and, unbeknown to us, governs our thought processes and behavior.

Many of Freud's theoretical speculations and therapeutic claims have been seriously questioned by mainstream theoreticians and clinicians. However, his general model of the psyche, limited as it is to postnatal biography and the individual unconscious, has been adopted by modern psychology and psychiatry. In the work with holotropic states of consciousness induced by psychedelics and various non-drug means, as well as those occurring spontaneously, this model proves to be painfully inadequate. To account for all the phenomena occurring in these states, we must drastically revise our understanding of the dimensions of the human psyche. Besides the postnatal biographical level that it shares with traditional psychology, the new expanded cartography includes two additional large domains.

The first of these domains can be referred to as perinatal, because of its close connection with the trauma of biological birth. This region of the unconscious contains the memories of what the fetus experienced in the consecutive stages of the birth process, including the emotions and physical sensations involved. These memories form four distinct experiential clusters, each of which is related to one of the stages of childbirth. I have coined for them the term Basic Perinatal Matrices (BPM I-IV). BPM I consists of memories of the advanced prenatal state just before the onset of the delivery. BPM II is related to the first stage of the birth process when the uterus contracts, but the cervix is not yet open. BPM III reflects the struggle to be born after the uterine cervix dilates. And finally, BPM IV holds the memory of emerging into the world, the birth itself. The content of these matrices is not limited to fetal memories; each of them also represents a selective opening into the areas of the historical and archetypal collective unconscious that contain motifs of similar experiential quality. Detailed description of the phenomenology and dynamics of perinatal matrices can be found in my various publications.[10]

The official position of academic psychiatry is that biological birth is not recorded in memory and does not constitute a psychotrauma. The usual reason for denying the possibility of birth memory is that the cerebral cortex of the newborn is not mature enough to mediate experiencing and recording of this event. More specifically, the cortical neurons are not yet completely "myelinized"—covered with protective sheaths of a fatty substance called myelin. Surprisingly, the same argument is not used to deny the existence and importance of memories from the time of nursing, a period that immediately follows birth. The psychological significance of the experiences in the oral period and even "bonding"— the exchange of looks and physical contact between the mother and child immediately after birth—is generally recognized and acknowledged by mainstream obstetricians, pediatricians, and child psychiatrists.[11]

The myelinization argument makes no sense and is in conflict with scientific evidence of various kinds. It is well known that memory exists in organisms that do not have a cerebral cortex at all. In 2001, American neuroscientist of Austrian origin, Erik Kandel, received a Nobel Prize in physiology for his research on memory mechanisms of the sea slug *Aplysia*, an organism incomparably more primitive than the newborn child. The assertion that the newborn is not aware of being born and is not capable of forming a memory of this event is also in sharp conflict with extensive fetal research showing the extreme sensitivity of the fetus already in the prenatal stage.[12] The most likely explanation of this striking logical inconsistency in the thinking of clinicians and academicians with rigorous scientific training is psychological repression and resistance in regard to the terrifying memory of biological birth.

The second transbiographical domain of the new cartography can best be called transpersonal, because it includes a rich array of experiences in which consciousness transcends the boundaries of the body/ego and the usual limitations of linear time and three-dimensional space. This results in experiential identification with other people, groups of people, other life forms, and even elements of the inorganic world. Transcendence of time provides experiential access to ancestral, racial, collective, phylogenetic, and karmic memories. Yet another category of transpersonal experiences can take us into the realm of the collective unconscious that the Swiss psychiatrist C. G. Jung called archetypal. This region harbors mythological figures, themes, and realms of all the cultures and ages, even those of which we have no intellectual knowledge.[13]

In its farthest reaches, individual consciousness can identify with the Universal Mind or Cosmic Consciousness, the creative principle of the universe. Probably the most profound experience available in holotropic states is identification with the Supracosmic and Metacosmic Void, with the Primordial Emptiness and Nothingness that is conscious of itself. The Void has a paradoxical nature; it is a vacuum, because it is devoid of any concrete forms, but it is also a plenum, since it seems to contain all of creation in a potential form. This experience seems to be related to the concept of the PSI or Akashic field formulated by world-famous system theorist and philosopher Ervin Laszlo. According to him, it is a subquantum field that is the source of all creation and in which everything that happens remains holographically recorded. Laszlo equates this field with the concept of quantum vacuum that has emerged from modern physics.[14] The existence and nature of transpersonal experiences violates some of the most basic assumptions of materialistic science. They imply such seemingly absurd notions as the relativity and arbitrary nature of all physical boundaries, nonlocal connections in the universe, communication through unknown means and channels, memory without a material substrate, nonlinearity of time, and consciousness associated with all living organisms and even inorganic matter. Many transpersonal experiences involve events from the microcosm and the macrocosm, realms that cannot normally be reached by unaided human senses, or from historical periods that precede the origin of the solar system, formation of planet Earth, appearance of living organisms, development of the nervous system, and emergence of homo sapiens.

Having spent more than half a century studying transpersonal experiences, I have no doubt that many, if not most of them, are ontologically real and are not products of metaphysical speculation, human imagination, or pathological processes in the brain. It would be erroneous to dismiss them as products of fantasy, primitive superstition, or a manifestation of mental disease, as has so frequently been done. Anybody attempting to do that would have to offer a plausible explanation why these experiences have in the past been described so consistently by people of various races, cultures, and historical periods. He or she would also have to account for the fact that these experiences continue to emerge in modern populations under such diverse circumstances as sessions with various psychedelic substances, during experiential psychotherapy, in meditation of people involved in systematic spiritual practice, in near-death experiences, and in the course of spontaneous episodes of psychospiritual crisis. Detailed discussion of the transpersonal domain, including descriptions and examples of various types of transpersonal experiences can be found in my various publications.[15]

In view of this vastly expanded model of the psyche, we could now paraphrase Freud's simile of the psyche as an iceberg. We could say that everything Freudian analysis has discovered about the psyche represents just the top of the iceberg showing above the water. Research of holotropic states has made it possible to explore the colossal rest of the iceberg hidden under water, which has escaped the attention of Freud and his followers, with the exception of the remarkable renegades Otto Rank and C. G. Jung. Mythologist Joseph Campbell, known for his incisive Irish humor, used a different metaphor: "Freud was fishing while sitting on a whale."

## THE ROLE OF SPIRITUALITY IN HUMAN LIFE

The leading philosophy of Western science has been monistic materialism. Various scientific disciplines have described the history of the universe as a history of developing matter, and they accept as real only what can be measured and weighed. Life, consciousness, and intelligence are then seen as more or less accidental side-products of material processes. Physicists, biologists, and chemists recognize the existence of dimensions of reality that are not accessible to our senses, but only those that are physical in nature and can be revealed and explored with the use of various extensions of our senses, such as microscopes, telescopes, and specially designed recording devices, or laboratory experiments.

In a universe understood this way, there is no place for spirituality of any kind. The existence of God, the idea that there are invisible dimensions of reality inhabited by nonmaterial beings, the possibility of survival of consciousness after death, and the concept of reincarnation and karma have been relegated to fairy tales and psychiatry handbooks. From a psychiatric perspective to take such things seriously means to be ignorant, unfamiliar with the discoveries of science, superstitious, and subject to primitive magical thinking. If the belief in God or Goddess occurs in intelligent persons, it is seen as an indication that they have not come to terms with infantile images of their parents as omnipotent beings they had created in their infancy and childhood and project into the Beyond. Moreover, direct experiences of spiritual realities, including encounters with mythological beings and visits to archetypal realms are considered manifestations of serious mental diseases—psychoses.

The study of holotropic states has thrown new light on the problem of spirituality and religion. The key to this new understanding is the discovery that in these states it is possible to encounter a rich array of experiences that are very similar to those that inspired the great religions of the world—visions of God and various divine and demonic beings, encounters with discarnate entities, episodes of psychospiritual death and rebirth, visits to Heaven and Hell, past life experiences, and many others. Modern research has shown beyond any doubt that these experiences are not products of fantasy or pathological processes afflicting the brain, but manifestations of archetypal material from the collective unconscious, and thus germane and essential constituents of the human psyche.

For example, Jung's concept of the archetypal collective unconscious was inspired by the fact that the dreams of his neurotic patients and visions of his psychotic patients often contained mythological motifs from cultures of which they had no intellectual knowledge. I have been able to confirm Jung's observation in my own work with psychedelic substances, with Holotropic Breathwork, and with individuals experiencing spiritual emergency.[16] Similarly, past life experiences often involve specific information about historical periods and countries about which the subjects previously had no intellectual knowledge. Out-of-body experiences in near-death situations have all the characteristics that the Tibetan Book of the Dead attributes to the bardo body, the immaterial essence that one becomes at the time of death. Although these experiences are accessed intrapsychically, in a process of experiential self-exploration and introspection, they have objective existence outside of the everyday personality of the subject.

To distinguish transpersonal experiences from imaginary products of individual human fantasy or psychopathology, Jungians refer to this domain as *imaginal*. French scholar, philosopher, and mystic, Henri Corbin, who first used the term *mundus imaginalis,* got the inspiration for this concept from his study of Islamic mystical literature.[17] Islamic theosophers call the imaginal world, where everything existing in the sensory world has its analogue, *'alam a mithal,'* or the "eighth climate," to distinguish it from the "seven climates," regions of traditional Islamic geography. The imaginal world possesses extension and dimensions, forms and colors, but these are not perceptible to our senses as they would be when they are properties of physical objects. However, this realm is in every respect as fully ontologically real as the material world perceived by our sensory organs and experiences of it can be verified by consensual validation by other people.

As I mentioned earlier, an astonishing aspect of transpersonal experiences occurring in holotropic states of various kinds is that their content can be drawn from the mythologies of any culture of the world, including those of which the individual has no intellectual knowledge. C. G. Jung demonstrated this extraordinary fact for mythological experiences occurring in the dreams and psychotic experiences of his patients. On the basis of these observations, he realized that the human psyche has access not only to the Freudian individual unconscious, but also to the collective unconscious, which is a repository of the entire cultural heritage of humanity.[18] Knowledge of comparative mythology is thus more than a matter of personal interest or an academic exercise. It is a very important and useful guide for individuals involved in experiential therapy and self-exploration and an indispensable tool for those who support and accompany them on their journeys.[19]

The experiences originating on deeper levels of the psyche, in the collective unconscious, have a certain quality that Jung referred to as numinosity. The word numinous—first used by Rudolf Otto—is relatively new and neutral and thus preferable to other similar expressions, such as religious, mystical, magical, holy, or sacred, which have often been used in problematic contexts and are easily misleading. The term numinosity applied to transpersonal experiences describes direct perception of their extraordinary nature; they represent *"mysterium tremendum et fascinans"* or the "wholly other"—something that cannot be usually experienced in our everyday states of consciousness. They convey a very convincing sense that they belong to a higher order of reality, a realm that is sacred.

In view of the ontological reality of the imaginal realm, spirituality is a very important and natural dimension of the human psyche and the spiritual quest is a legitimate and fully justified human endeavor. However, it is necessary to emphasize that this statement applies to genuine spirituality based on personal experience and does not provide support for ideologies and dogmas of organized religions. To prevent misunderstanding and confusion that in the past compromised many similar discussions, it is critical to make a clear distinction between spirituality and religion.

Spirituality involves a special kind of relationship between the individual and the cosmos and is, in its essence, a personal and private affair. By comparison, organized religion is institutionalized group activity that takes place in a designated location, such as a temple or a church, and involves a system of appointed officials who might or might not have had personal experiences of spiritual realities themselves. Once a religion becomes organized, it often completely loses the connection with its spiritual source and becomes a secular institution that exploits human spiritual needs without satisfying them.

Organized religions tend to create hierarchical systems focusing on the pursuit of power, control, politics, money, possessions, and other worldly concerns. Under these circumstances, religious hierarchy often dislikes and discourages direct spiritual experiences in its members, because they foster independence and cannot be effectively controlled. When this is the case, genuine spiritual life continues only in the mystical branches, monastic orders, and ecstatic sects of the religions involved. People who have experiences of the immanent or transcendent divine open up to spirituality found in the mystical branches of the great religions of the world or in their monastic orders, but not necessarily in their mainstream organizations. A deep mystical experience tends to dissolve the boundaries between religions and reveals deep connections between them, while the dogmatism of organized religions tends to emphasize differences between various creeds and engender antagonism and hostility.

There is no doubt that the dogmas of organized religions are generally in fundamental conflict with science, whether this science uses the mechanistic-materialistic model or is anchored in the emerging paradigm. However, the situation is very different in regard to authentic mysticism based on spiritual experiences. The great mystical traditions have amassed extensive knowledge about human consciousness and about the spiritual realms in a way that is similar to the method that scientists use in acquiring knowledge about the material world. It involves methodology for inducing transpersonal experiences, systematic collection of data, and intersubjective validation.

Spiritual experiences, like any other aspect of reality, can be subjected to careful, open-minded research and studied scientifically. There is nothing unscientific about unbiased and rigorous study of transpersonal phenomena and of the challenges they present for a materialistic understanding of the world. Only such an approach can answer the critical question about the ontological status of mystical experiences: Do they reveal deep truth about some basic aspects of existence, as maintained by various systems of perennial philosophy and transpersonal psychology, or are they products of superstition, fantasy, or mental disease, as Western materialistic science sees them?

Official psychiatry makes no distinction between a mystical experience and a psychotic experience and sees both as manifestations of mental disease. In its rejection of religion, it does not differentiate between primitive folk beliefs or the fundamentalist literal interpretations of religious scriptures and sophisticated mystical traditions or the great Eastern spiritual philosophies based on centuries of systematic introspective exploration of the psyche. Modern consciousness research has brought convincing evidence for the objective existence of the imaginal realm and has thus validated the main metaphysical assumptions of the mystical worldview, of the Eastern spiritual philosophies, and even certain beliefs of native cultures.

## CHAPTER SEVEN

# Amplified Subject

## Leonard Gibson

ABSTRACT: *After reviewing the historical importance of non-ordinary and psychedelic experiences, this essay suggests that the primary function of psychedelics is the amplification of certain aspects of subjective process. The deactivation of hub structures described by Carhart-Harris and its role in disrupting neurological activity is explored, as well as the importance of cathartic experience in psycho-spiritual healing. Finally, the essay considers, from a Whiteheadian perspective, some of the metaphysical dimensions that are revealed during intense non-ordinary states, including the death-rebirth experience, the relativity of lived time, the presence of the past, and the intrinsic value of each moment.*

T HE ONTOLOGY of the modern worldview, and much of the science allied with it, has not gone beyond many outdated footnotes to Plato.[1] The Aristotelian footnote that interpreted Platonic Being as substance developed into Descartes's notions of substance. Modern science then conceived Descartes's material substance as preeminently real and ontologically primary, a conception that still significantly informs natural and social science. This conception, according to Alfred North Whitehead, gives ontological prominence to abstractions as objective realities in preference to the subjective deliverances of actual experience. The promise of mathematics envisioned by Plato, but unappreciated by Aristotle, did not begin to be realized much before Galileo. Then it became deployed mistakenly in service of Cartesian matter rather than mind, yielding what Whitehead calls the "fallacy of misplaced concreteness."[2] The end result of these footnote missteps is today's metaphysical bias towards mechanistic materialism, with no place in science for subjective realities.

Chemical creations and anthropological discoveries in the twentieth century have presented radically new possibilities to Western philosophy for rediscovering subjective experience as fundamental to the con-sideration of ontology. Since Plotinus, no Western philosopher spoke about this—except to some extent Meister Eckhart—until William James. By discussing his "anesthetic revelations," James demonstrated for modern philosophy that his subjective experience was fundamental to ontology. James showed that psychedelic substances offer an exceptional means for experiential ontological investigation. Here is his testimony:

> Some years ago I myself made observations [regarding] nitrous oxide intoxication, and reported them in print. One conclusion was forced upon my mind at that time, and my impression of its truth has ever since remained unshaken. It is that our normal waking consciousness, rational consciousness as we call it, is but one special type of consciousness, whilst all about it, parted from it by the filmiest of screens, there lie potential forms of consciousness entirely different. We may go through life without suspecting their existence; but apply the requisite stimulus, and at a touch they are there in all their completeness, definite types of mentality which probably somewhere have their field of application and adaptation. No account of the universe in its totality can be final which leaves these other forms of consciousness quite disregarded. How to regard them is the question—for they are so discontinuous with ordinary consciousness. Yet they may determine attitudes though they cannot furnish formulas, and open a region though they fail to give a map. At any rate, they forbid a premature closing of our accounts with reality.[3]

This chapter maintains that Alfred North Whitehead's metaphysical scheme can facilitate keeping open our accounts with reality, as James suggests, because it is sufficiently broad to encompass psychedelic experience, both philosophically and scientifically. Appreciating Whitehead's framework is timely, as recent developments in psychological research offer the promise of relaxing restrictions on professional psychedelic experimentation. Legitimizing the use of psychedelics by validating their uses in psychotherapy is a first step towards making them an available avenue for philosophical, scientific, artistic, and other professional research.

HISTORY

James's report of mystical experience related to use of a psychedelic substance did not attract much philosophic attention until the cultural awakening to psychedelic substances that began in the middle of the twentieth century. Two discoveries led to that awakening. One was American ethnomycologist Gordon Wasson's disclosure of the psilocybin mushroom practice among indigenous peoples in Mexico. The other was the revelation of the psychological effects of LSD by the Swiss chemist Albert Hoffman. Although Hoffman's discovery was earlier, Wasson's was the first to attract attention when it was published in the popular magazine *Life*.[4]

Most of the attention subsequently paid to psychedelic experience has been by anthropology and psychology, although much of that has been out of the mainstream. Historically, mystical experiences have been pursued primarily through long and arduous practices such as meditation, yoga, fasting, extended chanting, *lectio divina*, Sufi whirling, flagellation, Voodoo, bloodletting (a notable Mayan technique), Mandan (American Plains Indian) Sun Dance, San Dance (Kalahari Bushman), and a variety of shamanic techniques, some of which have employed psychedelic substances. Primarily, anthropology has studied indigenous practices, including psychedelic ones. Psychology has given only marginal attention to psychedelic studies, and these studies have largely been relegated to the post-humanistic field of transpersonal psychology, which has yet to find significant attention in the academic world.

Mainstream philosophy has not paid much attention to James's report, nor has it ever paid much attention to suggestions that psychedelic experience was important to ancient philosophy. Plato, along with many other significant figures in ancient culture, was an initiate in the Eleusinian mysteries, which apparently used a psychedelic substance called kykeon.[5] These rites were of sufficient significance to endure for almost two millennia. Cicero singled them out as the only cult that he would permit in his ideal republic.

Plato's experience with the mysteries is a likely basis for the method he attributes to Diotima in the *Symposium*. Porphyry attests to the effectiveness of the method by reporting that Plotinus used "Plato's method" to lift himself "to the first and all-transcendent divinity."[6] Plotinus was the last ancient documented to practice Plato's method, but other methods, both Western and Eastern, avail themselves of meditation programs that analogously practice ascension through successive stages to attain mystical experience.

## PSYCHEDELIC AMPLIFICATION OF PROCESS

In what follows we will first review some material from psychology, including brain neurophysiology, as a background for discussing the ontology of psychedelic experience and as a prelude to explicating this experience through Whitehead's metaphysical scheme. Our focus in Whitehead's metaphysics will be on the concept of the event and the thread of events identified as the *final percipient occasions* (FPO) of human experience. Although Whitehead considers events in terms of entities ranging from animals down to subatomic happenings, our discussion will concern human perception and experience and its central events. Whitehead calls these events the "soul"[7] or "living person." He characterizes these events as a thread of occasions wandering through the interstices of the brain.[8]

An event, in the most general Whiteheadian sense, prehends the entire past. As humans in ordinary life, our awareness of prehensions is limited. If we were acutely aware, for instance, of the motions of air molecules, we would likely be so distracted that we could not even make our way across a room. And if we were acutely aware of all our past psychological history and trauma, we might be overwhelmed to the point of catatonic immobility.

The particulars of psychedelic experience vary widely. The terms *set* and *setting* are used in psychedelic literature to characterize the main factors relevant to those particulars. *Setting* refers to a person's physical, social, and cultural environment. *Set* refers to a person's psychological makeup, personality, psychosocial history, etc. Understanding these parameters can help prevent difficult and unpleasant experiences, which are most likely to occur in uncontrolled situations. For instance, if a person having a psychedelic experience goes out on a public street, the intensity of being around the noise and movement of traffic can be frightening. Unexamined religious beliefs or attitudes about what is real can create anxiety in the face of psychedelic challenge. Memories of traumatic psychological experiences may become amplified in psychedelic experience to the point that the associated feelings begin to pervade a person's experience. Because of such possibilities, psychedelic experience should take place in a situation that is physically and socially safe and where capable support is readily available for any psychological issues that arise.

The effect of LSD and similar psychedelic substances can be characterized as *nonspecific intensification* or *amplification of process,* explicitly the process that is manifest in each event in the thread of the FPO compromising a living person, that is, the psyche or soul. The psychedelic effect is mediated by human physiology, primarily brain physiology, but its ultimate consequence is realized in that society of events that comprise the "living person." This chapter understands the living person to be the ultimate subject in human experience.

Although Whitehead uses the term "subject" differently from ordinary language and coins an alternative term "subject-superject" to counter the connotation of passivity sometimes associated with "subject," we will use the simpler term "subject" in our discussion here. We will, however, understand "subject" to incorporate Whitehead's notion of superject as actively influencing the future, very different from the connotation of a passive recipient of experience that dominates contemporary neuropsychology.

To begin to understand what the amplification of process involves, we will first consider the eliminative aspect of brain functions. The idea of brain functions as eliminative is overtly at odds with the idea of amplification. We will attempt to resolve this paradox by first considering the work of Carhart-Harris and Friston with brain imaging.[9] Their work establishes a useful neurological background for discussing psychedelic experience in terms of the *eliminative* aspect of brain function. The next step to resolving the paradox is to see that the brain's function serves to eliminate the chaos otherwise resulting from the welter of unorganized feelings and data that present themselves as possible ingredients for an event's becoming. When this organizing brain function loosens under psychedelic influence, repressed material begins to come to the fore— both repressed experience in personal history and avoided existential dilemmas. The effort demanded by the process of becoming (formation of subjective experience) is profoundly amplified by the requirement to cope with all this previously repressed material. If one manages this integrative task well, the result is catharsis. The chaos of prehended contradictions is transmuted into unified contrasts, and amplification gives way to intensity and depth of experience. Thereby, one discovers the intrinsic value of the subject-superject, that is, of each moment of existence.

## NEUROPHYSIOLOGY

In the YouTube video, *Dr. Robin Carhart-Harris-Psilocybin and the Psychedelic State*, the doctor describes psilocybin as deactivating "hub structures" in the brain.[10] If these hub structures are thought of as shepherds keeping flocks of perceptions coherent or conductors insuring coordination between musicians, psilocybin in effect causes the shepherd or conductor to disappear. Consequently the sheep separate and stray, and the music slips toward chaos. On this analogy, the capacity of the brain to bring things together into familiar patterns is eliminated. Predictability falls by the wayside.

In the normal visual system, the results of photons falling on the retina are processed up into the visual nuclei of the thalamus, a hub in the center of the brain, then on to the primary visual cortex at the back of the brain, then on up to higher-level representations. At each stage the associated brain function makes predictions about the way material from the preceding stage might be organized, with the function eliminating less likely predictions, somewhat like the refinement of Bayesian logic. What might start out as a grouping of photons of certain frequencies becomes intimations of features at a successive level. At higher levels those intimations of features get organized into predictions of faces, and the process culminates in the recognition of a friend or suspicion of a stranger.

As hierarchical mental organization breaks down under the influence of psychedelics, the deliverances of individual layers of organization manifest without coordination, like each sheep wandering in its own direction without the oversight of the shepherd. Thus, the psychedelic experience may visually present simultaneous displays of flowing colors, sudden appearances of abstract shapes, bits of furniture flying about, fantastic animals crawling by, faces appearing and disappearing, or a variety of mishmashes.

The extent to which apparently perceived reality is a construction of the brain becomes obvious when one understands that the predictions produced at various stages can appear as disparate overlaps rather than getting integrated into a coherent whole. Psychedelic experience often provides a vivid demonstration of this phenomenon.

Considering the effect of psychedelic substances on the brain is crucial for understanding the mind aspect of psychedelic experience manifest in the final percipient occasion. Brain is messenger to mind. Psychedelic disruption of brain function impacts the gradation of relevance respecting prehension, that is, the criteria guiding patterns of unconscious selection and integration. Normally the hierarchical organization of the brain eliminates conflicting messages, leading it to function, according to Huxley, as a sort of cerebral reducing valve.[11]

In terms of Huxley's eliminative characterization, the brain's filtering can be compared with "negative prehension," that is, entirely excluding data and feeling from psychological processing. As the brain's filtering weakens, the final percipient occasion is faced with a burgeoning welter of data, many of which are *prima facie* contradictory and so would be eliminated by ordinary functioning.

The process of the FPO can be considered in terms of Whitehead's modes of perception as well as the terms set and setting, noted above. Practice has taught that psychedelic experience is best pursued in a safe and comfortable setting with the subject wearing eyeshades and earphones, over which carefully chosen, wordless instrumental music is played. This reduces the *presentational immediacy* (conscious sensory perception) of the visual and auditory *setting*. The blocking function of the eyeshades is obvious. Noise blocking earphones have only recently become widely available, so historically nonspecific music was the best alternative for auditory blocking. The psychedelic disruption of brain function particularly impacts the mode of *symbolic reference* (meaning formation), so diminishing the stimulus of presentational immediacy reduces the possibilities of identifying imagination with external loci in a hallucinatory way. The subject's attention thus turns mainly to the mode of *causal efficacy*—a direct intuitive perception of past events.

Even though the mode of presentational immediacy is discouraged, causal efficacy still yields a welter of data inherited as the set of the subject. Conventionally, set has been interpreted as the personality and psychological character of a person, what Whitehead might roughly call *personal identity.* That is indeed the most immediate inheritance of the FPO, but Whitehead's idea of inheritance goes well beyond just personal history. It involves inheritance from the entire past universe. This larger conception of inheritance suggests an enormous array of prehensive data. It could include phenomena unexplainable by mainstream science and psychology, such as "past lives" or direct intuitive contact not only of human beings, but of animals, even bacteria—that is, any nexus of occasions with personal identity.

## THE CHALLENGE OF PSYCHEDELIC EXPERIENCE

In some extremities of psychedelic experience, dealing with the confusion and extent of contradictory data can become a supreme metaphysical challenge. Failing the challenge, a person may succumb to a quasi-psychotic episode.

The standard clinical response to a psychotic episode is to administer powerful antipsychotic medications to arrest the episode. From the alternative perspective of spiritual emergence, this strategy is a mistake.[12] Where mainstream psychiatry sees a psychotic disease, this alternative sees a self-limiting, healing process where a breakdown of the ego clears away psychic flaws, inhibitions, and constraints. Once the breakdown bottoms out, like a forest of serotinus pines whose seeds release after fire, the mind begins to reconstitute. The nature of the process characterized by the clinical mainstream as psychotic is usually self-limiting by virtue of the "perpetually perishing" nature of events—as evocatively described by Whitehead.[13] Perpetual perishing underlies the psychological experience of death and rebirth, which is often how a person experiences the resolution of metaphysical challenge in the course of psychedelic experience.

Because psychedelic substances have a finite physiological duration, quasi-psychotic episodes, even if not fully resolved, usually dissipate along with the physiological effect of the substances. Unresolved challenges are most apt to happen in an uncontrolled, unsupported setting.

Unresolved psychological material is best not left untreated—and it is best treated by subsequent nonordinary experience in a controlled, safe, and supportive setting.

Clinical and physiological considerations notwithstanding, what is most interesting philosophically about a quasi-psychotic experience with psychedelics is its metaphysical challenge. The challenge is an existential crisis. The disappearance of one's normal mental organization can render the question of identity profoundly and acutely. There is no formula for resolving this crisis, but in James's terms, such an experience definitively forestalls closing one's accounts with reality.[14]

Though there is no blueprint for resolution of such an overwhelming predicament, many people have given retrospective accounts of experiences of wrestling with angels or passing through the dark night of the soul in contexts other than psychedelic experience. Those experiences are fundamentally commensurate with the ones that psychedelic experience can precipitate. The resolution of such crises is understood differently in different contexts. In a Christian context, it may be called salvation. In Buddhism it is called enlightenment. Whitehead calls it "Peace."

## CATHARSIS AND SUBJECTIVE FORM

The organizing brain function identified by Carhart-Harris performs the cerebral filtering that Huxley and Broad speak to. Psychedelic substances act to inhibit this organizing and filtering. Consequently, the FPO must deal with an extraordinarily chaotic welter of data that begets an extreme amplification and intensification of prehension or feeling. What we ordinarily conceive as the objective world recedes in the face of this welter, and subjective elements of experience become pronounced. Moving beyond these aspects of brain function, let us consider psychedelic experience in terms of a person's general psychological functioning.

Modern philosophy begins with Descartes conceiving himself most fundamentally as a *thinking subject*: I think, therefore I am. Then, opposite this basic subjectivity, he posits an objective, material world devoid of mentality. Modern psychology, pursuant to Descartes's conception, abstracts the individual subject from the more global Aristotelian paradigm that prevailed for millennia. Aristotle understood the individual comprehensively within the context of nature, morality, and community. Freud espoused Descartes's abstraction by focusing psychology on a delimited, individual biography. He thought of a person in terms of developmental stages and theorized that psychological illness originated in objective trauma whose effect depended on the stage of development it impacted.

To blunt the effect of trauma, according to Freud, people put up psychic defenses to repress memories related to this experience. These defenses, however, do not remove trauma. They merely redirect psychic attention and give rise to neuroses or even psychoses. Psychedelic psycho-therapy can be interpreted in the Freudian context under the rubric of catharsis. Psychedelic experience can be thought of as loosening the defensive aspect of cerebral filtering that represses memories of trauma. Experiencing the flood of traumatic memories that are released when repression is loosened is characterized clinically by Freudians as *regression*.

The consequences of "regressed" experience of this kind can be diverse. On the one hand, extreme regression can seem psychotic. On the other hand, it can be understood in terms of Kris's concept of "regression in service of the ego." [15] If such regression in service of the ego is supported and followed up therapeutically, it can lead to catharsis. Loosening the defenses, and thus opening the psyche, can foster suppleness and receptiveness to normally suppressed intuition, feeling, and insight and can significantly promote creativity. As the organization of normal mental life breaks down and thinking becomes less analytic, more magical, and fantasy-based, not only can trauma be healed, but the creativity of both personal insight and artistic production can be enhanced.

The psychedelic experience itself poses few dangers for an adequately supported, normal, healthy individual. Difficulties arise mainly if the experience does not take place in a safe and supportive environment, and if follow-up is inadequate. A capable therapist provides support and encouragement so that the person can experience the intensity of the past traumatic experiences, while at the same time feeling safe in a kind of psychological quantum superposition. The resolution of this superposition provides catharsis.

Whitehead's concept of *subjective form* is central to understanding psychological catharsis:

> The process through which a feeling passes in constituting itself, also records itself in the subjective form of the integral

feeling. The negative prehensions have their own subjective forms which they contribute to the process. *A feeling bears on itself the scars of its birth* [italics added]; it recollects as a subjective emotion its struggle for existence; it retains the impress of what it might have been, but is not. It is for this reason that what an actual entity has avoided as a datum for feeling may yet be an important part of its equipment. The actual cannot be reduced to mere matter of fact in divorce from the potential.[16]

In both repression and catharsis the scar of trauma is felt. The difference between repression and catharsis is in the *way* they are felt. Therapeutically supported, the recollection of trauma is transmuted from feeling the trauma as a mere matter of fact—which is a gross evil—to a tragic evil:

> As soon as high consciousness is reached, the enjoyment of existence is entwined with pain, frustration, loss, tragedy. Amid the passing of so much beauty, so much heroism, so much daring, Peace is then the intuition of permanence. It keeps vivid the sensitiveness to the tragedy; and it sees the tragedy as a living agent persuading the world to aim at fineness beyond the faded level of surrounding fact. Each tragedy is the disclosure of an ideal;—What might have been, and was not: What can be. The tragedy was not in vain. This survival power in motive force, by reason of appeal to reserves of Beauty, marks the difference between the tragic evil and the gross evil. The inner feeling belonging to this grasp of the service of tragedy is Peace—the purification of the emotions.[17]

Cathartic healing rescues a traumatized person from feeling like a victim to experiencing life as a hero's journey—and to understanding personal trauma, in the large context of existence, as pursuit of an ideal. The ideal necessarily lies beyond any final achievement. Life is a process always aiming beyond itself to elevate itself to transcendence. Catharsis is a critical key to unlocking psychological growth: "The right coordination of negative prehensions is one secret of mental progress; but unless some systematic scheme of relatedness characterizes the environment, there will be nothing left whereby to constitute vivid prehension of the world."[18]

Catharsis lifts existence from a psychic environment of hopelessness in the face of trauma and struggle to a feeling of life as causally efficacious in persuading the world to aim for beauty yet to be realized.

## SUBJECTIVITY AND SOLITARINESS

So far we have been considering catharsis in terms of individual psychological growth. Beyond psychological growth lies the potential for spiritual growth, which takes us into transpersonal territory. The psychedelic spiritual journey can begin with the surprising, forceful experience of having one's ordinarily experienced "objective" world disintegrate into perceptual chaos, as Carhart-Harris's description has it.[19] Beyond perceptual chaos, however, one's experience can slip to ideational chaos, conceptual chaos, and into existential chaos that raises questions of purpose, identity, and the nature of reality. Abreast this chaos, one comes face to face with one's utter subjectivity, one's solitariness:

> The great religious conceptions which haunt the imaginations of civilized mankind are scenes of solitariness: Prometheus chained to his rock, Mohomet [sic] brooding in the desert, the meditations of the Buddha, the solitary man on the Cross. It belongs to the depth of the religious spirit to have felt forsaken, even by God.[20]

Whitehead is careful to distinguish between religion as a social fact and religion as spiritual endeavor, which is religion as solitariness, and he traces one map of the spiritual journey: "Religion is what the individual does with his own solitariness. It runs through three stages, if it evolves to its final satisfaction. It is the transition from God the void to God the enemy, and from God the enemy to God the companion."[21]

One passes through all these stages in the subjectivity of becoming, which is the fundament of one's solitariness.

## METAPHYSICS AND THE PSYCHEDELIC SPIRITUAL JOURNEY

Whitehead's metaphysics supplies notable topics and concepts germane to the psychedelic spiritual journey. In turn, psychedelic experience can bring felt understanding to what otherwise might be only intellectual concepts. This is not to minimize the importance of intellectual understanding and facility with Whitehead's concepts, but felt understanding based on direct experience opens a deepened appreciation for the ontological significance of the concepts. Psychedelic experience does not guarantee felt understanding. The possibility of discovering such understanding is helped by having a reasonable intellectual familiarity with Whitehead's ideas. Also, unresolved personal psychological issues can distract from metaphysical investigation. One should first approach psychedelic exploration with psychological preparation and therapeutic support, rather than with the immediate intention of metaphysical exploration.

Let us now consider four of Whitehead's topics to which psychedelic experience can bring deep feeling:

I.     The notion that time is an abstraction, not an actuality. Thinking that time is an actuality is an error of "misplaced concreteness."

II.    The immanence of the past in the present, which illuminates the concept of subjective form.

III.   The transience of experience, at the heart of which is perpetual perishing. The process of becoming and perishing is a micro-cosmic analog of the experience of death and rebirth, which is spiritually quintessential.

IV.    The enjoyment of *value*, which is the word Whitehead uses "for the intrinsic reality of an event."[22] Value arises out of the intensity that develops when the contradictions associated with feelings of psychological trauma or metaphysical crisis are resolved into contrasts—that is, by bringing previously conflicting elements together within a greater harmony that subsumes these elements.

Whitehead's explanation of an actual occasion involves all of these concepts and provides a unique and powerful means to understand the metaphysical significance of psychedelic experience. It resolves problems that cannot be understood within ordinary discourse and the mechanist-materialist framework dominant in Western science and culture.

I. TIME

Carhart-Harris and Friston note that "Freud considered timelessness to be a major characteristic of the id, and time perception to be a function of the ego."[23] They suggest that the sense of timelessness in psychedelic experience results from impairment in temporal perception due to the breakdown of associative brain function that produces ego disintegration and brings primary process to the fore.

This notion of impairment of time perception involves the concept that time is an objective reality. Freud, influenced by the success of contemporary physics, uncritically accepted the materialist-mechanist idea that Whitehead deems a fallacy of misplaced concreteness. The derivative notion of time perception impairment applied to psychedelic experience rules out the possibility that the experience may reveal reality more truly than does ordinary perception. The feeling of timelessness that can obtain in psychedelic experience bodes awareness that the actual event is internally timeless, that eternity is at the heart of experience. In this respect it is ordinary perception that is deficient regarding a fundamental dimension of experience.

For Whitehead, time is an abstraction from actual experience. The psychic amplification provided by profound psychedelic experience promotes intense focus on the immediate present occasion. It magnifies that occasion to the extent that one experiences fully and completely its timelessness, which is eternity. That experience is sacred, the foundation of reverence: "The foundation of reverence is this perception, that the present holds within itself the complete sum of existence, backwards and forwards that whole amplitude of time, which is eternity."[24]

Interpreted from Whitehead's perspective, intense psychedelic experience does not entail a deficiency of perception. The deepening of experience under psychedelic influence brings a person experientially into the timelessness of the actual event, which is a single, present occasion in the society that exhibits the person's thread of identity. That experience yields felt understanding that time is an abstraction, or more poetically stated, an illusion. In that same moment of experience the Void is manifest.

"Personal identity is the thing which receives all occasions of a man's existence . . . as a natural matrix for all the transitions of life," Whitehead says, comparing it to Plato's Receptacle, which, since it "receives all manner of experiences into its own unity . . . must be bare of all forms . . . [It] is invisible, formless, and all receptive."[25] Personal identity is not actual in and of itself, because only occasions of experience are actual, but it is the thread of continuity that runs through the society of occasions that are the ultimate instances of perception (prehension) of human life. As it compares to the Receptacle, it also compares to the Void of Eastern philosophy.

Plato's description in the *Timaeus* of time as "the moving image of eternity"[26] establishes the basis for Whitehead's characterization of the actual event as internally timeless. This understanding is vividly supported in the moment of peak psychedelic experience. Not only is timelessness magnified into eternity in this moment, but the whole immanence of the past in the present is intensely immediate in its subjective form. It manifests as a profound feeling of pervasive oneness in which the "suchness" Zen Buddhism speaks of is revealed. So the poet is given:

> To see a world in a grain of sand,
> And a heaven in a wild flower,
> Hold infinity in the palm of your hand,
> And eternity in an hour.[27]

## II. SUBJECTIVE FORM

Concomitant with the timelessness in the psychedelic peak experience—ultimately deep experience of the present moment in one's society of actual occasions—one feels the force of subjective form from even the most distant past occasions. This is the basis of the mystical comprehension of *oneness*.

"In living persons, the subjective feelings of one occasion are reenacted in its successors with a certain immediacy, but this quickly fades."[28] In extraordinary, profound psychedelic experience that deepens to eternity, all prior subjective form is present in a manner that reflects what Whitehead calls the consequent nature of God. Not only then does the experience elicit oneness with all of creation, but also oneness with the Divine, as signified by *tat tvam asi*, the renowned Hindu expression for the relationship between the individual and the Absolute. How quickly the experience of oneness fades for a person depends on the degree of commitment to living in awareness of it.

This ultimate awareness is most difficult to entertain humbly. In the aftermath of psychedelic experience one may come to believe oneself as God-like and devoid of ego. In that mistaken belief one may unfortunately adopt the mantle of divinity as a substitute for genuine self-understanding. This error is a spiritual bypass likely taken to avoid coming to terms with unresolved biographical material. Therapeutic engagement and committed personal work are important means of averting this error.

## III. PERPETUAL PERISHING

Just as powerfully as experience is immersed in the bliss of eternity and oneness, however, the perishing that is perpetual irrevocably follows, and mortal fear may erupt at the prospect of death of the ego. "I found myself all at once on the brink of panic."[29]

To overcome this fear requires momentous effort. It may mean giving oneself to be devoured by the bear that has suddenly emerged from a dark cave of one's Jungian shadow or cracking under the pressure of some impossible paradox of existential logic. Support from someone who understands the experience is critical in this situation. When courage is summoned, however, and one makes the plunge into the emptiness of the Void, the next occasion will be born. But it cannot be born before the previous moment perishes. At the most intense level this sequence of experience yields the human feeling of death, rebirth, and salvation. At lesser levels the doors of perception get a temporary cleansing.

## IV. VALUE

Contrasts are very important ingredients in the becoming of actual occasions, as contrasts are able to unify opposing feelings and information without eliminating their unique contributions to the whole. Consider how the contrasting colors in classical painting create heightened intensity of effect within an overarching harmony. Effective contrasts help to overcome discrepancies, conflicts, and contradictions in the welter of ingredients an actual occasion must comprehend. There are contrasts between the ways previous actual occasions are prehended, contrasts between characteristics common to groups of actual occasions, and contrasts between potentials. These are contrasts described in metaphysical terminology. In conventional terms there are contrasts between perceptions, feelings, ideas, judgments, previous experiences, and more. Ordinarily a person may not be significantly aware of them. Psychologically, for instance, a person may repress memories of the contradictions faced as a child. A child, dependent upon a mother for its vital sustenance, may also have suffered anger at the mother's neglect. The conflict between need and anger may issue in neurotic inhibition with intimate persons in later life. Conflicted attitudes toward authority may be another source of difficulty in adult life. Such conflicts diminish achievement, satisfaction, and enjoyment in life.

In modern psychology, psychoanalysis was conceived as a means to bring these conflicts into awareness, to make the unconscious conscious, with the goal of resolving the conflicted and contradictory feelings that beget neurosis. A person finds resolution by transmuting the contradictions of past experience into contrasts in present experience. To do so is a profound achievement in the subjectivity of becoming. The result of this achievement in respect to the actual event is greater intensity and realization of value, which was inhibited previously by unresolved contradictions from the past. A person who can come to see the mother of their childhood as a fallible individual—capable of love, neglect, and occasional cruelty—by transforming these conflicting qualities into the contrasting facets that make up every whole human being, will be in a much better position to create an intimate, adult relationship made up of the emotional vicissitudes that constitute all human connection.

Classical psychoanalysis is a very slow process. It takes years of work to get through repressive defenses. It is expensive and requires significant intellectual capacity in a client. Psychedelic amplification of psychological process operates much more quickly, but support and guidance is utterly essential to secure beneficial outcomes.

The intensity of experience with psychedelics is somewhat dose dependent, but intensification may develop for reasons that have no direct relation to dosage or even the substances themselves. Environmental factors in an uncontrolled setting may pose puzzles that are distressingly difficult for a person in a non-ordinary state to sort through. Great psychological effort may be required for a person to cope with the impact of repressed material that comes into awareness with its unresolved conflicts and dilemmas. Mild conflicts initially brought to the fore by psychedelic amplification beget intensity that amplifies further conflicts and even deep contradictions, engaging a self-reinforcing, autocatalytic process. Intensity builds on intensity, ultimately leading to profound existential and metaphysical quandaries. If the process proceeds to the full intensity engendered by profoundly confronting the contradictions that give rise to these quandaries, they can resolve into a harmony of contrasts. In that harmony the FPO reveals its being as an event for its own sake, the intrinsic reality which Whitehead calls "value."[30] It compares to what Plato calls "being" and what Zen Buddhism calls "suchness."

## CONCLUSION

The success of modern Western science, especially its technology, has promoted an ontology that conceives the fundamental nature of the world to consist of discrete bits of enduring matter that are related only by external mechanisms. This ontology relegates subjectivity to a secondary phenomenon that should be explainable by electrochemical interaction. Whitehead proposes a radically different ontology. His fundamental realities are self-created, transitory occasions of subjective experience that become objectively immortal in their perishing—that is, they continue to influence future events. Agency resides in the self-creative becoming of occasions as subjects that intend themselves.

Psychedelic substances, which have come to the fore since the mid-twentieth century, foster exceptional experience that amplifies the subjective process of the occasion's becoming that is the final percipient of the thread of events called a "living person" or "soul" by Whitehead. The modern discovery of psychedelic substances makes it possible to bring the amplification of the subjective process of becoming under the rubric of an experimental ontology. The deliverances of that experimentation both support Whitehead's speculative philosophy and serve his categoreal scheme as a framework for explication of exceptional human experience. These results offer the prospect of returning the subjectivity conceived by Plato and other ancient philosophers—which disappeared in the modern era—back to science and the world.

## CHAPTER EIGHT

# David Ray Griffin on Steiner
# and Whitehead

*Robert McDermott*

ABSTRACT: *This chapter is an appreciative response to David Ray Griffin's previously published essay, "Steiner's Anthroposophy and Whitehead's Philosophy." The first section explores commonalities between Steiner's and Whitehead's philosophies, including their roots in Goethe and their shared rejection of the Cartesian dualism of matter-spirit and subject-object. They both provide strenuous philosophical affirmation of freedom and a panentheistic conception of God. In the second section Griffin offers Whiteheadian support to Steiner's description of the evolution of consciousness. In the third section, Griffin explains that Whitehead would withhold support for Steiner's confident account of the distant future. In the fourth section Griffin generously shows several ways that Steiner's esotericism and spiritual discipline can support Whitehead's philosophy, including his metaphysics and philosophical approach to religion, culture, and education.*

A T A SEMINAR titled "Steiner and American Philosophy" in January 1991, David Ray Griffin presented a paper, "Steiner's Anthroposophy and Whitehead's Philosophy."[1] Frank Oppenheim, S.J., presented an equally thorough and generous essay on Steiner and Josiah Royce. I presented on Steiner and William James. The seminar also included comparisons between Steiner and John Dewey, and Steiner and feminism. These essays were first published in a double issue of *Revision: A Quarterly*

149

*Journal for Consciousness and Transformation*,[2] and subsequently published in a book I edited, *Steiner and American Philosophy*.[3] For the past forty years I have been studying and expositing Steiner's writings in a way comparable to Griffin's lifelong commitment to Whitehead and Oppenheim's commitment to Royce. Although Griffin's essay is available in two publications, I assume that it has not received the attention it deserves. Consequently, I have written this essay in service to Griffin, Whitehead, and Steiner. With impressive thoroughness and clarity, Griffin brought Steiner's philosophical writing (and to some extent his esoteric research) into comparison with Whitehead's philosophy in four categories: commonalities, contrasts, possible advantages of Whitehead, and possible advantages of Steiner. The purpose of the present chapter is to comment on Griffin's essay. This limited purpose is due to the excellence of Griffin's interpretation of Steiner; there is very little to contest. It is precise, insightful, and characteristic David Ray Griffin.

My replies to Griffin's essay, mostly from a Steinerian perspective, are intended to be as fair to Whitehead as Griffin is to Steiner. I offer commentary as an expression of gratitude and an invitation to further speculation. This exercise seems to me well justified because Steiner remains largely ignored by philosophers and because Griffin's essay has probably not been widely read and discussed. It should be enlightening for students of Whitehead to consider Rudolf Steiner, a mostly ignored 20th-century European philosopher and esotericist, shown to be in so many points comparable to Whitehead.

Scholars of Whitehead frequently lament that his philosophy has not gained the prominence nor exercised the influence that it should. This complaint issues from a conviction that Whitehead's vision, analyses, solutions, insights, and intellectual generosity are needed more urgently since their publication in the first half of the twentieth century. Whitehead's warnings against inert ideas, separation of humans from nature, restrictive epistemology, and a lack of vision are ever more corrective for dysfunctional societies and a planet in jeopardy. In a similar way, individuals devoted to Steiner lament that his esoteric ideas, practical advice, and contributions to philosophy and religion, historical vision, education, economics, societal structures, agriculture, and the arts have thus far failed to attract widespread attention among the intellectual class.

Steiner and Whitehead were born within weeks of each other in 1861. David Ray Griffin and I were born within days of each other in

1939. Given Steiner's research in astrology (or what he referred to as astro-
sophy), these two sets of shared birth times will undoubtedly be of greater
interest to students of Steiner than to students of Whitehead. Whitehead
spent his entire career as a professor. In his twenties, Steiner worked as
the editor-in-chief of the national edition of the scientific writings of
Goethe, then as an instructor at an evening school for workers, then
as a philosopher without a position, and beginning at age thirty-nine,
and until his death at age sixty-five, as an esoteric teacher, first for the
Theosophical Society (1902–1912) and then for the rest of his life for the
Anthroposophical Society. Whereas Whitehead's influence is probably
hindered by his use of neologisms—e.g., "prehension," "actual occasion,"
"eternal object,"—Steiner's influence is surely limited by his ideas, not his
terms but the claims themselves: knowledge of the prehistoric past, of
the dead, of angels, of etheric forces in nature; unusual interpretations of
the events revealed in the New Testament; and the cosmic dimensions
of biodynamic (BD) agriculture that takes account of the movement of
planets in planting and harvesting.

The almost complete neglect of Steiner by academic philosophers
after his lifetime is likely due to his esoteric writings following his brief
career as a philosopher. His first proper philosophy book, *Truth and
Knowledge,*[4] which was his doctoral dissertation at Rostock University
in 1891, defended an epistemology based on Johann Gottlieb Fichte.
His major work in philosophy, *Die Philosophie der Freiheit* [*Philosophy
of Freedom*] (1894)[5] falls into two parts. The first is a defense of original
thinking, or thinking based on one's inner life rather than on inherited
or sense-based ideas; the second makes a case for the ideal of a free deed,
one free of external or habitual influences. Steiner also wrote *Riddles of
Philosophy,* a history of Western philosophy beginning with the Greeks
and concentrating on nineteenth-century German philosophy. These
three volumes, and the six thousand lectures (collected in three-hundred-
fifty volumes) that followed, contain only slight references to Emerson
and William James, and no references to other American philosophers.
That Steiner does not mention Whitehead is not surprising, considering
that Steiner died in 1925, just one year after Whitehead went to Harvard
to begin his philosophical career.

Griffin opens his essay with a basic or general contrast: Whitehead
is concerned with truth, Steiner with transformation. Griffin places
this contrast at the front of the essay instead of in section three, on

contrasts, because it is basic to all four sections as well as to Whitehead's and Steiner's philosophies. While this contrast is valid and helpful up to a point, it gives the impression that Steiner is exclusively a spiritual and esoteric teacher, as indeed he was for the last quarter of his life, but from age twenty-one to thirty-nine he was primarily a philosopher and interpreter of contemporary culture. His intellectual concerns compare with the topics on which Whitehead focused during his philosophical career. While Steiner's dissertation shows the dominant influence of German idealism, his other writings show the influence of Goethe, whose worldview is closer to Whitehead's than to German idealism. Steiner's devotion to truth, like Whitehead's, issues from his conviction that false ideas lead to a faulty culture.

Similarly, Whitehead is devoted to transformation as well as to truth. In correspondence on this point my colleague Matthew David Segall, a Whitehead scholar, sent a reply worth quoting in full:

> I wouldn't say Whitehead is uninterested in transformation, since for him every act of cognition irreversibly transforms the knower ("no thinker thinks twice," as he puts it in *Process and Reality*.)[6] In regard to truth, I am reminded of Whitehead's statement: "It is more important that a proposition be interesting than that it be true. This statement is almost a tautology. For the energy of operation of a proposition in an occasion of experience is its interest, and its importance. But of course a true proposition is more apt to be interesting than a false one."[7]

Like Plato's and Aristotle's philosophies, both Steiner and Whitehead focused on *paideia*, the ideals of the culture. They were both convinced that only the truth could lead to lasting transformation. Whitehead's *Process and Reality* (1929) is a metaphysics, and, especially, a cosmology, whereas *Adventures of Ideas* (1933) and *Modes of Thought* (1938) are better understood as *paideia*. Similarly, while Steiner published three books that are properly philosophical—written by a philosopher for professors and students of philosophy—most of his other writings and most of his lectures are focused, as Griffin notes, on transformation. Consequently, Griffin's point holds, but it is worth noting that Steiner considers a true philosophy, as well as true spiritual and esoteric knowledge, to be essential for the ideal transformation of individuals and cultures.

When referring to the writings of Whitehead and Steiner, this essay uses present tense. When referring to the circumstances of the writings, past tense seems more appropriate.

## SIMILARITIES BETWEEN STEINER'S AND WHITEHEAD'S POSITIONS

*Steiner and Whitehead agree on the centrality of the reconciliation of science and religion.*

Whitehead joins science and religion by Creativity; Steiner joins them by imagination. Whitehead's concern with the relation between science and religion was focused primarily on Christianity and secondarily on Buddhism. In *Process and Reality,* Whitehead compares his cosmology to Buddhism and in *Religion in the Making,* he lists Buddhism and Christianity as the only two "rational religions" and praises both for their "clarity of idea, generality of thought, moral respectability, survival power, and width of extension over the world."[8] Because Steiner was a teacher in the Theosophical Society from 1902 until 1912, he lectured extensively on Krishna and the *Bhagavad Gita* as well as on Buddha, but he was focused on spirituality and Western esotericism rather than on historical religions. Steiner was eager to lead his readers past religion to spiritual science, i.e., to a scientific way of knowing spirit in its myriad manifestations.

*Steiner and Whitehead both achieved reconciliation by a more inclusive scheme of thought.*

In Whitehead's third period, after 1) mathematics and logic at Cambridge and 2) philosophy of science at the University of London, he addressed most of the topics necessary for "an inclusive scheme of thought," including philosophy, religion, education, and ideals of a culture, or what is properly referred to as *paideia.* Steiner performed a similar service. To the topics covered by Whitehead, Steiner adds arts, agriculture, economics, and the institution of the Anthroposophical Society for the spread of his esoteric research and methodology.

*For both Steiner and Whitehead the starting point for constructing a worldview is immediate experience.*

Whitehead (in this respect following William James) and Steiner (following Goethe) avoided unwarranted assumptions and built their philosophies from immediate experience. In this respect, they both exhibit a strong affinity with phenomenology. Steiner's affinity with phenomenology extends the idealistic sensibility of Husserl whereas Whitehead in this regard has much in common with the more embodied phenomenology of Merleau-Ponty. Steiner bases his *Philosophy of Freedom* on the reality of his immediate experience of himself as an "I" thinking a relationship between itself and the universe.

*Both Steiner and Whitehead affirm the reality of genuine freedom.*

Freedom is a core presupposition of Whitehead's philosophy. For Steiner, freedom is a goal of the evolution of consciousness. It is also a precondition for love. Steiner sees the future differently from Whitehead, who asserted that "there are no future facts." The difference is not as strong a contrast as I once thought. Griffin's contrast of Whitehead's and Steiner's view of the future, especially their willingness to predict, is complex, subtle, and important. Not surprisingly, the difference hinges on their respective ontologies, essentially idealist and organic. Whitehead's commitment to continuity and relationality works against a prediction not well grounded in the present. Because Steiner predicts events in the very far future, tens of thousands of years, it surely appears that his imagination has outdistanced any relationship between present and future. This might be so, but it is also possible, as Steiner and his followers surely believe, that Steiner actually saw at least some relations of continuity, perhaps some very plausible ones between present and future. He might also have seen the influence of the past through the present to future.

Steiner's position on the possibility of knowing the distant future presupposes claims for a vast and detailed esoteric knowledge of lines of development of the cosmos and of human history. Whitehead's view of the future is based on the more recent past. For Whitehead, future possibilities emerge from the present (inclusive of the past that it has taken up and transformed) in a way that combines both novelty and some degree of predictability. The temporal for Whitehead is organic, not determined or mechanical, but it is not entirely unpredictable if a prediction includes novelty and a measure of indeterminacy.

*Both Steiner and Whitehead reject three dominant modern*
*Western worldviews: Cartesian dualism of matter and spirit, and*
*two forms of monism—materialism and spiritualism.*

Whitehead's metaphysics is a model of *pan-en-theism*. Griffin regards
Steiner as a monist and pantheist but, depending on how these terms are
defined, there is room for argument on this characterization. What is
clear is that for both thinkers, the divine permeates but is not exhausted
by (i.e., not coextensive with) creation. God is both imminent and transcendent. They both reject the pantheism of Spinoza. Granting Griffin's
point, Steiner sees the whole of creation issuing from and necessarily
returning to the divine. In Steiner's view, which seems identical to
Whitehead's concept of the consequent nature of God, initial aims of
finite creatures return to God. Steiner believes that human aims and
deeds, including all thoughts, are saved in God's infinite and eternal
nature. In some of Steiner's lectures he refers to Christ as the Lord of
Karma, that is, as the divine being, one with the Father/Ground of
Being, who gathers all of creation, from the cosmos to a fleeting thought,
into Himself. All of the past (which will include the future) is destined
to be saved by and in God through Christ. The creation that comes
to be through the Logos returns to God through the saving agency of
Christ. Steiner holds that the penetration of matter by spirit is constantly
evolving, ideally leading to complete transformation, or more precisely
the complete spiritualization of matter. For both Whitehead and Steiner,
materialism fails to acknowledge the reality of spirit, and spiritualism
fails to acknowledge the reality of matter.

*Both Steiner and Whitehead reaffirm a macrocosm-microcosm metaphor: Each*
*member depends on every other, so that interdependence is the basic fact of existence.*

Along with the philosophies of Friedrich Schelling, William James,
and Henri Bergson, Whitehead's is one of the prime examples of a
thoroughly organic philosophy. Every particular is connected to
every other, no particular is in complete isolation, and none is lost.
Steiner similarly affirms mutual interdependence of the four spheres
of being he describes: the physical, etheric (life principle), soul (astral),
and spirit (the enduring spiritual "I"). Further, nature and humanity
are dependent on divine hierarchies who in turn are dependent on
humanity to realize the shared goals of freedom and love on Earth.

The hierarchies desire this achievement but are powerless to create it without human collaboration.

*Both Steiner and Whitehead are concerned with overcoming the subject-object split.*

For Whitehead, process is foundational and inclusive of "subject" and "object." Similarly, Steiner's phenomenology affirms a recursive loop: subject-object-subject-object. Both philosophies are comprehensively multi-perspectival: every subject serves as an object for at least one other subject. Every object has its own interiority, and no subject stands entirely alone and unattended. The object to which a subject is related is also a subject observed by an object, *ad infinitum,* without limit.

*Both Steiner and Whitehead are influenced by Romanticism.*

As Whitehead's philosophy echoes the poetic sensibility of Wordsworth, Steiner's philosophy expresses the artistic imagination of Goethe.

*Both Steiner and Whitehead reject the dominant
modern denial of divine presence in the world.*

As Griffin explains:

> Whitehead, after having been an agnostic for most of his profes-
> sional life, came to affirm the reality of a deity who provides an
> "initial aim" to every event, thereby grounding the teleology of
> the universe. "The world lives by its incarnation of God in itself."[9]

Creativity both pushes and lures creation in general and in every detail. Steiner similarly affirms (and strives to know) the influence on cosmos and humanity of an imminent divine reality. From the beginning of creation and presumably until its end, the nine divine hierarchies (nine levels of creativity from Seraphim and Cherubim to Archangels and Angels) have poured their substance into the cosmos. These hier-archies figure prominently in Steiner's spiritual cosmology.

Whitehead does not affirm, and probably did not consider, these divine hierarchies, at least not at length and not in scriptural terms, but he does approvingly mention Plato's conception of "subordinate deities" as "the animating principles" of "certain departments of nature."[10]

Both Whitehead and Steiner believe that divine influence is

necessary. Consequently they reject the Darwinian theory of biological evolution as an inadequate basis for a metaphysics of creation. Evolution is central to their thinking, but they differ from a Darwinian version in their affirmation of divine cause and purpose in creation. Evolution of consciousness is implicit in Whitehead's philosophy whereas for Steiner it is a central commitment, one that he developed comprehensively. As John Cobb and David Ray Griffin developed the evolutionary dimension of Whitehead's philosophy, Owen Barfield further developed evolution of consciousness as espoused by Steiner.

*Both Steiner and Whitehead provide a Christian cosmology.*

Far more than Whitehead, Steiner's cosmology affirms Christ at the center throughout the evolution of consciousness, and it does so in the kind of detail that has been difficult for most readers to accept. Whitehead insists that the divine element must be persuasive (not coercive); Steiner would seem to agree but he also sees Christ as a force, perhaps not coercive, but certainly a comprehensive and powerful intervention on the side of love.

Whitehead reconciles theism with both evolution and evil. By attributing limited power to God, a position first proposed by William James, Whitehead solves the problem that occupied Christian theologians for centuries, namely, the conflict between the unlimited power attributed to God and the failure of such an all-powerful God to prevent evil and suffering. By attributing to God total goodness but limited power, Whitehead frees the concept of God from responsibility for evil and suffering. According to Steiner, God does not directly cause evil but because God did set, and continues to influence, the evolution of creation, God apparently intends that evil serve as a stimulant to the more meaningful eventual triumph of good over evil, of love over hatred.

*Both Steiner and Whitehead hold a "dipolar" doctrine of*
*God: God affects the world, the world affects God.*

In contrast to the traditional Christian theological conception of God, Whitehead holds that God's consequent nature evolves thanks to collaborative striving of all creation, most particularly human beings. According to Steiner, all beings evolve dependent on the effort of humans, the only free hierarchy.

*Both Steiner and Whitehead reject the sensationist doctrine of perception.*

Whitehead insists, against the British empiricists—particularly John Locke and David Hume—that human experience is not limited to sensory perception. His philosophy is sufficiently Platonic and Romantic to affirm multiple ways of knowing, including intuition. Steiner's philosophy affirms sensory perception as the lowest of four ways of knowing. The three higher ways, all in need of development, are imagination, inspiration, and intuition. Steiner's *Philosophy of Freedom* is essentially an epistemological argument for intuitive thinking, and his *How to Know Higher Worlds* (1904),[11] is essentially a guidebook for the acquisition of esoteric knowledge.

*Both Steiner and Whitehead espoused "epistemological monism" (the comprehensive perception of "facts," "qualities," and "values") thanks to their acceptance of nonsensory perception through which the affective and valuational features of reality can be directly perceived.*

## WHITEHEADIAN SUPPORT FOR SOME OF STEINER'S OCCULT NOTIONS

In direct opposition to the dominant modern Western epistemology and metaphysics, Whitehead and Steiner affirm secondary qualities or properties, also called "occult." Since the eighteenth century and, specifically the philosophy of John Locke, secondary qualities—color, taste, smell, sound—have been generally rejected as a source of objective knowledge. Most philosophers since Locke have accepted his argument that objective knowledge is derived only from sense experience of primary qualities, i.e., measurable, quantifiable dimensions. By this argument, primary qualities (which are better understood as quantities) provide facts independent of an observer, whereas secondary qualities are subjective. Whitehead and Steiner (following Goethe) recognize that all facts are theory laden, and all objective knowledge has a subjective dimension hidden to sensory perception and intellectual reasoning. This epistemological position enables Whitehead and Steiner to affirm five realities not shared by the main line of Western philosophy, and are rather developed in the field of parapsychology, or what might more accurately be called paraphilosophy.[12]

*Occult Qualities and Powers*

Whitehead opposes the standard modern Western view of nature as "lifeless," and urges readers to get beyond that view to "nature alive" (with enjoyment, aim, and creativity), through recognition that perception is not limited to the senses. Whitehead explains:

> Sense perception for all its practical importance is very superficial in its disclosure of the nature of things. . . . My quarrel with modern epistemology concerns its exclusive stress upon sense perception for the provision of data respecting nature.[13]

The problem with this sensationalist doctrine of perception is that it "only deals with half the evidence provided by human experience."[14]

Whitehead, the defender of Romantic poets, mocks this view of nature in an oft-quoted passage from *Science and the Modern World*, in which he spells out the consequences of Locke's epistemology, according to which sensory qualities, which are "purely the offspring of the mind," are "projected by the mind so as to clothe appropriate bodies in external nature." Writes Whitehead:

> Thus nature [for Locke] gets credit, which should in truth be reserved for ourselves; the rose for its scent; the nightingale for its song; and the sun for its radiance. The poets are entirely mistaken. They should address their lyrics to themselves, and should turn them into odes of self-congratulation on the excellency of the human mind. Nature is a dull affair, soulless, scentless, colorless; merely the hurrying of material, endlessly, meaninglessly.[15]

Whitehead agrees with Locke that "secondary qualities" are a function of the perceiver, but disagrees that a secondary quality is produced solely from a primary quality. Whitehead holds that secondary qualities are produced out of tertiary qualities, i.e., values (e.g., red), which are a "subjective form of feeling."[16] Whitehead recognizes the creativity of the human mind in sensory perception, thereby avoiding naive realism, without succumbing to the view that nature in itself is devoid of qualitative values.

Similarly, by "occult," Steiner means knowledge that is not grasped by means of the senses aand not derived from the senses by the intellect. His *Philosophy of Freedom* is an attempt to steer the same middle way as Whitehead: Following Aristotle, Thomas Aquinas, and especially Goethe, he argues against naive realism (the tree is there, it is as simple as that) and subjective idealism (the tree is in the mind) in favor of critical idealism. This position could also be called critical realism. His epistemology is a realism because nature is the necessary ingredient in knowledge; it is critical in that it requires a way of knowing above sense perception. It requires actual thinking made possible by will and affect.

*Extrasensory Perception*

Griffin defines extrasensory perception as the direct, conscious perceptual experience of actualities beyond one's own body without employment of the bodily senses. According to Whitehead, perception includes the prehension of the entire past, not just contiguous past: The "many become one" and the "many" is comprised of the entire past of the entire universe. Therefore it is possible to prehend distant objects: "In this form of perception we directly perceive (contra Hume) other actualities, and we (contra Hume and Kant) directly perceive their causal efficacy upon us."[17] Thus we experience interconnectedness. Direct perception (apart from sensory organs) is telepathic or clairvoyant. According to Steiner, extrasensory perceptions are usually smothered by sensory perceptions but they can be "supersensible" i.e., perceptions of real events and entities at a distance.

*The Akashic Record*

For both Whitehead and Steiner, the past exists and is accessible. "Retrocognition," or perception at temporal distance, is controversial because of the (mistaken) notion that the past no longer exists. Steiner insists that "the facts even of the remote past have not disappeared."[18] Similarly, Whitehead states, "The consequent nature of God is the fluent world become 'everlasting' by its objective immortality in God."[19] Because individuals of the world prehend the consequent nature of God, one can have knowledge of the truth about the past and about its influence on the world. Steiner states, and develops by countless examples, knowledge derived by this direct access to the Akashic Record.[20]

*Divine Influence*

Whitehead holds that God's primordial nature provides an initial subjective aim for the realization of eternal objects in the world in due season. The finite occasion has the power of self-determination even vis-a-vis God. Similarly, according to Steiner, God, and more specifically the nine hierarchies, provide the impetus for the realization of ideal destinies of individuals.

*Life After Death*

Late modern, materialistic thought (distinct from early modern, dualistic thought) considers the idea of life after death impossible because perception is thought to be wholly dependent upon the physical body. Whereas theism is dualistic (Creator and creation), both Whitehead and Steiner are panpsychist: Creation is permeated by consciousness. Although Whitehead did not believe life after death to be actual, he acknowledged its possibility because psyche is potentially free to exist and perceive apart from its physical body. Steiner argued for the existence of personal life after death based on both his clairvoyance and his philosophical reflections, specifically, as with Whitehead, on the independence of psyche from sense perception.

## WHITEHEADIAN BASES FOR WITHHOLDING
## AFFIRMATION FROM SOME OF STEINER'S IDEAS

*Monism*

According to Griffin, Whitehead and Steiner both hold that we are composed of the same stuff as the divine and that "being" is to be predicated univocally of God and creation. But Griffin also states that Whitehead distinguishes God from being whereas, according to Griffin, Steiner equated God and being. This might be so, but it should be noted that Steiner seldom wrote or lectured on being as such, or on God. He was concerned to know and describe the nine hierarchies, beings below the level of God. He was not writing metaphysics, or ontology, but phenomenology, a description and analysis of his experience of mental and spiritual life.

For Whitehead, being is identical with creativity. God is the primordial embodiment of creativity: "All actual entities share with

God this characteristic of self-causation."[21] Finite events are self-determining. Because all human beings (true individuals as opposed to stones, for example) are able to deviate from divine initial aim, it must be maintained that God and being are distinct.

While it is possible that Steiner would disagree with this position that Griffin attributes to Whitehead, I am not sure why Steiner would do so. As I mentioned above, Steiner did not develop an ontology with respect to God or being. If he were to respond to Griffin on this point, however, it seems to me that he would add that such a deviation from God characterizes every hierarchical level to a greater or lesser extent. Satan or Lucifer, in Steiner's esoteric tracking and extensive descriptions, is a particularly powerful example of an influential spiritual being who opposes God. In their thinking and behavior, humans obviously thwart divine intention—i.e., they act out of ignorance, fear, and hatred and not out of knowledge, courage, and love.

Griffin characterizes Steiner's philosophy as monistic "and thereby pantheistic." In the discussion above I agree with Griffin's characterization of Steiner's philosophy as panpsychist—consciousness permeates the whole of creation. (For Whitehead, "experience" permeates the whole of creation.) But Griffin's characterization of Steiner as pantheist seems to me unclear, and in certain respects misleading. Griffin quotes Steiner's rhetorical question: "Would anyone contend that a drop of water is the sea when he says that the drop is of the same essence or substance as the sea?" Steiner also states that "the drop of water has the same relationship to the sea that the I has to the Divine." And again: "our innermost being is drawn from the Divine."[22]

Based on these statements by Steiner, Griffin is entirely justified in his attribution of pantheism as well as monism to Steiner. These passages seem to support Griffin's contention that according to Steiner "we are simply parts of God." Steiner might want to agree, however, with Whitehead's position, which Griffin characterizes as pan-en-theist, i.e., "that it distinguishes between God and being itself." I also think Steiner would partly agree with Griffin's statement on behalf of Whitehead "that we and God both transcend each other by virtue of having our own creativity."[23] Because Steiner discussed Christ, but very seldom discussed God, it is difficult to assess the extent of the agreement on this topic. Overall, it seems to me that Steiner's position is closer, perhaps decisively so, to Hegel's than to Whitehead's.

Because Steiner's account of the origin and evolution of the cosmos and of humanity involves the nine hierarchies and the profound struggle to return to God, the adjective "simply" seems misleading at best. The Logos is distinct from the Father and Spirit but not "simply." In sum, the whole of creation is distinguishable from God, equally and ultimately, but not simply "parts of God." With respect to the Creator-creation relationship, "drawn from" is slightly different from "identical with" or the "same substance as" in that creation expresses itself freely and creatively, yet, always and necessarily not outside of God.

In Steiner's view, creation is from and of God but is free to express itself in an infinity of finite ways. For Steiner, God's substance is spirit, infinite and eternal; all else is finite and temporal. Steiner attributes to God as Trinity a nature that includes the world, but he almost certainly would not agree with Whitehead's statement that "the world transcends God."[24] The world expresses and changes God, but as part of God's being; it is not separable. Monism of spirit is a correct characterization of Steiner's position, but if pantheism denies a distinction between God and creation, then Steiner would not qualify. Instead, his position would seem to be panentheist, i.e., God, particularly in the influence of Christ and the Holy Spirit, is throughout creation, but God as Father/Ground of Being remains eternally not exhausted by creation.

## Problem of Evil

According to Griffin, Steiner's view of evil is implausible because it regards all evil, as indeed all events, as part of God's nature. What Griffin refers to as "Steiner's pantheistic tendency" prevents an evil deed from enduring as evil; all evils will eventually be redeemed by God and as such evil deeds must be understood to be merely temporally and instrumentally evil—in the long run not really evil after all. In agreement with Whitehead (and Griffin), Steiner holds that "the forces at work in the world are both destructive and constructive"[25] and that it is the moral duty of human beings to work for the constructive against the destructive. He would also agree with Whitehead and Griffin that the better does not happen because of human ignorance and flawed nature. Griffin claims that the view which expects God to gather up all evil thoughts and deeds inevitably leads the human who holds such a view to withhold necessary effort on behalf of the good or better.

While Steiner admits that evil should be understood to be in the service of a higher good, it is not for that reason less evil. It is still the enemy of good and better. God and creation are less, and less good, than they might have been. Steiner, a deeply committed Christian incarnationalist, considers Christ's entering human history, and in the end suffering as a human being, to be in direct opposition to evil. Redemption by Christ transforms evil but does not eradicate it. Torture, suffering, loss of meaning, and other forms of physical and mental evil actively negate whatever might have been better. They can lead to what might be better, but in themselves evil thoughts and deeds really occurred in all of their negativity, and they await transformation but not eradication.

*Philosophy*

According to Whitehead, philosophy "embodies the method of the 'working hypothesis.'" Such a philosophy is speculative: "Our thoughts are not God's thoughts."[26] Steiner viewed his claims, both philosophical and esoteric, as fallible, but rather unfortunately he also reported esoteric claims with a confidence suggesting certainty. Given Steiner's comprehensive view of the evolution of consciousness, he should always have reported results of esoteric research tentatively: Whatever might be true at present needn't have been true in the past and needn't prove to be true in the future. While his specific esoteric claims might be true to the circumstance or situation, a philosophy that attempts to place and explain such claims (however true they might be in the moment) will eventually undergo a change of circumstance and therefore a diminishment of truth. Claims might also gain in truth. Steiner granted that other esoteric researchers would see differently from him the events he saw preserved in the Akashic Record, and even that he would read it more clearly at a later time, but unfortunately he also gave the impression that his reading was certain and would endure as such.

Griffin is skeptical of Steiner's claim to be able to distinguish genuine spiritual perception from self-produced vision, the kind that Owen Barfield describes as the "specious given."[27] These perceptions seem given as spiritual truth when in fact they are self-produced. Steiner should have been willing to treat his claims as hypotheses to be evaluated according to the criteria Griffin suggest here, namely, self-consistency, adequacy, and illuminating power. It is sad to agree, as one must, that both Steiner and his followers are generally uncritical about the reliability of his spiritual knowledge. Griffin also introduces a fascinating, obvious, and yet surprising complication: Given that the Akashic Record includes the essential memory of all events in the past, it must include "a wild mixture of fact and fancy." If one were to tap into the Akashic, as Steiner presumably did to a remarkable degree, false and evil ideas would be retrieved along with truth. This conundrum awaits further consideration.

*Freedom and Knowledge of the Future*

Griffin attributes to Steiner the view that at least in some important respects the future is knowable. This is so because the future is determined: in Steiner's view, "what must happen will happen." It is also  true, however, that Steiner holds that human freedom alters what might happen. Steiner would seem to agree that human self-determination and creativity in the present forever change future possibilities. The difference between Whitehead-Griffin and Steiner is due to Steiner's affirmation of human freedom while holding to some degree of necessity with respect to nonhuman events. Griffin argues that there is no dualism between human and natural events: In his view, they are either all necessary or all contingent. And nature is not as independent of human freedom as Steiner supposed (e.g., global warming and natural disasters have now come to be caused by human freedom). The most challenging part of Steiner's view is his confident description of events and qualities of consciousness in the distant future.

## STEINER'S SUGGESTION OF A SPIRITUAL DISCIPLINE APPROPRIATE TO WHITEHEADIANS

*Transformation*

Griffin correctly identifies Steiner's "central concern," as the evolution of humanity. In Griffin's view, Steiner holds that the human being "has it in his power to perfect himself and, in time, completely to transform himself."[29] A fuller characterization of Steiner's central concern would include the realization of freedom and love. As Griffin notes, Whitehead affirms a similar concern but does not offer a method of transformation. For Steiner, the attempt at perfection through spiritual discipline is an accomplishment for both oneself and the world. Whitehead similarly affirms the influence, both direct and indirect, of one's soul activity on others, but Whitehead does not delineate such a transformative process nor prescribe exercises for its attainment.

## Self-Consciousness

Both Steiner and Whitehead sought to overcome the subject/object split that gained dominance beginning in the seventeenth century and increased in its control of human consciousness up to the present. Following Steiner, Owen Barfield describes this mode of consciousness as "the maximum point of self-consciousness the point at which the individual feels entirely cut off from the cosmos."[30] Similarly, in Whitehead's account of consciousness, the modern Western person lives at a remove from causal efficacy. But, again, Whitehead's method for reducing this isolation is philosophic thought. Griffin would have done well to emphasize what, to a far greater degree than Whitehead, Steiner espouses and advises, namely, that all arts—including painting, poetry, sculpture, architecture, and music—are crucial anthroposophical methods of human transformation.

## Problem of Modern Philosophy

Both Steiner and Whitehead are critical of the extent to which modern Western philosophy clings to the illusion that philosophy, and thinking more generally, can progress without attention to "the physical perception of other actualities." Whitehead holds that in their affirmation of mind as independent of physical realities, Descartes, Locke, Hume, and Kant all accepted this subjectivist and, in fact, solipsistic view. Because Steiner's epistemology is rooted in the nature philosophy of Goethe (a critical antidote to German idealism, in which Steiner was equally rooted) he was able to develop a realist metaphysics and epistemology fully affirmative of the physical world. Griffin could have expanded his treatment of this dimension of Steiner's thought, particularly his contribution to a new method of agriculture, remedies for illnesses, theories of heat and light, and the functioning of the human body.

In this regard, Steiner could easily agree with Whitehead's characterization of philosophy as "the self-correction by consciousness of its own initial excess of subjectivity."[31] Griffin rightly asks whether this ideal function of philosophy is a sufficient foundation for transformation. Can contemporary consciousness be healed, i.e., rendered more integral and organic, by making the correction in "rational experience"? Steiner's reply would be "of course not": Transformation at such a fundamental level in direct opposition to modern Western consciousness requires a comprehensive spiritual discipline, including arts, sciences, personal relations, and a comprehensive schooling in thought and action. Griffin might have noted that while Whitehead embodied reverence and humility, the two qualities that Steiner places at the foundation of spiritual practice, Whitehead did not attempt to teach others the way to realize the excellence he exemplified.

## *Disciplines of Transformation*

Griffin effectively pairs Whitehead's and Steiner's commitment to morality based on the unity of the human and the cosmos, the whole of reality. The experienced "sense of connection with 'the totality' ... can lead, as most religions stress, to a transformation from egoism to a sense of love and concern for others, even for all things." Griffin notes that "Whitehead sees this goal as the only solution to the problem of morality." Whitehead emphasizes that the occasions of experience act as a whole such that knowing is not divorced from feeling. Griffin writes: "If we could become fully conscious of the feelings at the base of our experience in each moment, we would know 'the deepest mysteries.'"[32]

Griffin offers a passage from Steiner's *Philosophy of Freedom* that supports and, perhaps, extends Whitehead's metaphysically based ethics:

> The individual ... ceases to contemplate things from his own separate standpoint. The limits of his narrow self, which fetter him to this outlook, disappear. ... This is liberation. ... It is from this personal manner of regarding things, that the ... student must become independent and free. [33]

Griffin correctly states that according to Steiner, the first step in this process is the student's "basic feeling of devotion for everything which is truly venerable ... Just as the sun's rays vivify all feelings of the soul."[34] Griffin quotes two passages from Steiner's *Philosophy of Freedom* concerning reverence:

It is not easy, at first, to believe that feelings like reverence and respect have anything to do with cognition. This is due to the fact that we are inclined to set cognition aside as a faculty by itself—one that stands in no relation to what otherwise occurs in the soul. In so thinking, we do not bear in mind that it is the soul which exercises the faculty of cognition; and feelings are for the soul what food is for the body.

If we give the body stones in place of bread, its activity will cease. It is the same with the soul. Veneration, homage, devotion are like nutriment making it healthy and strong, especially strong for the activity of cognition. Disrespect, antipathy, underestimation of what deserves recognition, all exert a paralyzing and withering effect on this faculty of cognition . . . A soul which harbors feelings of reverence and devotion . . . receives intelligence of facts in its environment of which it had hitherto no idea. Reverence awakens in the soul a sympathetic power through which we attract qualities in the beings around us, which would otherwise remain concealed.[35]

These passages effectively summarize the primary way that Steiner, in terms of this section, offers a spiritual discipline appropriate for Whiteheadians.[36] Complementarily, Whitehead himself is an inspiring model of precisely these virtues, and irrespective of Whitehead's relationship to such a discipline, his philosophy shows the positive effects of his character.

CONCLUSION

David Ray Griffin's essay stands as a positive contribution to comparative philosophy, as another perspective on the philosophy of A. N. Whitehead, and as one of only a few studies of Steiner by a non-anthroposophist. It is also a model of textual scholarship, sound philosophical judgment, and precise thinking and exposition. Steiner would have been pleased to have his thought rendered intelligible and comparable by a first-rate American philosopher and a representative of the American philosophical tradition, which, except for his reading of Emerson, Steiner generally ignored and neglected.

This essay mostly agrees with Griffin's interpretation and presentation of Steiner's thought. It merely adds detail, occasional clarification, and two points of substance: It questions, without satisfactorily settling, Griffin's characterization of Steiner's thought as pantheist, and also questions Griffin's interpretation of Steiner's position on evil. Steiner holds that evil will be atoned by God but that it will also continue to exist in its original negativity. The resulting unity within God apparently will not eradicate the initial opposition of good and evil, hatred and love. This essay agrees with Griffin's characterization of Whitehead's focus on truth and Steiner's on transformation, and then emphasizes that Steiner's commitment to a dozen arts contributes to the attainment of truth as well as adds to the process of transformation. Finally, I recommend that students of Whitehead, Griffin, and Steiner return to Griffin's essay available in *American Philosophy and Rudolf Steiner*.[37]

## CHAPTER NINE

# A Phenomenology
# of the Ecological Self

*Christopher M. Aanstoos*

ABSTRACT: *This chapter explores the question "Who are we?" from an ecopsy-chological perspective. Combining insights and ideas from classical and current phenomenologists—such as Maurice Merleau-Ponty and David Abram—along with the metaphysics of Alfred North Whitehead, this essay develops and promotes a view of concrete lived existence that is holistic, interconnected, and ecological to the core. This new way of understanding existence is vital for overcoming the objectification of self and nature, which results from modernity's anachronistic commitment to a mechanistic worl-dview. This new holistic understanding involves what the author has described as the "long body" of lived experience, which flows seamlessly into nature as the "ecological self."*

## SO, WHAT'S THE PROBLEM?

STEPHEN TOULMIN cleverly noted that the problem with our modern age is that it's over, but this demise has not yet been duly understood.[1] That "modern" view of the nature of reality has been governed by science ever since it displaced religion four centuries ago as the less corruptible source of authority after a century of religious sectarian warfare in Europe had culminated in the devastating Thirty Years War. But, as philosophers of science have long recognized, science itself is governed by sets of fundamental assumptions about reality that frame its own world picture. Edwin Burtt called these the "metaphysical foundations of modern physical science."[2] Toulmin called them the "hidden agenda of modernity," because they are typically presupposed rather than recognized as such. As Thomas Kuhn famously observed, these basic assumptions form an implicit "paradigm."[3] They tend to become evident only when a sufficiently alarming number of anomalies accumulate—phenomena that cannot be reconciled to the prevailing paradigmatic model. The ongoing failure of the paradigm to account for these anomalous phenomena eventually leads to deeper questions about the basic assumptions of the paradigm itself, and then to its eventual overturning by a successor paradigm better able to account for the anomalies. The ways that relativity theory and quantum mechanics eventually displaced the Newtonian paradigm in physics in the twentieth century might stand as an exemplar case.

Now, as we navigate the dilemmas of the twenty-first century, we find ourselves confronted by unprecedented challenges to our former ways of looking at reality. Basically, the dilemma of looming ecological disasters presents us with the most fundamental challenge to our former way of conceiving of the world as a storehouse of energy reserves to be exploited. The utter unsustainability of that conception of our world relations, now evident in light of its catastrophic ecological consequences, has finally led to the emergence of deep critical questions about the basic assumptions of the current paradigm. It is finally time to "seize an alternative," to build an "ecological civilization." I take this to be an extremely urgent task, and ecology to be the key to the next century. Just as the twentieth century began with the need to understand the depth of our psyche (from the Greek *psükhe* meaning breath, life, soul), now we are faced, at the twenty-first, with the task to become aware of the breadth of our *eco* (from the Greek *oikos,* meaning home). Or, to put this emergence into a longer historical context, we can consider that the discipline of eco-nomics—the regulation of the eco—came into prominence as we began the modern world. At the end of the seventeenth century, we began to conceive of the world as a machine, a vast storehouse of resources to be exploited by our mechanistic approach to it, which became the Industrial Revolution. And it is only now, as we arrive at the far side of that industrial mentality and reap the whirlwind of its true ecological cost, that the discipline of ecology—the logos of the eco—has now found its prime time.[4]

I think it is no coincidence that zombies have become the culture's current face of the inimical Other, having displaced the vampire that had previously held sway in that regard. Vampires at least still had desire, could be aroused, and felt fear for their own and others' vulnerability. Zombies, on the other hand, are the true "walking dead." A zombie will devour its own brother, its own mother, and its own child, with no concern, with no awareness even, for the destructive consequences of its actions. We are now being faced, through the work of our artists, with the stark, unsustainable ecological consequences of our zombie-being.

Only now? But wasn't this crisis already well-known before this century dawned? Didn't John Cobb warn that it might already be "too late"—in 1972? Didn't the 60s' counterculture promote the first "Earth Day" to raise consciousness of environmental crises—in 1970? Didn't Rachel Carson warn us of "silent springs"—in 1962? And didn't Aldo Leopold depict the eco-logos—in 1947? Oh, yes, we have had lots and lots of warning. So why are we still living unsustainably? Why are we still being zombies? Because, ultimately, this crisis is not a technological problem. Ultimately, it is a crisis of *vision*. It is a crisis of perception, a mindset that we need to change if we are to transcend this crisis.

And that is the realm of psychology. If only psychology, still in thrall to the natural science paradigm, would rise in stature to take this on. So far, mainstream cognitivist and behaviorist-based experimental studies on environmental thinking and acting remain too abstract from the real world to have any helpful impact. However, psychology's humanistic and transpersonal branches, marginalized though these still are, have been at this task for a generation now. Ted Roszak coined the term "ecopsychology" in 1992 to portray this emerging trend, and then literally edited the book on it, featuring the work of these pioneers.[5] I teach a course with that title at the University of West Georgia and, although it is not a required course, it fills up as quickly as any in the university. The students are there. They come, hungry for a new vision.

SO, WHAT'S THE ALTERNATIVE?

What perceptual shift, what paradigmatic change, is needed? What new vision is called for, to which the old paradigm has blinded us? The paradigm of the past few centuries has enframed the world as a big pile of objects having only extrinsic relations, governed by causal, mechanical forces—a "standing reserve" of resources, potential energy to be harnessed for power.[6] At first, this vision seemed to place people as the "lords and masters" of reality—as the harnessers of the power. But, as Marx and other political economists of the nineteenth century began to note (and Heidegger to later articulate very deeply), in this conception, humans too, become part of that standing reserve to be used. As corporate power now realizes quite well, the "human resources" must be especially exploited for maximal gain.

While retrieving the human from its alienation as "stuff" is surely a step in the right direction, this crisis is deeper than that. It will not be solved by separating the human as something apart from the world. In this retrieval project, we must recover the whole natural world as well. As noted already, the current trajectory is simply unsustainable: we need a new vision of the world.

## BUT WHAT IS THE SOLUTION?

Shame? Guilt? Loud as they have become, they don't seem to be working very well. Appeals to self-interest? They do sound very rational, but these have tended to fall prey to the classic "freeloader dilemma": one's own self-interest is best served by getting others to change their ways while you get to continue living unsustainably. (This can be applied to whole countries.) Some, such as Roszak, have proposed encouraging a sense of "bio-phila"—teaching people to love the natural world.[7] And certainly this is a very good step. But my point here is that we must—and can—go further than that. Or, if you like, we can, and must, take "biophilia" to its deepest, experiential taproots and implications. What we need to do is to renew a deeper way of experiencing the world. Specifically, we need to get beyond encountering the world as an Other, as something "out there" to either exploit or to appreciate. We need to encounter the world not through merely extrinsic relations, but as intrinsically related to us. In short, what this ecological crisis requires is for us to fully and finally experience our nondual relationship with the world. A deep connectedness.

It is that crippling legacy of dualism—of the separation of consciousness from the world—that is the fatal flaw of the dominant paradigm. Bequeathed to us at the seventeenth-century birth of modern physical science by Galileo, Descartes, and Newton, it definitely had its uses. By steering its vision of nature in the image of a machine, a pile to exploit, it enabled Europe to achieve the Industrial Revolution, augmenting its own power so exponentially that, within two centuries, it had colonized all the other great civilizations in the world. But dualism, like Newtonian physics more generally, is a vision that is accurate only in rough approximation. Examined more closely (i.e., at the very small or very large scale), dualism conceals a deeper reality: an implicate order of intrinsic, interrelated wholeness. If we are to see our way beyond the ecological crisis, it is this vision of the whole that we so urgently need.

## SO, WHAT DOES THIS NEW VISION OFFER?

To discover what this holistic vision can show us, I will now sketch its implications in two ways: first, via the philosophy of Alfred North Whitehead, and second, via that of phenomenological ecopsychology. Asian traditions, especially the Buddhist and Vedic paths, have, of course, also contributed enormously to the development of philosophies of nonduality.[8] But as a Western legacy, I would like to examine contemporary Western attempts to overcome this dualism. And within contemporary Western thought on the theme of nonduality, I find these two approaches to be the most fertile and the most promising. I also find these two paths remarkably convergent, and the overlap in the philosophies of Whitehead and Husserl's phenomenology is striking, as noted by various scholars (Enzo Paci, Jean-Marie Breuvart, Matthew Segall, Evan Thompson, and Charles Hartshorne, for example).[9] Their major works were often written at the same time, though completely independently of each other. They did not even know of each other! (Surely this is an example of the sorts of synchronicities in the new philosophies of science of the 1920s that Toulmin and Burtt both noted.)

With Whitehead and Husserl as our interlocutors, we can decisively challenge and overturn the mechanistic paradigm by finally and fully accounting for its anomalies. Let's start with Whitehead. He very sharply criticized the traditional subject-object dualism as being an abstraction from reality, for shooting "beyond" reality, as it were, and ending in what he called "the fallacy of misplaced concreteness." For example, he wrote about the

> fixed scientific cosmology which presupposes the ultimate fact
> of an irreducible brute matter, or material, spread throughout

space ... this assumption that I call 'scientific materialism' ... it is not wrong if properly construed. If we confine ourselves to certain types of facts, abstracted from the complete circumstances in which they occur, the materialistic assumption expresses these facts to perfection. But when we pass beyond the abstraction ... the scheme breaks down at once.[10]

The enormous success of the scientific abstractions ... has foisted onto philosophy the task of accepting them as the most concrete rendering of fact ... Thereby modern philosophy has been ruined ... this juggling with abstractions can never overcome the inherent confusion introduced by the ascription of misplaced concreteness to the scientific scheme.[11]

For Whitehead, the trap is thinking in terms of subject-object dualism, and the way out of this trap was to return to unitary reality as experienced—experience being the ultimate event, the actualization of reality.[12]

This is all extraordinarily similar to what Edmund Husserl was saying at the same time. He developed phenomenology as an approach to philosophy and to the sciences:

we must note something of the highest importance that occurred even as early as Galileo: the surreptitious substitution of the mathematically substructed world of idealities for the only real world, the one that is actually given through perception, that is ever experienced and experiencible—our everyday life-world.[13]

Both Husserl and Whitehead sought to ground philosophy not speculatively but in actual data. These data, to be actual, are events, experienced reality. It is our actual living experience that is anterior to any conceptions of subjects and objects. Return to the things themselves!, said both Whitehead and Husserl. That is where we will find our mean- ingfully lived experiences—beneath the separate concepts of subject and object—as experienced units of bodily, lived interconnectedness. As Whitehead said, this "unity of the perceptual field must be a unity of bodily experience" and "the withness of the body" in all perception.[14] The same is true for Husserl, a key point to which I will return later. For now, one last key Whiteheadian concept: Nature.

For Whitehead, nature was no collection of objects, but a

concrescence of events. Indeed, his most sardonic refutation of the dominant paradigm was for what he called its mistaken concept of "simple location"—that each putative object was defined as such because it occupied a singular point or location. This point is part of his larger critique that each bit of matter is individually independent and thus fully describable, apart from any reference to any other portion of matter. Whitehead's refutation was to show instead that, basically, "everything is everywhere at all times."[15]

For both Husserl and Whitehead, Nature is crucial as the locus of intersubjective experiencing, as the concrescence of nonduality, and thus the way to decisively overcome Cartesian dualism. In other words, it is in the eventing of Nature that we can perceive, actually perceive, the everything-goes-with-everything vision. A vision, I would add, of mutual interdependency that underlies the deep ecology vision that we need in order to get beyond our current ecological crisis.

Here is Whitehead's very concrete example. Note that it is not an experience of Nature in the abstract, but as experienced very concretely. It is an experience of a tree:

> A single tree by itself is dependent upon all the adverse chances of shifting circumstances. The wind stunts it, variations in temperature check its foliage, the rains denude its soil, its leaves are blown away and are lost for the purpose of fertilization. You may obtain individual specimens of fine trees either to exceptional circumstances, or where human cultivation has intervened. But in nature the normal way in which trees flourish is by their association in a forest. Each tree may lose something of its individual perfection of growth, but they mutually assist each other in preserving the conditions for survival. The soil is preserved and shaded, and the microbes necessary for its fertility are neither scorched, nor frozen, nor washed away. A forest is the triumph of the organization of mutually dependent species.[16]

So, if this is the alternative vision, then, how do we develop an ecological civilization? How do we develop a phenomenological ecopsychology? Fortunately, this adventure is already underway. Inspired especially by the work of Merleau-Ponty, one of Husserl's French followers in the next generation, a current group of phenomenologists are elaborating a very profound vision of interconnectedness, of person-and-nature, which they are calling our "participatory psyche"—and, even, nature's "partic-ipatory psyche." I will begin with Merleau-Ponty's phenomenology, then introduce the work of two of these new ecophenomenologists. Here is a very succinct thought by Merleau-Ponty (1968) to our thesis:

> Given that relations among things are always mediated by our body, then the setting of our own life must in fact be all of nature; nature must be our interlocutor in a sort of dialogue ... The thing can never be separated from someone who perceives it, nor can it ever actually be in itself because its articulations are the very ones of our existence ... To this extent, every perception is a communication or a communion ... a coupling of our body with the things.[17]

Note, again, that this commingling of person-world does not take place as a subject and object dualism but as an embodied experiencing. In other words, the wholeness of the world is not something apart from us "over there," which we observe: it includes us. But what sort of body is it that has intercourse with the world?

The body conceived by Cartesian dualism, after all, was just another lump—an object capable of only mechanistic, extrinsic, causal interac-tions with its likewise objective environmental stimuli. Ah, but this is NOT the body we *live*—that concept of the body-as-object is another example of what Whitehead called "misplaced concreteness."

Now I don't mean to imply here that we cannot consider the body as an object. It sometimes does present itself to our reflective awareness in that way as well. And, indeed, sometimes it can be very useful to see it so—as in the case of much of modern medicine. But when we do, we are overlooking another, deeper, more concrete experienced body—namely, the body as we live it, as we actually live our embodied relations with each other and with the world.

It is not that we have two bodies, but two ways of approaching the body: one, to conceive it abstracted from our experience, as if it were a mere object; the other to conceive it concretely, that is, as we actually live it. And, when we do that, then we become capable of comprehending those lived relationships of mutual interdependence—of embodied-con-sciousness-in-the-world that are the basis for our alternative vision of ecological civilization.

So, let's give it a go—let's put some "flesh" on this vision. First, we should recognize that this body-as-we-live-it is very different from that conceived by the physiologist, who will break it down into neurons, cells, molecules, and DNA. When was the last time you experienced your DNA Now, I would argue, as John Cobb (echoing Whitehead) and Medard Boss (echoing Husserl) do, that even this activity of our neurons, cells, and DNA is as events. Even at that level, we are engaged intrinsically with a meaningful world, rather than simply mechanistically reacting to extrinsic causes. For example, our DNA may be triggered to activate or to remain latent. And what triggers DNA? The meanings we are experiencing. The same goes for the neuronal activity of the brain. As Stan Grof has said so well, "consciousness is mediated by the brain, but it is not generated by the brain."[18] Put another way, the brain registers our experience; it does not cause it.

So yes, if we want to, we could even develop a neurophenomenology, and there are those who are currently involved in doing just that. Likewise, for medical conditions from heart attacks to cancer recovery, we could have a phenomenological cardiology or a phenomenological oncology. But, for our purposes today, there are more accessible examples of how the lived body and the lived world form a unity of lived experience. Even extrasensory perception is perception, and perception is the work of my embodied presence in the world on an ordinary, ongoing, everyday basis. Enabling me to be in relation with all other presences: Wholeness.

Contemporary ecophenomenologists, such as David Abram and Will Adams, have drawn on this key point very fruitfully. They begin by noting, with Merleau-Ponty, that the body I live is not the object closed on itself, but rather is open, permeable, indeterminate, unbounded. As Grof has repeatedly shown, the objective boundaries of space and time are not the limits of our actually embodied experiencing.[19]

For Merleau-Ponty, to be embodied consciousness means that we are a network of relationships, a reciprocity, an ongoing interchange between my body and what is around it.[20] He writes that we are experiences, we are a field of interrelationships that, even in our most ordinary perceptual relations, there is an astonishing "adhesion" of the seer and the visible, the toucher and the tangible: an inherent, inhabited, lived relationship, such that "each is only the rejoinder of the other and which therefore form a couple, a couple more real than either of them."[21] Merleau-Ponty said that this is possible because, finally, my flesh and the flesh of the world are one flesh. So that, when touching, what begins as a thing ends as consciousness and what begins as consciousness ends as a thing.[22] Yet, as Will Adams points out, "neither consciousness nor thing initiates this interchange. Rather they co-arise reciprocally as one unified phenomenon." [23] Adams concludes his summary of Merleau-Ponty by noting that:

> This path led him to describe an ontologically primary, nondual interrelational phenomenon that he variously named 'flesh,' 'the intertwining,' and 'the chiasm.' He was intrigued by the chiasmatic, crisscrossing, interresponsive ecoparticipation of our lived body with the rest of the world . . . our flesh and the flesh of the world are discovered as one participatory flesh, in and as its interrelational chiasm.

> "Grasp this chiasm . . . That is the mind."[24]

So says Merleau-Ponty in this profound imperative from his personal working notes. Thus, he was beginning to appreciate mind as chiasmic participation. He emphasized that

> "it is a matter of understanding that the 'subjectivity' and the 'object' are one sole whole."[25]

This insight is awe-inspiring: the worldliness of the mind, the earthliness of the mind. These phrases deepen our appreciation of mind and invoke an experience that—when consciously integrated—helps foster a mutually convivial human-nature relationship. Thus, we all have the opportunity to become reasonably aware of what is given ontologically but usually lived prereflectively, unconsciously: our nondual, interresponsive, participatory mind.[26]

David Abram also describes this participatory psyche in wonderfully descriptive examples. For instance:

> My life and the world's life are deeply intertwined; when I wake up one morning to find that a week-long illness has subsided and that my strength has returned, the world, when I step outside, fairly sparkles with energy and activity: swallows are swooping by in vivid flight; waves of heat rise from the newly paved road smelling strongly of tar; the old red barn across the

field juts into the sky at an intense angle. Likewise, when a haze descends upon the valley in which I dwell, it descends upon my awareness as well, muddling my thoughts, making my muscles yearn for sleep. The world and I reciprocate one another. The landscape as I directly experience it is hardly a determinate object; it is an ambiguous realm that responds to my emotions and calls forth feelings from me in turn.[27]

Thus, the flesh is, in Abram's evocative depiction:

The mysterious matrix that underlies and gives rise to both the perceiver and the perceived as interdependent aspects of its own spontaneous activity. It is the reciprocal presence of the sentient in the sensible and of the sensible in the sentient...a mystery of which we have always been at least tacitly aware.[28]

In an earlier iteration, in which I sought to reflect phenomenologically on parapsychological experience, I coined the term "the long body" to depict this deeply embodied interconnectedness, and it might be useful here, to give us some examples.[29] For example...cold feet...pain in the neck ... gut feeling ... heartache ... these are easy, everyday examples that show us that the body is, as we live it, a commingling with the meaningful world we are experiencing. We could go farther than that. Consider the case of the expectant father, whose fingers and toes swelled up much as his pregnant wife's did. Or when he had to nap more often, urinate more often, as the pregnancy progressed. Yes, that was me. I, in my way, was also embodying the experience of being pregnant. In some cultures, even giving birth can be a bodily-shared experience, as the man writhes in shared birth pain—and the women's pain is lessened. Several studies, especially those of Michael Murphy,[30] have noted that extraordinary athletic performances are anomalous experiences to the conception of the body as an object. Yes, they sure are, but I have shown that even our ordinary ones reveal this structure of the "long body."[31]

In conclusion, a phenomenology of embodiment can disclose our deeper ecological interrelatedness with the whole. For example, I regularly communicate with my wife's pet rabbit. Our conversations, quite lengthy, of course, take place with the movements of our noses rather than our mouths. I learned how to "speak rabbit" when I allowed my body to get in synch with the gestural, postural inhabiting of the world by which the rabbit was engaged. It really wasn't that hard—once I let it happen. But how often do we allow such permeability, such reciprocity, to happen? More typically, we close it off, by surrounding ourselves within our own artefactual bubble of things. How many even know what phase the moon is in? Or when it set? Such a loss, for as Abram tells us:

> Humans are tuned for relationship ... for the largest part of our species existence, humans have [related with] every aspect of the sensuous surroundings ... a shifting web of meanings that we felt on our skin or inhaled through our nostrils or focused with our listening ears . . . the color of the sky, the rush of waves—every aspect of the earthly sensuous could draw us into a relationship ... every sound was a voice, every scrapevwas a meeting—with Thunder, with Oak, with Dragonfly. And from all these relationships our collective sensibilities were nourished (ix) ... A genuinely ecological approach does not work to attain a mentally envisioned future, but strives to enter, ever more deeply, into the sensorial present ... to become ever more awake to the . . . other forms of sentience and sensibility that surround us in the open field of the present moment . . . gradually, then, our senses awaken to the world. We become aware of the thoughts that are thinking around us—in the bushes, under the tumbled stones. As we watch the crows, our own limbs begin to feel the intelligence of feathered muscles adjusting to the wind...walking along the beach, we notice the ground itself responding to our footfalls—the hermit crabs all diving for cover ... slowly a bank of clouds approaches, drawing its bulged and billowing texture over the earth, enclosing the heron and the alder trees and my gazing body into the depths of a vast breathing being, enfolding us all within a common flesh, a common story bursting with rain.[32]

## CHAPTER TEN

# All Tangled Up:
# Life in a Quantum World

*Larry Dossey*

ABSTRACT: *This essay argues that the modern worldview is bereft of value and meaning. This spiritual malaise, in turn, has put our entire civilization and the planet itself in jeopardy. One source of this crisis can be traced back to the early days of modern science, when the theories of nature that involved subjectivity and value were brutally and needlessly suppressed. That said, anomalous phenomena in various scientific fields suggest an emerging revolution in how science and philosophy understand reality. New and surprising findings in the field of quantum entanglement and nonlocality are cited. Importantly, these anomalies seem to be occurring at the macroscopic level as well, seen clearly in the herd behavior of buffalo and in swarming birds, and even at the human level with parapsychological phenomena. These developments have strained modern science's materialistic-mechanistic model of nature to the breaking point. As a result, a new science and worldview based on subjectivity and intrinsic value are taking hold.*

Any local agitation shakes the whole universe ... There is no possibility of a detached, self-contained existence ... Matter has been identified with energy, and energy is sheer activity. The modern point of view is expressed in terms of energy, activity, and the vibratory differentiations of space-time. Any local agitation shakes the whole universe. The distant effects are minute, but they are there. The concept of matter presupposed simple location ... but in the modern concept the group of agitations which we term matter is fused into its environment. There is no possibility of a detached, self-contained existence.[1] ~ Alfred North Whitehead

Inconceivable as it seems to ordinary reason, you and all other conscious beings as such—are all in all. Hence this life of yours which you are living is not merely a piece of the entire existence, but is in a certain sense the *whole*; only this whole is not so constituted that it can be surveyed in one single glance.[2] ~ Erwin Schrödinger

THERE ARE CONVERSATIONS one never forgets. One I'll always remember occurred around ten years ago, in which a good friend of mine, who is a physicist, and I were discussing remote viewing. In one version of this procedure, an individual somehow conveys complex, detailed information to a distant person, even though the two have no sensory contact with each other.[3] My physicist friend is a leading researcher in this field and has published several experiments that demonstrate these phenomena beyond reasonable doubt. I asked him whether quantum-physical effects might be involved in these long-distance exchanges of information. I had in mind the 1964 theorem of CERN physicist John Stewart Bell and subsequent experiments showing that subatomic particles, once in contact, remain connected thereafter, no matter how far apart they are, so that a change in one is correlated with a change in its remote partner, instantly and to the same degree.[4, 5] Such particles are said to be "entangled," a term introduced into physics in 1935 by Nobel physicist Erwin Schrödinger. Schrödinger said, "I would not call [entanglement] *one* but rather *the* characteristic trait of quantum mechanics, the one that forces its entire departure from classical lines of thought."[6] Might the nonlocal connectedness of distant subatomic particles underlie the linkage between humans who share thoughts remotely?

"Impossible!" my physicist friend said emphatically. Quantum effects, he maintained, are limited to the invisible, subatomic microworld; they don't matter in big objects such as brains and bodies. Quantum information, he insisted, would be quickly degraded in warm, wet brains in a process called decoherence; it would fizzle, get lost, vanish like a snowball in an oven. Besides, he added, distant, nonlocal connections can't be used to send messages. Therefore quantum phenomena in brains cannot conceivably underlie the connectedness of distant humans seen in remote viewing experiments.

"But there are respected physicists who see things a bit differently," I offered hesitantly. As a non-physicist, I was trying to mind my manners. I cautiously mentioned physicist Nick Herbert who said, in discussing distant, nonlocal connections in his 1987 book *Quantum Reality*, "Bell's theorem . . . takes non-locality out of the inaccessible microworld and situates it squarely in the familiar world of cats and bathtubs."[7] If cats and bathtubs, why not humans? "Wishful thinking," my physicist friend said with unmistakable irritation. "Can't happen. Doesn't happen." Our conversation was over, and we moved on to less touchy talk.

LIVING IN A QUANTUM WORLD

My friend's view mirrored the message in standard physics textbooks. The mid-sized world of bricks, brains, and beasts, and the colossal world of planets, stars, and galaxies, the texts say, are the domains of classical physics and are described by Newton's laws and Einstein's theories of relativity. But as we descend in scale to subatomic particles and atoms, we cross an invisible boundary where classical physics no longer applies, and the strangeness of quantum behavior takes charge. The framework provided by quantum mechanics governs this microscopic, invisible level.

How things change! The June 2011 cover of the journal *Scientific American* displays a human head made of tiny particles and the caption "Living in a quantum world: small-scale physics has a 'spooky' power over the world at large." In his lead article, Oxford physicist Vlatko Vedral explains what this fuss is all about:

> Quantum mechanics is not just about teeny particles. It applies to things of all sizes: birds, plants, maybe even people . . . Quantum mechanics is commonly said to be a theory of microscopic things: molecules, atoms, subatomic particles . . . This convenient partitioning of the world is a myth . . . It is but a useful approximation of a world that is quantum at all scales . . . Over the past several years experimentalists have seen quantum effects in a growing number of macroscopic systems. The quintessential

quantum effect, entanglement, can occur in large systems as well as warm ones—including living organisms—even though molecular jiggling might be expected to disrupt entanglement... Until the past decade, experimentalists had not confirmed that quantum behavior persists on a macroscopic scale. Today, however, they routinely do. These effects are more pervasive than anyone ever suspected. They may operate in the cells of our body ... We can't simply write [quantum effects] off as mere details that matter only on the very smallest scales ... The entanglements are primary.[8]

There are apparently no limits to the extent of entanglement. As physicist N. David Mermin has shown, quantum entanglement grows exponentially with the number of particles involved in the original quantum state, and that there is no theoretical limit on the number of these entangled particles.[9] "If this is the case," say physicist Menas Kafatos and science historian Robert Nadeau in their book *The Conscious Universe: Parts and Wholes in Physical Reality*, "the universe on a very basic level could be a vast web of particles that remain in contact with one another over any distance in no time in the absence of the transfer of energy or information."[10]

When I saw this issue of *Scientific American* endorsing the macroscopic status of quantum effects, I had the urge to mail a copy to my physicist friend. But if he and I are entangled, as the article implies, I figured he might already be picking up on what I'm thinking. Save the postage.

## ENTANGLEMENT AND NONLOCALITY

"Entanglement" and "nonlocality" are often used interchangeably, but they are not identical.

An object is said to be entangled if it cannot be fully described without considering one or more additional objects. It is as if the separate, distant entities comprise a single system. Entanglement has been experimentally verified many times over the past three decades and is accepted by the majority of physicists as a fundamental feature of nature.[11]

Nonlocality is widely considered to be a mechanism for the effects of entanglement. As Kafatos and Nadeau describe, "When particles originate under certain conditions, a measurement of one particle will correlate with the state of another particle even if the distance between the particles is millions of light-years. And … even though no signal can travel faster than light, the correlations will occur instantaneously, or in 'no time.'"[12] These instantaneous connections are said to be nonlocal, and particles displaying nonlocally correlated behavior are said to be entangled.

Three types of nonlocality have been described: spatial or type I nonlocality; temporal or type II nonlocality; and type III nonlocality, a combination of type I and type II, which takes in the unified whole of space and time.[13]

According to physicist Nick Herbert, "A non-local connection links up one location with another without crossing space, without decay, and without delay." These connections have three identifying characteristics, says Herbert. They are *unmediated* (no connecting signal is involved), *unmitigated* (the strength of the correlations do not fade with increasing distance), and *immediate* (they are instantaneous).[14]

In order for distant particles to demonstrate nonlocal connections, they must have once been in contact. According to the big bang theory, all the matter in the universe was originally in contact, concentrated in a "very hot dot" of matter-energy that exploded around 14 billion years ago, resulting in the universe we see.[15] So, if the big bang theory is valid, a requirement for nonlocal connections—original contact—was met early on.

A NEW WORLD

We are witnessing one of the most important transitions in the history of human thought: entanglement and nonlocality, once thought limited to the invisible, microscopic world, are now demonstrated to be a feature of the biology of living creatures, apparently including ourselves.[16, 17] This realization will profoundly affect our concept of our place in the universe and what it means to be human.

There seems to be no going back to a divided world. "Few physicists now think that classical physics will ever really make a comeback at any scale," Vedral says.[18] That doesn't mean classical physics is finished, headed for the junk-heap of obsolete ideas. It remains an excellent approximation of how things work in the see-touch-feel world of visible, large-scale objects. Any scientific model that can put satellites into space and men on the moon can hardly be considered irrelevant.

The incursion of entanglement and nonlocality into the biological domain is not a fringe movement. Neither is it based on a mere handful of studies. A Google search for "biological nonlocality" yields over a million hits; a search for "biological entanglement" identifies nearly a million sites. The basic ideas have been around for some time. Nobel physicist Brian D. Josephson and physicist Fotini Pallikari-Viras saw where this field was headed two decades ago in their seminal paper "Biological Utilisation of Quantum Nonlocality," published in *Foundations of Physics* in 1991.[19] For a lay-oriented update on the robust research on entanglement in biological systems, see science journalist Mark Anderson's intriguing article "Is Quantum Mechanics Controlling Your Thoughts?" in *Discover,* where Anderson asserts, "Science's weirdest realm may be responsible for photosynthesis, our sense of smell, and even consciousness."[20]

Just how profoundly and in what ways we will be affected by these discoveries, no one knows for sure. It is early days, and physicists are still recovering from their astonishment. "The implications of macroscopic objects such as us being in quantum limbo is mind-blowing enough that we physicists are still in an entangled state of confusion and wonderment," Vedral acknowledges. "Even those of us who make a career of studying these effects have yet to assimilate what they are telling us about the workings of nature."[21]

Could these "mind-blowing" discoveries tell us something about distant communication between humans, which my physicist friend and I discussed? Dean Radin, co-editor-in-chief of *Explore,* thinks so. Radin has thoughtfully examined the implications of entanglement in his superb book *Entangled Minds: Extrasensory Experiences in a Quantum Reality.* He says:

> Some may regard all the excitement about entanglement a fad, or as mere hyperbole designed to annoy physicists and beguile new agers. But it goes deeper than that. Experiments have demonstrated that the worldview implied by classical physics is wrong. Not just slightly incorrect in minor ways, but fundamentally wrong in just the right way to support the reality of psi.[22]

Some physicists sense the momentous nature of nonlocality and entanglement. Among them are University of California, Berkeley theoretical physicist Henry P. Stapp, who says that nonlocality could be the "most profound discovery in all of science."[23] Columbia University physicist Brian Greene echoes the sentiment, saying, "There can be strange, weird, and 'spooky' quantum connections between things over here and things over there[24] . . . This is an earth-shattering result. This is the kind of result that should take your breath away."[25] And as Kafatos and Nadeau assert in their book *The Non-Local Universe*, the implications are "quite staggering." They see "a new view of the relationship between mind and world" coming into view, in which "mind, or human consciousness . . . is seamlessly interconnected [with the] whole called the cosmos."[26]

Consciousness loose in the world? The idea evokes snickers from materialists who are convinced the brain somehow makes consciousness, like the liver makes bile, and that consciousness is confined to the brain and body. Other scientists disagree. Among them is anesthesiologist Stuart Hameroff, who started the Center for Consciousness Studies at the University of Arizona in 1998. The center sponsors biannual conferences titled "Toward a Science of Consciousness." For years Hameroff has collaborated with Oxford mathematical physicist Roger Penrose in rethinking the origin and nature of consciousness. In summing up his view, Hameroff states, "Most people think that consciousness emerged over eons as a byproduct of random mutations and the inherent complexity of natural selection, but I look at it the other way around. I think a fundamental field of protoconscious experience has been embedded all along—since the big bang . . . and that biology evolved and adapted in order to access it and to maximize the qualities and potentials implicit in it."[27] Penrose is also dubious of the conventional brain-makes-consciousness view, saying, "My position [on consciousness] demands a major revolution in physics . . . I've come to believe that there is something very fundamental missing from current science . . . Our understanding at this time is not adequate and we're going to have to move to new regions of science."[28]

But what is consciousness? Although fully adequate definitions do not exist, I follow the definition offered by Robert G. Jahn and Brenda J. Dunne, who for three decades researched the nonlocal manifestations of consciousness at PEAR, the Princeton Anomalies Research lab: "[Consciousness is] the capacity to react to, attend to, and be aware of self and other. Consciousness subsumes all categories of experience, including perception, cognition, intuition, instinct, will and emotion, at all levels, including those commonly termed 'conscious,' 'subconscious,' 'superconscious,' or 'unconscious,' 'intention,' and 'attention,' without presumption of specific psychological or physiological mechanisms. Neither consciousness nor its environment exists in isolation; they can be represented only in interaction and exchange of information."[29]

## ENTANGLED BEHAVIOR IN ANIMALS

If, as Hameroff and others suggest, consciousness has been embedded in the world from the beginning, and biological systems evolved to adapt and take advantage of it, and if consciousness is nonlocal, entangling the creatures who possess it, how would it manifest? What would it look like? Where would we look for evidence?

We would naturally look at the behaviors and experiences of humans, of course. Abundant evidence strongly suggests that human consciousness is nonlocal, unconfined to specific points in space, such as brains and bodies, or in time, such as the present. This evidence affirms, compellingly in my view, the validity of what psychologist and psi researcher Charles Tart calls the Big Five: telepathy, clairvoyance, psychokinesis, precognition, and remote healing.[30] I've reviewed this evidence often.[31, 32, 33] Those wanting a comprehensive review of this field may also consult Dean Radin's groundbreaking books *The Conscious Universe*[34] and *Entangled Minds*,[35] as mentioned, or the authoritative book *Consciousness and the Source of Reality* by Princeton researchers Robert G. Jahn and Brenda J. Dunne.[36]

But what about nonhumans? Could other creatures possess a form of proto- or precursor consciousness that is not as highly evolved as in humans, but which might qualify as rudimentary consciousness nonetheless? If so, might it behave nonlocally, and might it entangle the creatures who possess it? I suggest the answer is yes, and that the evidence may be all around us in the natural world. Let's consider a tantalizing example: the magnificent American bison or buffalo. In the following, I'll provide examples of their behavior that suggest that individual animals are perhaps entangled and united as a larger organism.

Every spring and fall bison were on the move, vast herds of them stretching as far as the eye could see. No one really knew how many there were, for they were countless and uncountable. Estimates ranged from fifty to one-hundred-and-fifty million. Their running created a faint vibration and a deep rumble in the earth that announced their coming to any living thing in their path. The animals would stop to rest and feed periodically and bed down at night. Then they were up at dawn to renew their journey toward the horizon and to destinations that had beckoned them for millennia. On cold mornings their breath formed a giant frosty cloud that hung like a halo over the mammoth herd, a sign sought by every hunter.

The animals moved as a single being and with a unified will that caused many to die, because there could be no careful testing of danger or weighing of risk by single individuals when the group mind took charge. When they approached a river, the leading animals would venture hesitantly into the water, probing for deep unseen holes and quicksand. But the herd behind them kept coming, pushing and shoving the leaders into drowning places and quicksand bogs. Thousands might be killed as a result, a sacrifice to the unbending single-mindedness of the colossal herd. Native Americans were bison mind readers. They understood the instincts that molded the masses into a single organism, and they used this knowledge to drive the bison off precipices such as Wyoming's Chugwater bluffs and Montana's Palisades cliffs.[37]

The herd behavior of bison is not an isolated pattern. Highly coordinated movements occur also in the famous wildebeest migrations in Africa, in the caribou herds of Alaska and the Canadian Yukon, and in other animals as well. Nor are these patterns limited to large mammals.

Early white settlers in America reported highly organized group behavior in passenger pigeons. Before the immense flocks were exterminated from wanton slaughter during the 1800s, it was said that their passage would block the sun for days at a time. Like the bison, they were so numerous that no one could imagine they *could* be exterminated.

One of the birds most adept at group behavior is the starling, whose acrobatic movements in huge flocks are a kind of aerial ballet. In England, during the winter months, thousands of starlings return in the evening from foraging to Ot Moor, a 400-acre grassy wetland in southeast England. Small flocks merge into larger flocks, at which point they begin to wheel and gyre in arrays that are among the most elegant in nature. For a visual treat, see the spectacular video "Starlings at Ot Moor" by video journalist Dylan Winter. [38]

Enormous schools of fish such as herring and sardines demonstrate similar group behavior, wheeling in breathtaking unison. An awe-inspiring example can be found in the BBC documentary series *Swarm: Nature's Incredible Invasions.*[39]

When creatures demonstrate group behavior, are they acting unthinkingly and blindly, or is something else involved? Might we be glimpsing mass entanglement of thousands or millions of creatures acting as a single unit as a consequence of nonlocally distributed protoconsciousness?

SWARM THEORY

Currently ethologists are not into entanglement, nonlocality, or protoconsciousness as explanations of these behaviors. When animals, birds, and fish manage to act in concerted, coordinated ways, the concept of "swarm intelligence" or "swarm theory" is generally invoked as an explanation. Swarm theory was introduced in the 1980s by researchers in artificial intelligence and robotics. According to this view, the individuals in a group interact locally with one another and with their environment via ordinary sensory means. Although there is no centralized controlling influence dictating how the individuals should behave, the local and often random interactions between the individuals somehow lead to the emergence of intelligent group behavior. In other words, the individual isn't particularly clever, but the group is. Swarm theory has been applied to naturally occurring phenomena such as animal herding, bird flocking, fish schooling, ant and termite colonies, beehives, and bacterial growth.[40] Swarm theory has practical applications. It has been used to determine how best to ticket and board passengers onto commercial aircraft, assign aircraft arrivals to airport gates, and route trucks in the most efficient way possible. Scientists have developed software for groups or "swarms" of robots, using simple rules that mimic the behavior of insect swarms. The goal is to use robots to intelligently perform dangerous minesweeping and search-and-rescue operations that would place human first responders at risk. Someday, scientists predict, robotic swarms might explore the surface of Mars.[41]

When animals, birds, fish, or insects swarm, how do they do it? If none of the herring in the school grasps the big picture, how do they change direction in a flash, like a single entity? One key, say swarm theorists, is that no one is in charge. There is no "general" giving orders, which would take time to disseminate information throughout the herd, flock, school, or hive. Instead of orders from the top, complex, unified behavior originates with the individual.

In 1986, Craig Reynolds, a computer graphics researcher, created a simple program he called "boids" in order to explore what these rules might be in flocking behavior. In his simulation, generic bird-like objects, the boids, were each given three instructions: (1) don't crowd nearby boids, (2) fly in the average direction of nearby boids, and (3) stay close to nearby boids. When he set the program in motion on a computer screen, there was a striking simulation of the unpredictable and lifelike movements seen in flocking.[42]

But why do creatures follow these rules, and why do they form immense herds, flocks, or schools in the first place? A standard answer from biology is that there is a survival advantage in doing so. A big group of animals, birds, or fish has more eyes with which to spot predators. When attacked, they can confuse a predator by coordinated mass movements. A mass of individuals has an advantage in locating a mate, finding food, or following a migration route. As a group member, each individual is more likely to stay alive and reproduce than if isolated and alone.

If only it were all so simple. Swarm intelligence "seem[s] miraculous even to the biologists who know them best," says National Geographic writer Peter Miller.[43] Some biologists who live in the wild for long periods and observe creatures up close have a gnawing suspicion that the neat formulations of swarm theory leave something out.

For five months in 2003, wildlife biologists Karsten Heuer and his wife Leanne Allison trailed the Porcupine caribou herd of 123,000 animals for more than a thousand miles in their migration from their winter range in Canada's northern Yukon Territory to calving grounds in Alaska's National Wildlife Refuge.[44] "It's difficult to describe in words, but when the herd was on the move it looked very much like a cloud shadow passing over the landscape, or a mass of dominoes toppling over at the same time and changing directions," Heuer said;—one domino hitting the next in line, a succession of falling dominos one after the other. Classical cause and effect? Not exactly. Heuer elaborates, "It was as though every animal knew what its neighbor was going to do, and the neighbor beside that and beside that. There was no anticipation or reaction. No cause and effect. It just was."[45]

No cause and effect? This sort of talk makes paid-up biologists crazy. There is no room in modern biology for "it just was" that bypasses cause and effect. The closest biologists come to "just is" is the concept of instincts, the inherent inclinations of a living organism toward a particular behavior. These fixed action patterns are not based on learning but are inherited, say biologists, by the passage of DNA from parent to offspring. DNA is the cause; instinctual behavior is the effect. Yet other kinds of knowing keep cropping up in animals that suggest entanglement and the nonlocal acquisition of information.

## ANIMAL-HUMAN ENTANGLEMENT?

During the 1920s, a two-year-old dog named Bobbie, mostly collie with a bit of English sheep dog, became a national sensation. His owners, Mr. and Mrs. Frank Brazier, restaurant owners in Silverton, Oregon, were vacationing in Indiana when Bobbie got lost. Despite intense efforts to locate the dog, the Braziers finally despaired of finding him. Brokenhearted, they resumed their trip westward, never expecting to see him again. Six months later Bobbie showed up, emaciated, at the family restaurant in Oregon. He ran upstairs to the second-floor living quarters and jumped on the bed, awakening Frank Brazier by licking his face.

No one could believe it. But when the Silverton *Appeal* published the story, it quickly spread to newspapers across the country, and hundreds of people sent letters to the Braziers claiming they'd seen Bobbie and were able to confirm his identity by several distinguishing marks. Still dubious, the Oregon Humane Society launched an investigation into the Braziers' claims. By interviewing people who claimed to have seen him, they reconstructed the route home, which they estimated was around 2,800 miles, much of which took place in the dead of winter. Bobbie did not follow his owners' route back to Oregon, but traveled an indirect course over land he had never seen nor could have been familiar with. This was no lookalike dog; his owners were able to identify him not only because of his loving behavior, but also by several unique marks and scars.

I've had the opportunity to discuss distant, nonlocal knowing with many audiences over the years, and I often use returning animals as examples. I find that the most frequent explanation that critics offer for Bobbie and similar instances is a highly developed sense of smell. This cropped up in a lecture I gave at the Smithsonian Institution in

Washington, D.C. I was interrupted by a man in the audience who confidently announced, "Pheromones! The dog sensed pheromones coming from his owners in Oregon. The prevailing winds blow west to east. The dog followed this chemical signal all the way to Oregon." Pheromones are chemicals produced by mammals and insects and are released in minute concentrations into the environment. They play a role in sexual attraction. "Nearly 3,000 miles," I said, "and between members of different species? Creatures sense pheromones from their own kind. In any case, these chemicals would get pretty diluted over 3,000 miles, don't you think?" Another man in the audience chimed in with another explanation. "Pure chance! The dog found the home in Oregon by dumb luck." "There are a lot of houses to the west of Indiana," I offered. "The odds against finding the right house by chance are pretty high." Both men were supremely confident and were unmoved by my comments. It was a reminder that, for many individuals, any explanation is preferable to one involving some sort of nonlocal communication.

Cynics still suggest that the entire Bobbie episode was a gigantic hoax or an exercise in massive self-delusion. Perhaps. But the evolving evidence for entanglement between biological systems, and for nonlocal operations of consciousness, suggest the possibility of cognitive entanglement between pets and their owners. If the owner possesses specific information—in this case, knowledge of the location of the home in Oregon—it might be available to the pet as well, because of the nonlocal linkages in consciousness bonding two living creatures.

Thousands of similar cases have been reported. No doubt some can be dismissed as involving look-alike animals, but not all; often the returning animal has its original collar and nametag, and can be further identified by distinguishing marks and scars.

Particularly fascinating are those cases in which the returning animal appears to be responding to the physical and emotional needs of some remote person. An example is that of an Irish soldier in World War I, whose wife and small dog, Prince, took up residence in 1914 in Hammersmith, London, while he was sent with one of the earliest contingents to the battlefields of France. After a period of service he was granted leave to visit his family, but when he returned to battle Prince was utterly disconsolate and refused all food. Then the dog disappeared. For ten days the wife tried desperately to trace him, to no avail. Finally she decided to break the news in a letter to her husband. She was astonished when she heard from him that the dog had joined him in the trenches at Armentières, under heavy bombardment. Somehow Prince had made his way through the streets of London, seventy miles of English countryside, hitched a ride across the English Channel, traveled over sixty miles of French soil, and then "smelt his master out amongst an army of half a million Englishmen and this despite the fact that the last mile or so of intervening ground was reeking with bursting shells, many of them charged with tear-gas."[46]

One of the most thorough investigators in this field is British biologist Rupert Sheldrake, who has done pioneering work with dogs who know when their owners are returning. Even when the experimenter tries to fake out the dogs by varying the time the owner returns, or varying the means of transportation, the dogs still seem to go on the alert by standing at a door or window minutes before the owner shows up. This occurs even when no one at home knows the time of the owner's return. Sheldrake's work is detailed in his fascinating book *Dogs That Know When Their Owners Are Coming Home.*[47]

## LIMBIC SCIENCE

Swarm intelligence and instinctual behaviors make sense until you start examining the niggling little exceptions that don't fit in. But the exceptions are crucial. William James, the father of American psychology, was a champion of misfit observations. As he put it, "When was not the science of the future stirred to its conquering activities by the rebellious little exceptions to the science of the present?"[48] And, "Any one will renovate his science who will steadily look after the irregular phenomena. And when the science is renewed, its formulations often have more of the voice of the exceptions in them than of what were supposed to be the rules."[49] I suggest that when biologists bump up against observations that evoke reactions such as the above comment—"No cause and effect. It just was."—they are sensing James's "rebellious little exceptions." They are entering a domain we might call "limbic science"—from *limbus*, the Latin word for "edge." Limbic science is science that is on the edge, on the borderline. It is science that is forward leaning, a probe into the future, a search for hypotheses and concepts that are better able to explain nature's mysteries than do our current ideas. It is science that points toward biological nonlocality and entanglement.

## BEYOND "QUANTUM"

There has been runaway enthusiasm in lay circles to give everything over to quantum physics, and to enshrine it as a kind of über religion at whose altar everyone should worship. This is unwise, because there are mysteries of consciousness that appear to be completely untouched by quantum physics.

One of them has to do with the communication of individuals at a distance, the topic of my conversation with my physicist friend. According to most physicists in the field of nonlocal quantum effects, nonlocal connections cannot be used to send intelligible messages from one object to another. As physicist Nick Herbert says, these connections, while real, involve "consciousness *without content.*" He states, "It is difficult to see what use we could make of such non-local connections. On the other hand, perhaps these connections are not there for us to 'use.'"[50]

But this cannot be the whole story, because hundreds of studies show that humans can and do use these connections to share intelligible information remotely with others, as in telepathy, precognition, and remote viewing.[51, 52, 53, 54] Moreover, emotional closeness is a major factor facilitating nonlocal communication between distant individuals, and emotional factors are completely missing in the equations of physics. Therefore, events involving distant communication between humans await a deeper explanatory model than that which is available in quantum physics, as currently understood.

The traditional response of many scientists has been to deny the existence of intelligible, information-packed, nonlocal exchanges, since they are not permitted in classical physics. A wiser approach is to not sacrifice empirical data in order to protect one's pet theory, but to revise current models or search for better ones that might explain the facts.

Physics may need to take a few lessons from biology. Although physicists maintain that entangled states between distant particles cannot be used to send meaningful information, evidence now suggests that separated individual human neurons in vitro are nonlocally linked.[55] If individual neurons can be nonlocally entangled, could bunches of them—whole brains—be nonlocally entangled as well? Several experiments using fMRI and EEG-based protocols suggest this is the case. In these experiments, the stimulation of one individual's brain appears to be registered simultaneously in a distant individual's brain, as demon-strated by fMRI or EEG.[56, 57, 58] These experiments suggest that the idea of united, linked minds is more than philosophical speculation.

## THE GHASTLY SILENCE

While some people have achieved a sense of unity with the cosmos based only on a scientific and intellectual worldview—Einstein is perhaps the great example—intellectual formulations are not enough for most individuals, because too much of the juice of life gets omitted. This deficiency in a purely scientific approach has long been noted by some of the greatest individuals in the history of science. Among them was Gottfried Wilhelm Leibniz (1646–1716), the German philosopher and mathematician. Leibniz, who invented the infinitesimal calculus independently of Isaac Newton, was considered one of the greatest minds of the eighteenth century. He refined the binary number system, which underlies virtually all digital computers, and invented mechanical calculators that were a marvel for their time. His intellectual reach touched all the major domains of learning. Even so, Leibniz could not find within science the satisfaction he was looking for. In a letter two years before his death, he wrote: "But when I looked for the ultimate reasons for mechanism, and even for the laws of motion, I was greatly surprised to see that they could not be found in mathematics but that I should have to return to metaphysics."[59]

Three centuries later, Nobel physicist Erwin Schrödinger would come to the same conclusion:

> The scientific picture of the real world around me is very defi-cient. It gives a lot of factual information, puts all our experience in a magnificently consistent order, but it is ghastly silent about all and sundry that is really near to our heart, that really matters to us. It cannot tell us a word about red and blue, bitter and sweet, physical pain and physical delight; it knows nothing of beautiful and ugly, good or bad, God and eternity. Science sometimes pretends to answer questions in these domains, but the answers are very often so silly that we are not inclined to take them seriously.[60]

The great Darwin also encountered the effects of the ghastly silence

Schrödinger spoke of. Late in life he lamented, "My mind seems to have become a machine for grinding general laws out of large collections of facts ... The loss of [the emotional] tastes is a loss of happiness, and may possibly be injurious to the intellect, and more probably to the moral character, by enfeebling the emotional part of our nature ... The loss of these tastes is a loss of happiness." His solution: "If I had to live my life again, I would have made a rule to read some poetry and listen to some music at least once every week."[61]

Something more is needed—something that can marshal not only an intellectual appreciation of the wholeness implied in biological entanglement and nonlocality, but also something that can quicken the pulse and stir an ethic toward the earth that can counter the unbridled greed and plunder that threaten us.

Currently there are excellent exemplars of this awakening, including numerous scientists. But many scientists, it must be said, are reluctant to speak out in favor of wholeness, unity, and oneness because they fear being labeled as having "gone mystic." It is as if there are hooded inquisitors lurking within science who are keeping score, and who are continually oiling the rack and heating the pincers, just waiting for a scientist to step out of line.

Fear has never silenced great poets and artists, however. Poets have been yammering away about wholeness for centuries. As author Philip Goldberg points out in his important book *American Veda*,[62] there are superb examples among the Romantic poets, particularly William Blake, Percy Bysshe Shelley, William Wordsworth, and Samuel Taylor Coleridge. These poets sensed the interconnectedness and unity that are a feature of an entangled, nonlocal world. Thus Blake, in "Augeries of Innocence": "To see a world in a grain of sand / And a heaven in a wild flower, / Hold infinity in the palm of your hand / And eternity in an hour"[63]; Shelley, in "Adonais": "The One remains, the many change and pass"[64]; Wordsworth, in "Tintern Abbey": "A motion and a spirit, that impels / All thinking things, all objects of all thought, / And rolls through all things"[65]; and Coleridge, who wrote of "the translucence of the eternal through and in the temporal."[66]

In his book *Opening to the Infinite*, *Explore* columnist Stephan A. Schwartz describes how the personal experience of a nonlocal event can carry the emotional wallop of an epiphany. Schwartz, who practically invented the science of remote viewing, has taught thousands of individuals in workshops to have these experiences. He concludes that nonlocal experiences, of which remote viewing is only one example, bestow an "ineffable sense of connection" and a "sense of empowerment" that is so profound it can permanently and radically alter one's world-view and conduct.[67]

The felt experience of being nonlocally connected—all tangled up with all there is—may be a way out of the mess created by self-centered, greed-obsessed individuals who have no sense of wholeness and no concern for the integrity of the world. As Goldberg puts it, when we realize the unitary nature of consciousness,

> one's sense of "I" and "we" opens out from the narrow identifi-
> cation with family, tribe, race, political affiliation, religion, and
> so on, to encompass a broader swath of humanity. With that
> comes a corresponding expansion of the moral compass. This
> is not a fanciful imagining of "we are the world" harmony but
> a living experience of unity with other humans, with nature,
> and ultimately with the cosmos.[68]

## "SOMETHING WENT BADLY WRONG"

The undivided wholeness portended by an entangled, nonlocal world may seem like a chic, modern discovery, but it is an old theme pre-dating the origins of science. For two millennia this perspective was known as the Hermetic worldview, explicated in the ancient *Hermeticum,* a collection of writings ascribed to the legendary sage Hermes Trismegistus.[69] Hermiticism deeply influenced the life and work of the great early scientists—Bacon, Brahe, Kepler, Copernicus, Bruno, Galileo, Newton, Leibniz, Boyle, and many others, as Lynn Picknett and Clive Prince show in their brilliant book *The Forbidden Universe: The Occult Origins of Science and the Search for the Mind of God.*[70] "In the beginning all science was Hermetic science," they say. "But something went badly wrong." Thus we see Giordano Bruno burned at the stake, Galileo barely avoiding execution for heresy and condemned to lifelong domestic imprisonment, and the other great pioneers going underground and off record with their Hermetic views of how the world works.

The reasons for these developments are too complex to examine in detail, but they occurred chiefly because the Church considered the

Hermetic view a threat to its very existence. The Hermetic tradition maintained that humans are godlike, born with an innate connection with the divine, and in no need of clerical intermediaries to facilitate this relationship. The Church stood for the exact opposite, maintaining that all humans are born as weak, miserable, sinful, hell-bound creatures unless salvation, mediated by the Church, intervenes. The Church was horrified by Hermiticism and its potential to turn its institutional power upside down. It feared the Hermetic view of the intrinsic goodness of all humans and their inherent freedom to think for themselves about any subject that stirred their mind and heart, without the approval and guidance of their priest.

Even though the Renaissance was Hermetic to the core, as Picknett and Prince show, the Hermetic principle of natural unity between God and humankind, and of the unity between human and world and all its creatures, was rejected with all the vehemence the Church could summon. Its wrath fell with full force on many of the early scientists of that period. They were demonized, excommunicated, threatened, and sometimes imprisoned, tortured, and executed. For reasons largely having to do with survival, the early scientists not surprisingly went along, and science was whipped into shape. Although science at first disowned and disinherited Hermetic views out of expediency, this rejection gradually became an ingrained prejudice. And so it remains. To this day, the enforcers of the ban are all too common—the irritating, voluble, militant atheist-scientists, the meaning-haters, and the psi and consciousness deniers who are blind to the faith-based nature of their scientism. The reputations of the early Hermetic scientists have been scrubbed; the victors always re-write the histories. The Hermetic force— it was never just a thread—in early science is now concealed. When it does crop up—Newton's profound interest in alchemy is an example still on the books—it is often ridiculed, as in the recurring suggestion that poor Newton's brain was temporarily deranged by sniffing too much mercury vapor in his alchemical experiments.

Thus the remnants of Hermetic belief were eventually hounded into the private domain, resulting in clandestine, veiled communications between adherents, and the formation of secret societies that have cropped up periodically ever since, as Dan Brown's novels remind us.

Meaning, direction, and purpose in the universe, and the divine worthiness of the world's creatures, are now considered silly superstitions by buttoned-up scientists. We are living with the results. As Picknett and Prince write, "When it junked the Hermetic philosophy, science began to preach that we owe our existence to a long series of accidents and that ultimately our lives have no meaning. The sense of unlimited horizons and the joy of being alive were eroded. When the scientific wisdom was plucked from Hermeticism to fuel the engines of progress for today's world and the underlying transcendentalism rejected, the whole tradition lost its soul—specifically the feminine aspect of its soul. . . . And in the ironic replay of the excision of the sacred feminine from Christianity, here science lost not only its soul but also its heart."[71]

It could have turned out differently. Again, Picknett and Prince:

> If science had been uninterruptedly Hermetic, would the environment be in the same terrifying condition we find it in today? Almost certainly not. Without oversentimentalizing, the Earth itself would have been cherished as a living being. There would be no question of having to fight for human rights or the right of animals to be treated gently and with respect. If every human and every beast is an integral part of all creation, then they are all part of us in a very real way. Hurting them would be hurting ourselves. The Hermetic system adds a moral centre to science, which is largely lacking.[72]

There are stunning similarities between the wholeness and unity implied by the discovery of widespread entanglement and nonlocality, and the Hermetic principle of an unlimited, universal connectedness that unites all humans with the Absolute or Transcendent, however named. Straight-laced scientists deny these similarities, fearing the contamination of modern science by "the occult," one of their favorite epithets. But science desperately *needs* contamination by several factors that are missing from its equations, if we are to survive—a moral center, an Earth ethic, a sense of responsibility for all of life—those qualities whose absence has led to an abyss that is becoming impossible to ignore. A one-sided science is not only incomplete: it can be deadly. As Dr. Samuel Johnson put it nearly three centuries ago, "Integrity without knowledge is weak and useless, and knowledge without integrity is dangerous and dreadful."[73]

Dr. Johnson also observed, "When a man knows he is to be hanged in a fortnight, it concentrates his mind wonderfully."[74] Perhaps our sense of impending global disasters—I won't enumerate them—is concentrating our collective mind as a species, resulting in the return of ancient wisdom in the form of modern scientific insights, of which biological entanglement and nonlocality are an urgent example.

What we commonly call empathy, compassion, and love may be human entanglement banging on the doors of consciousness to gain entry. Albert Schweitzer, the legendary physician, missionary, priest, philanthropist, theologian, pacifist, musicologist, and winner of the 1952 Nobel Peace Prize, is an example of someone who opened those doors, and in so doing made the world a better place. In a kind of manifesto of wholeness, he wrote:

> What we call love is in its essence Reverence for Life[75]... Profound love demands a deep conception and out of this develops reverence for the mystery of life. It brings us close to all beings. To the poorest and smallest, as well as all others ... The idea of Reverence for Life gives us something more profound and mightier than the idea of humanism. It includes all living beings.[76]

At this stage of humankind's existence, the best we can wish for one another is not that we achieve success, clarity of purpose, or even happiness in life, but that we each realize that we're all tangled up with each other and everything, and that we find the courage to allow this realization to make a difference in how we live our life.

# Notes

## FOREWORD

1   Alan Watts, *The Book: On the Taboo Against Knowing Who You Are* (New York: Pantheon, 1966).

2   David Bohm, "A New Theory of Mind and Matter," *Journal of the American Society for Psychical Research* 80 (1986): 113–35.

3   Jeremy Narby, *Intelligence in Nature: An Inquiry into Knowledge* (New York: Tarcher/Prager, 2005).

4   Stanley Krippner, "The Plateau Experience: A. H. Maslow and Others," *Journal of Transpersonal Psychology* 4 (1972): 107–20.

5   Johnathan Shear, *Explaining Consciousness: The Hard Problem* (Cambridge: The MIT Press, 1997).

6   Susan Gordon, "Existential Time and the Meaning Of Human Development," *The Humanistic Psychologist* 40 (2012): 79–86.

7   Julia Mossbridge and Imants Baruss, *Transcendent Mind: Rethinking the Science of Consciousness* (Washington, DC: American Psychological Association, 2017).

## INTRODUCTION

1   This essay is a condensed version of an article from the *Journal of*

*Transpersonal Psychology,* which generously gave permission for its use in this collection. Some entire sections of the original paper have been omitted due to space considerations. "Revision and Reencahntment of Psychology: Legacy of a Half a Century of Consciousness Research," *Journal of Transpersonal Psychology* 44.2 (2012): 137–63.

## CHAPTER TWO

1  Alan Gauld, *The Founders of Psychical Research* (New York: Shocken Books, 1978), 138.

2  "Introduction to Psychical Research and Parapsychology," *Society for Psychical Research,* 2009, http://www.spr.ac.uk/page /introduction-psychical-research-and-parapsychology.

3  Richard J. Westfall, *Never at Rest: A Biography of Isaac Newton* (Cambridge: Cambridge University Press, 1980), 381.

4  Richard J. Westfall, "The Influence of Alchemy on Newton," in *Science, Pseudo-Science, and Society,* eds. Marsha P. Hanen et al. (Waterloo, Ontario: Wilfrid Laurier University Press, 1980), 145–70.

5  Westfall, *Never at Rest,* 464.

6  James E. Alcock, *Parapsychology: Science or Magic? A Psychological Perspective* (Oxford: Pergamon Press, 1981), 196.

7  Martin Gardner and John Archibald Wheeler, "Quantum Theory and Quack Theory," *New York Review of Books,* 17 May, 1979; Richard S. Broughton, *Parapsychology: The Controversial Science* (New York: Ballantine Books, 1991), 75. Having charged during the AAAS session that J. B. Rhine had falsified an experiment, he later, learning that his charge was false, wrote a retraction in *Science* 13 (May 1979): 144.

8  Antony Flew, "Parapsychology: Science or Pseudoscience?" in *A Skeptic's Handbook of Parapsychology,* ed. Paul Kurtz (Buffalo, NY: Prometheus Press, 1985), 519–36, at 529.

9  William James, *Essays in Radical Empiricism,* ed. Ralph Barton Perry, published in one volume with James's *A Pluralistic Universe* (New York: E. P. Dutton, 1971), 270, 271.

10  William James, *William James on Psychical Research,* ed. Gardner Murphy and Robert O. Ballou (Clifton, NY: Augustus M. Kelley, 1973), 42.

11 Mary Hesse, *Forces and Fields: The Concept of Action at a Distance in the History of Physics* (Totowa, NJ: Littlefield, Adams, and Co., 1965), 118, 125, 291.

12 Alfred North Whitehead, *Process and Reality*, corr. ed., ed. David Ray Griffin and Donald W. Sherburne (New York: Free Press, 1978), 308.

13 Whitehead, *Process and Reality*, 236.

14 William James, "Preface" in *The Meaning of Truth* (1909), http://fair-use.org/william-james/the-meaning-of-truth/preface.

15 David Hume, *A Treatise of Human Nature*, vols. 1 and 2, in *The Philosophical Works of David Hume* (1739), III: II.

16 Ian Stevenson, *Telepathic Impressions* (Charlottesville: University Press of Virginia, 1970), 10–11.

17 Broughton, *Parapsychology*, 91.

18 Broughton, *Parapsychology*, 121; Marilyn Schlitz and Elmar Gruber, "Transcontinental Remote Viewing," *Journal of Parapsychology* 44 (December 1980): 305–17.

19 Broughton, *Parapsychology*, 121; Schlitz and Gruber, "Transcontinental Remote Viewing," 305–17.

20 Broughton, *Parapsychology*, 101.

21 Broughton, *Parapsychology*, 101.

22 Broughton, *Parapsychology*, 113.

23 Rita Atkinson et al., *Introduction to Psychology*, 10th ed. (San Diego: Harcourt Brace Jovanovich, 1990), v, 235.

24 Atkinson et al., *Introduction to Psychology*, 235.

25 Rachel Laudan, ed., *The Demarcation between Science and Pseudo-Science* (Blacksburg, VA: Center for the Study of Science & Society, 1983); Patrick Grim, ed., *Philosophy of Science and the Occult* (Albany: State University of New York Press, 1982).

26 Ray Hyman, *The Elusive Quarry: A Scientific Appraisal of Psychical Research* (Buffalo, NY: Prometheus Books, 1989), 176.

27 James E. Alcock, *Science and Supernature: A Critical Appraisal of Parapsychology* (Buffalo, NY: Prometheus Books, 1990), 19.

28 Paul Kurtz, "Is Parapsychology a Science?" in *A Skeptic's Handbook*

*of Parapsychology*, ed. Paul Kurtz (Buffalo, NY: Prometheus Press, 1985), 503–18, at 510.

29 George Price, "Science and the Supernatural," in *Philosophy and Parapsychology*, ed. Jan Ludwig (Buffalo: Prometheus Books, 1978), 145–71.

30 Price, "Science and the Supernatural," 152–53; Flew, "Parapsychology: Science or Pseudoscience?" 532; D. O. Hebb, "The Role of Neurological Ideas in Psychology," *Journal of Personality* 20.1 (September 1951): 39–55, at 45.

31 C. D. Broad, *Religion, Philosophy and Psychical Research* (New York: Humanities Press, 1969), 9.

32 Jane Duran, "Philosophical Difficulties with Paranormal Knowledge Claims," in *Philosophy of Science and the Occult*, ed. Patrick Grim (Albany: State University of New York Press, 1982), 196–206, at 202.

33 See, for example, Bob Brier, *Precognition and the Philosophy of Science* (New York: Humanities Press, 1974), 174; J. G. Pratt, *Parapsychology: An Insider's View of ESP* (Garden City, NJ: Doubleday, 1964), 167.

34 Alfred North Whitehead, *Adventures of Ideas* (New York: Free Press, 1933, 1967), 193.

35 Charles Hartshorne, *Omnipotence and Other Theological Mistakes* (Albany: State University of New York Press, 1984), 39.

36 J. B. Rhine, *The Reach of the Mind* (New York: William Sloan, 1947), 66.

37 Antony Flew, "Comment" on Ray Hyman's essay "Pathological Science: Towards a Proper Diagnosis and Remedy," *Zetetic Scholar* 6 (1980).

38 Flew, "Parapsychology: Science or Pseudoscience," 533.

39 Stephen Braude, *The Limits of Influence: Psychokinesis and the Philosophy of Science* (New York: Routledge, 1986), 261–74.

40 Although some physicists have suggested that events occurring today could influence the creation of the universe many billions of years ago, the fact such an idea is suggested by a physicist does not make it any less ridiculous.

41 See my "Parapsychology and Philosophy: A Whiteheadian Postmodern Perspective," *Journal of the American Society for Psychical Research* 87, 3 (July 1993): 217–88, especially the sections on "Parapsychology

as not Ultra-Revolutionary" and "Apparent Precognition," (http://www.anthonyflood.com/griffinparapsychology.htm).

42  Robert L. Morris, "Assessing Experimental Support for True Precognition," *Journal of Parapsychology* 46 (1982): 321–36, at 334.

43  Stephen Braude, review for Jule Eisenbud, *Parapsychology and the Unconscious* (Berkeley, CA: North Atlantic Books, 1983).

44  Jule Eisenbud, *Parapsychology and the Unconscious* (Berkeley, CA: North Atlantic Books, 1983), 46.

45  William James, *William James on Psychical Research*, ed. Gardner Murphy and Robert O. Ballou (Clifton, NY: Augustus M. Kelley, 1973), 42.

46  See David Ray Griffin, "Parapsychology and Philosophy: A Whiteheadian Postmodern Perspective," and "Parapsychology, Science, and Religion," in David Ray Griffin, *Religion and Scientific Naturalism: Overcoming the Conflicts* (Albany: State University of New York Press, 2000).

47  Edward F. Kelly, Emily Watson Kelly, et al., *Irreducible Mind: Toward a Psychology for the 21ˢᵗ Century* (Lanham, MD: Rowman & Littlefield, 2007).

48  Kelly, et al., *Irreducible Mind*, 633.

49  Kelly, et al., *Irreducible Mind*, 577; quoting Alfred North Whitehead, *The Function of Reason* (Boston: Beacon Press, 1929, 1958), 61.

50  Alfred North Whitehead, *Modes of Thought* (New York: Free Press, 1938 1968), 2.

51  Whitehead, *Modes of Thought*, 639.

52  Whitehead, *Modes of Thought*, 2.

## CHAPTER THREE

1  C. E. M. Hansel, *ESP and Parapsychology: A Critical Re-evaluation* (Buffalo, NY: Prometheus, 1980).

2  Ray Hyman, "Further Comments on Schmidt's PK Experiments," *Skeptical Inquirer* 5, 3 (1981): 34–40.

3  John Palmer, "Implicit Anomalous Cognition," in *Parapsychology: A Handbook for the 21st Century*, eds. Etzel Cardeña, John Palmer,

and David Marcusson-Clavertz, (Jefferson, NC: McFarland, 2015), 215–29.

4   Lance Storm, Patrizio E. Tressoldi, and Lorenzo Di Risio, "Meta-analysis of Free-response Studies, 1992–2008: Assessing the Noise Reduction Model in Parapsychology," *Psychological Bulletin* 136 (2010): 471–85; Jessica Utts, "An Assessment of the Evidence for Psychic Functioning," *Journal of Scientific Exploration* 10 (1996): 3–30.

5   Dean Radin and Roger Nelson, "Consciousness Related Effects in Random Physical Systems," *Foundations of Physics* 19 (1989): 1499–514.

6   Stefan Schmidt, Rainer Schneider, Jessica M. Utts, and Harald Walach, "Distant Intentionality and the Feeling of Being Stared at: Two Meta-analyses." *British Journal of Psychology* 95 (2004): 235–47

7   John Palmer, "Conceptualizing the Psi Controversy," *Parapsychology Review* 19.1 (1988): 1–5.

8   J.G. Pratt, "Statement," *Proceedings of the Society for Psychical Research* 56 (1978): 279–81.

9   Thomas S. Kuhn, *The Structure of Scientific Revolutions,* 3rd ed. (Chicago: University of Chicago Press, 1996).

10  Edwin C. May, S. James, P. Spottiswoode, Jessica M. Utts, and Christine L. James, "Applications of Decision Augmentation Theory," *Journal of Parapsychology* 59 (1995): 221–50.

11  John Palmer and Brian Millar, "Experimenter Effects in Parapsychology Research," in *Parapsychology: A Handbook for the 21st Century*, eds. Etzel Cardeña, John Palmer, and David Marcusson-Clavertz (Jefferson, NC: McFarland, 2015), 293–300.

12  Roger D. Nelson, "Implicit Physical Psi: The Global Consciousness Project," in *Parapsychology: A Handbook for the 21st Century*, eds. Etzel Cardeña, John Palmer, and David Marcusson-Clavertz (Jefferson, NC: McFarland, 2015), 282–92.

13  Julie Beischel and Nancy L. Zingrone, "Mental Mediumship," in *Parapsychology: A Handbook for the 21st Century*, eds. Etzel Cardeña, John Palmer, and David Marcusson-Clavertz (Jefferson, NC: McFarland, 2015), 301–13.

14  Mental mediumship is contrasted with physical mediumship, in

which the operative psi is PK. Table tipping is the classic example of such physical phenomena. The argument that these manifestations are the work of a discarnate spirit rather than the medium is particularly weak, and thus I will not review this research.

15 Ian Stevenson, *Twenty Cases Suggestive of Reincarnation*, 2nd rev. ed. (Charlottesville: University Press of Virginia, 1974).

16 Emily W. Kelly and Diane Arcangel, "An Investigation of Mediums Who Claim to Give Information about Deceased Persons," *Journal of Nervous and Mental Disease* 199 (2011): 11–17.

17 Edward F. Kelly, Emily W. Kelly, Adam Crabtree, Alan Gauld, Michael Grosso, and Bruce Greyson, *Irreducible Mind: Toward a Psychology for the 21st Century* (Lanham, MD: Rowman & Littlefield, 2007).

18 Michael B. Sabom, *Recollections of Death: A Medical Investigation* (New York: Harper & Row, 1982).

19 Eben A. Alexander, *Proof of Heaven: A Neurosurgeon's Journey into the Afterlife* (New York: Simon & Schuster, 2012).

20 Elizabeth A. Rauscher and Russell Targ, "The Speed of Thought: Investigation of a Complex Space-time Metric to Describe Physical Phenomena," *Journal of Scientific Exploration* 15 (2001): 331–54

21 Dean Radin, *Entangled Minds: Extrasensory Experiences in a Quantum Reality.* (New York: Paraview Pocket Books, 2006).

22 Brian Millar, "The Observational Theories: A Primer," *European Journal of Parapsychology* 2 (1978): 304–32.

23 Helmut Schmidt and Henry Stapp, "Study of Psychokinesis with Pre-recorded Random Events and the Effect of Pre-observation," *Journal of Parapsychology* 57 (1993): 331–48.

24 Dean Radin, Leena Michel, Karla Galdamez, Paul Wendland, Robert Rickenbach, and Arnaud Delorme, "Consciousness and the Double-slit Interference Pattern: Six Experiments," *Physics Letters* 25 (2012): 157–71.

25 Henry P. Stapp, *The Mindful Universe: Quantum Mechanics and the Participating Observer,* http://www-physics.lbl.gov/~stapp/stappfiles. html.

26 Stuart Hameroff and Roger Penrose, "Consciousness in the Universe: A Review of the 'Orch OR' Theory," *Physics in Life Reviews* 11 (2014):

39–78.

27  Robert Nadeau and Menas Kafatos, *The Non-Local Universe: The New Physics and Matters of the Mind* (Oxford: Oxford University Press, 2001).


CHAPTER FOUR


1   Edwin C. May and Sonali Bhatt Marwaha, eds., *Extrasensory Perception: Support, Skepticism and Science* (Santa Barbara, CA: Praeger, 2015).

2   Charles Richet, "Further Experiments in Hypnotic Lucidity or Clairvoyance," *Journal of the Society for Psychical Research* (1889): 66–83; Richet, "La suggestion mentale et le calcul des probabilités," *Revue philosophique de la France et de l'étranger* 18 (1884): 609–74.

3   H. I. F. M. Brugmans, "A Report on Telepathic Experiments Done in the Psychology Laboratory at Groningen," *Le Compte rendu officiel du Premier Congrès International des Recherches Psychiques,* 1922; I. Jephson, "Evidence for Clairvoyance in Card Guessing," *Journal of the Society for Psychical Research* (1929): 223–68; and G. H. Estabrooks, "A Contribution to Experimental Telepathy," *Bulletin of the Boston Society for Psychical Research* (1927): 1–30.

4   J. B. Rhine, *Extrasensory Perception* (Boston: Boston Society for Psychical Research, 1934).

5   G. Schmeidler, "Separating the Sheep from the Goat," *Journal of the American Society for Psychical Research* (1945): 47–49.

6   J. McMoneagle, *The Stargate Chronicles: Memoirs of a Psychic Spy* (Charlottesville, VA: Hampton Roads Publishing, 2002).

7   Daryl Bem, Patrizio Tressoldi, Thomas Rabeyron, and Michael Duggan, "Feeling the Future: A Meta-Analysis of 90 Experiments on the Anomalous Anticipation of Random Future Events." *F1000Research* (2015): 1188, doi: 10.12688/f1000research.7177.1.

8   "The decline effect may occur when scientific claims receive decreasing support over time. The term was first described by parapsychologist Joseph Banks Rhine in the 1930s to describe the disappearing of extrasensory perception (ESP) of psychic experiments conducted by Rhine over the course of study or time," https://en.wikipedia.org /wiki/Decline_effect.

9    James C. Carpenter, *First Sight: ESP and Parapsychology in Everyday Life* (Landover, MD: Rowman & Littlefield, 2012).

10   D. Bohm and B. J. Hiley, *The Undivided Universe: An Ontological Interpretation of Quantum Theory* (London: Routledge, 1993); S. R. Hameroff and R. Penrose, "Consciousness in the Universe: A Review of the 'Orch Or' Theory," *Physics of Life Reviews* (2014): 39–78; Henry P. Stapp, *Mindful Universe: Quantum Mechanics and the Participating Observer* (New York: Springer, 2007).

11   Joseph F. Rychlak, *The Human Image in Postmodern America* (Washington, DC: American Psychological Association, 2003).

CHAPTER FIVE

1    William James, *A Pluralistic Universe: The Hibbert Lectures at Manchester College on the Present Situation in Philosophy* (Lincoln: University of Nebraska Press, 1996), 231.

2    Alfred North Whitehead, *Process and Reality: An Essay in Cosmology*, corr. ed., eds. David Ray Griffin and Donald W. Sherburne (New York: Free Press, 1929, 1978), 119.

3    Stanislav Grof, *Beyond the Brain: Birth, Death and Transcendence in Psychotherapy* (Albany: SUNY Press, 1985), 32.

4    Personal correspondence and James C. Carpenter, *First Sight: ESP and Parapsychology in Everyday Life* (Lanham, MD: Rowman and Littlefield Publishers, 2012), 106.

5    Carpenter, *First Sight: ESP and Parapsychology in Everyday Life*, 89.

6    Carpenter, *First Sight*, 48.

7    Carpenter, *First Sight*, 115.

8    Carpenter, *First Sight.*, 75.

9    Carpenter, *First Sight*, 115.

10   Carpenter, *First Sight*, 50.

11   Carpenter, *First Sight*, 49.

12   Carpenter, *First Sight*, 49–50.

13   Carpenter, *First Sight*, 42.

14   Carpenter, *First Sight*, 43–44. Carpenter does fully recognize the

importance of this issue.

15  Whitehead, *Process and Reality*, 236.

16  Carpenter, *First Sight*, 60–61; I see this as a separate issue from that of how loosening repression might facilitate psi data from entering into consciousness. The data that might pass through a more permeable repression "barrier" involve feelings that have already undergone significant unconscious processing, so it is not psi or physical prehensions *themselves* that would be entering conscious awareness.

17  Carpenter, *First Sight*, 27–29.

18  Carpenter, *First Sight*, 47.

19  Carpenter, *First Sight*, 20, 93.

20  This impression is supported by some recent email exchanges with Larry Dossey and Jim Carpenter.

21  Carpenter, *First Sight*, 200–01.

22  Carpenter, *First Sight*, 200–01

23  Carpenter, *First Sight*, 77.

24  David Ray Griffin, *Parapsychology, Philosophy, and Spirituality: A Postmodern Exploration* (Albany: SUNY Press, 1997), 90–95.

25  Carpenter, *First Sight*, 8, 56.

26  Carpenter, *First Sight*, 116.

27  Carpenter, *First Sight*, 399.

28  Carpenter, *First Sight*, 51.

29  Carpenter, *First Sight*, 236–37.

30  Carpenter, *First Sight*, 6.

31  Carpenter, *First Sight*, 312.

CHAPTER SIX

1   Stanislav Grof, *When the Impossible Happens: Adventures in Non-ordinary Realities* (Louisville, KY: Sounds True, 2006).

2   Stanislav Grof and Christina Grof, *Spiritual Emergency: When Personal Transformation Becomes a Crisis* (Los Angeles: J. P. Tarcher,

1989); *The Stormy Search for the Self: A Guide to Personal Growth through Transformational Crises* (Los Angeles: J. P. Tarcher, 1991).

3   Stanislav Grof, *The Cosmic Game: Explorations of the Frontiers of Human Consciousness* (Albany: State University of New York Press, 1998).

4   Stuart Hameroff, *Ultimate Computing* (North Holland: Elsevier Publishing, 1987).

5   Francis Crick, *The Astonishing Hypothesis: The Scientific Search for the Soul* (New York: Simon and Schuster, 1994).

6   Crick, *The Astonishing Hypothesis*, 3.

7   Immanuel Kant, *Critique of Pure Reason,* trans. and eds. Paul Guyer and Allen W. Wood (Cambridge: Cambridge University Press, 1999).

8   Kenneth Ring and Sharon Cooper, *Mindsight: Near-death and Out-of-Body Experiences in the Blind* (Palo Alto, CA: William James Center for Consciousness Studies, 1999); Kenneth Ring and Evelyn Elsaesser Valarino, *Lessons from the Light: What We can Learn from the Near-Death Experience* (New York: Plenum Press, 1998).

9   Stanislav Grof, *Psychology of the Future* (Albany: State University of New York Press, 2000).

10  Stanislav Grof, *Realms of the Human Unconscious: Observations from LSD Research* (New York: Viking Press, 1975); republished as *LSD: Doorway to the Numinous* (Rochester, VT: Inner Traditions, 2009).

11  Marhsall H. Klaus, John H. Kennell, and Phyllis H. Klaus, *Bonding: Building the Foundations of Secure Attachment and Independence* (Reading, MA: Addison Wesley, 1995); John H. Kennell and Marshall H. Klaus, "Bonding: Recent Observations that Alter Perinatal Care," *Pediatrics in Review* 19, 1 (1998): 4–12.

12  Christine Moon, Hugo Lagercrantz, and Patricia K. Kuhl, "Phonetic Learning in Utero," *The Journal of the Acoustical Society of America* 127, 3 (2010): 2017; Alfred A. Tomatis, *The Conscious Ear: My Life of Transformation Through Listening* (Barrytown, NY: Station Hill Press, 1991); Giselle E. Whitwell, "The Importance of Prenatal Sound and Music," *Journal of Prenatal and Perinatal Psychology and Health* 13, 3/4 (1999): 255–62.

13  Carl G. Jung, *The Archetypes and the Collective Unconscious*, collected works, vol. 9, part 1, Bollingen Series XX (Princeton: Princeton

University Press, 1959).

14  Ervin Laszlo, *The Connectivity Hypothesis: Foundations of an Integral Science of Quantum, Cosmos, Life, and Consciousness* (Albany: State University of New York Press, 2003); *Science and the Akashic Field: An Integral Theory of Everything* (Rochester, VT: Inner Traditions, 2004).

15  Grof, *Realms of the Human Unconscious*; *Psychology of the Future*; and *The Adventure of Self-Discovery* (Albany: State University of New York Press, 1987).

16  Grof, *When the Impossible Happens*.

17  Henry Corbin, "Mundus Imaginalis, or the Imaginary and the Imaginal," in *Working with Images: The Theoretical Base of Archetypal Psychology*, 71–89, ed. Benjamin Sells (Woodstock, CT: Spring Publications, 2000).

18  Carl G. Jung, *Symbols of Transformation*, collected works, vol. 5, Bollingen Series XX (Princeton: Princeton University Press, 1956); *The Archetypes and the Collective Unconscious*.

19  Grof, *When the Impossible Happens*.

CHAPTER SEVEN

1  Whitehead famously said that: "The safest general characterization of the European philosophical tradition is that it consists of a series of footnotes to Plato." In Alfred North Whitehead, *Process and Reality*, corr. ed., eds. David Ray Griffin and Donald W. Sherburne (New York: Free Press, 1978), 39.

2  Alfred North Whitehead, *Science and the Modern World* (New York: The Free Press, 1925), 51.

3  William James, *Varieties of Religious Experience: A Study in Human Nature* (New York: Longmans, Green, and Co, 1903), 387–88.

4  Robert Gordon Wasson, "Seeking the Magic Mushroom," *Life Magazine*, May 13, 1957, 100.

5  Robert Gordon Wasson, Albert Hoffman, and Carl Ruck, *The Road to Eleusis: Unraveling the Secret of the Mysteries* (Los Angeles: Hermes Press, 1998), 91.

6  Plotinus, *The Essential Plotinus*, trans. Elmer O'Brien (Indianapolis:

Hackett, 1975), 16.

7  Alfred North Whitehead, *Adventures of Ideas* (New York: The Macmillan Company, 1933), 11 ff.

8  Whitehead, *Process and Reality*, 105–7

9  Robin L. Carhart-Harris and Karl J. Friston, "The Default-Mode, Ego-Functions and Free-Energy," *Brain* 133, 4 (2010): 1265–83.

10  Dr. Robin Carhart-Harris, *Psilocybin and the Psychedelic State,* directed by Matt Faw, Youtube, December 2, 2012, https://www.youtube.com/watch?v=zrYl9krZksk&feature=youtu.be.

11  "We should do well to consider…the type of theory which Bergson put forward in connection with memory and sense perception. The suggestion is that the function of the brain and nervous system and sense organs is in the main eliminative and not productive. Each person is at each moment capable of remembering all that has ever happened to him and of perceiving everything that is happening everywhere in the universe. The function of the brain and nervous system is to protect us from being overwhelmed and confused by this mass of largely useless and irrelevant knowledge, by shutting out most of what we should otherwise perceive or remember at any moment, and leaving only that very small and special selection which is likely to be practically useful." In Aldous Huxley *The Doors of Perception* (New York: Harper & Row, 1963), 22–23.

12  Grof, Stanislav and Christina Grof, *Spiritual Emergency: When Personal Transformation Becomes a Crisis* (Los Angeles: Jeremy P. Tarcher, Inc, 1989).

13  Whitehead, *Process and Reality*, 29.

14  James, *Varieties of Religious Experience*, 386–88.

15  Ernst Kris, *Psychoanalytic Explorations in Art* (New York: The New American Library/Mentor, 1952).

16  Whitehead, *Process and Reality*, 226–27

17  Whitehead, *Adventures of Ideas* (New York: The Macmillan Company, 1933), 369.

18  Whitehead, *Process and Reality*, 254.

19  Carhart-Harris and Friston, "The Default-Mode, Ego-Functions and Free-Energy."

20  Whitehead, *Religion in the Making* (New York: The Macmillan Company, 1926), 19.

21  Whitehead, *Religion in the Making*, 16.

22  Whitehead, *Science and the Modern World*, 93.

23  Carhart-Harris and Friston, "The Default-Mode, Ego-Functions and Free-Energy," 1272.

24  Whitehead, *The Aims of Education*, (New York: Macmillan, 1929), 14.

25  Whitehead, *Adventure of Ideas*, 240–41.

26  Plato, *Timaeus* 36d, *Platonis opera quae extant omnia*, Henricus Stephanus (Geneva, 1578.)

27  William Blake, "Auguries of Innocence," *The Pickering Manuscript* (B.M. Pickering, 1866).

28  John B. Cobb, *Whitehead Word Book* (Claremont: P&F Press, 2008), 70.

29  Huxley, *The Doors of Perception*, 55.

30  Whitehead, *Science and the Modern World*, 93.

CHAPTER EIGHT

1   "Steiner and American Philosophy," the first of a three-part "Project for the Renewal of Thinking in Philosophy, Science, and Education," Wainwright House, Rye, New York, January 1991, directed by Robert McDermott with support from Laurance S. Rockefeller; the first part, "Renewal of Thinking in Philosophy," was published as "Rudolf Steiner and American Thought," in a double issue of *Revision*; for reference, see Robert McDermott, "Rudolf Steiner and American Thought," *Revision* 13.4 (Spring 1991): 155–83, and 14.1 (Summer 1991): 1–52.

2   McDermott, "Rudolf Steiner and American Thought."

3   McDermott, *American Philosophy and Rudolf Steiner* (Great Barrington, MA: Steinerbooks, 2012).

4   Rudolf Steiner, *Truth and Knowledge: An Introduction to "Philosophy of Spiritual Activity,"* trans. Rita Stebbing, ed. Paul M. Allen (Great Barrington, MA: Steinerbooks, 1981).

5    Translated as *Philosophy of Freedom: The Philosophy of Spiritual Activity*, trans. and intro Michael Wilson (London: Rudolf Steiner Press, 1986) and *Intuitive Thinking as a Spiritual Path: A Philosophy of Freedom,* trans. Michael Lipson (Great Barrington, MA: Steinerbooks, 1995).

6    Alfred North Whitehead, *Process and Reality*, corr. ed., eds. David Ray Griffin and Donald W. Sherburne (New York: Macmillan/Free Press, 1978), 29.

7    Alfred North Whitehead, *Adventures of Ideas* (New York: Free Press/ Macmillan, 1933), 244.

8    Whitehead, *Religion in the Making* (New York: World Publishing Company, 1926), 32–33.

9    David Ray Griffin, "Steiner's Anthroposophy and Whitehead's Philosophy," in McDermott, *American Philosophy and Rudolf Steiner*, 149.

10    Whitehead, *Process and Reality*, 94. I am grateful to Matthew David Segall for this reference.

11    Steiner, *How to Know Higher Worlds: A Modern Path of Initiation,* trans. Christopher Bamford (Great Barrington, MA: Steinerbooks, 1994).

12    For a thorough treatment of these topics, see Griffin, *Parapsychology, Philosophy, and Spirituality: A Postmodern Exploration* (New York: State University of New York Press, 1997).

13    Alfred North Whitehead, *Modes of Thought* (New York: The Free Press, 1938, 1966), 133

14    Whitehead, *Modes of Thought,* 154.

15    Alfred North Whitehead, *Science and the Modern World (New York: The Free Press,* 1967), 54

16    Griffin, "Steiner's Anthroposophy and Whitehead's Philosophy," 147–48.

17    Griffin, "Steiner's Anthroposophy and Whitehead's Philosophy," 152.

18    Rudolf Steiner, *An Outlline of Occcult Science* (Hudson, NY: Anthropsophic Press, 1972), 104.

19    Whitehead, *Process and Reality,* 347.

20  "Akashic Record" refers to the cosmic memory of all events, actions and thoughts.

21  Whitehead, *Process and Reality*, 222.

22  Steiner, *An Outline of Occult Science*, trans. Henry B. Monges and Lisa D. Monges (Spring Valley, NY: Anthroposophic Press, 1972), 35.

23  Griffin, "Steiner's Anthroposophy and Whitehead's Philosophy," 159.

24  Whitehead, *Process and Reality*, 348.

25  Griffin, "Steiner's Anthroposophy and Whitehead's Philosophy," 160, quoting Steiner, *The Philosophy of Spiritual Activity*, 75.

26  Griffin, "Steiner's Anthroposophy and Whitehead's Philosophy," 162.

27  Griffin, "Steiner's Anthroposophy and Whitehead's Philosophy," 163.

28  Griffin, "Steiner's Anthroposophy and Whitehead's Philosophy," 165.

29  Griffin, "Steiner's Anthroposophy and Whitehead's Philosophy," 170; quotation from Steiner, *The Philosophy of Spiritual Activity*, 10.

30  Owen Barfield, *Romaticism Comes of Age,* unk ed.

31  Griffin, "Steiner's Anthroposophy and Whitehead's Philosophy," 173; quotation from Whitehead, *Process and Reality*, 15.

32  Griffin, "Steiner's Anthroposophy and Whitehead's Philosophy," 180.

33  Steiner, *The Philosophy of Spiritual Activity* (Hudson, NY: Anthroposophic Press, 1986), 174.

34  Steiner, *The Philosophy of Spiritual Activity*, 12.

35  Steiner, *The Philosophy of Spiritual Activity*, 179.

36  Griffin, "Steiner's Anthroposophy and Whitehead's Philosophy," 180.

37  Griffin, "Steiner's Anthroposophy and Whitehead's Philosophy," 135–81.

CHAPTER NINE

1   Stephen Toulmin, *Cosmopolis: The Hidden Agenda of Modernity* (Chicago: University of Chicago Press, 1990).

2   Edwin A. Burtt, *The Metaphysical Foundations of Modern Science*, revised ed. (New York: Anchor, 1932), 15–35.

3   Thomas Kuhn, *The Structure of Scientific Revolutions*, 2nd ed. (Chicago: University of Chicago Press, 1970).

4   The simplest meaning of logos is "logic"; hence, "eco-logos" is the logic of the planet, our common home. In theology, the word is associated with the creative order of the universe.

5   Theodore Rozsak, Mary Gomes, and Allen D. Kanner, *Ecopsychology: Restoring the Earth, Healing the Mind* (San Francisco: Sierra Club Books, 1995).

6   Martin Heidegger, "The Question Concerning Technology," in *Martin Heidegger: Basic Writings*, trans. W. Lovitt (New York: Harper & Row, 1977), 287–317.

7   Theodore Roszak, "Where Psyche meets Gaia," in Theodore Roszak, Mary E. Gomes, and Allen D. Kanner, eds. *Ecopsychology: Restoring the Earth, Healing the Mind* (San Francisco: Sierra Club Books), 1–17.

8   David Loy, *Nonduality: A Study in Comparative Philosophy* (Amherst, MA: Humanity Books, 1996).

9   This is a very wide-ranging literature. For quick entry, the interested reader might consider consulting Enzo Paci's essay, "Whitehead and Husserl" in which he discusses "extraordinary analogies between some of Husserl's positions and those of Whitehead's." It was published in German in the *Reveu Internationale de Philosophie* (1961): 56–57. It is also available in a draft translation in English at: http://www.yorku.ca/lbianchi/paci/whitehead_and_husserl.html.

10   Alfred North Whitehead, *Science and the Modern World* (New York: Macmillan, 1925), 17.

11   Whitehead, *Science and the Modern World*, 55.

12   Whitehead, *Science and the Modern World*, 151–52.

13   Edmund Husserl, *The Crisis of European Sciences*, trans. David Carr (Evanston, IL: Northwestern University Press, 1970), 48–49.

14   Whitehead, *Science and the Modern World*, 91.

15   Whitehead, *Science and the Modern World*, 91.

16   Whitehead, *Science and the Modern World*, 206.

17   Maurice Merleau-Ponty, *The Visible and the Invisible*, trans. Alphonso Lingis (Evanston, IL: Northwestern University Press, 1968), 334. Originally published as *Le visible et l'invisible* (Paris: Gallimard, 1964).

18 Grof made this remark at the symposium we presented at the "Toward an Ecological Civilization" conference from which this book emerged. See his chapter in this book for further elaboration on this point.

19 Again, this was part of Grof's presentation. See his chapter in this book for further elaboration on this point.

20 This description is a central theme of Merleau-Ponty's. His best later writing on it is the chapter "The Intertwining—The Chiasm" from his last book *The Visible and the Invisible*, 130–55. But it was also central to his earlier (1945) magnum opus, *Phenomenology of Perception* (trans. D. Landes [New York: Routledge, 2012]).

21 Merleau-Ponty, *The Visible and the Invisible*, 139.

22 Merleau-Ponty, *Phenomenology of Perception*, 214–52.

23 Will W. Adams, "Nature's Participatory Psyche: A Study of Consciousness in the Shared Earth Community," *The Humanistic Psychologist* 38 (2010): 15–39, at 30.

24 Adams quoting Merleau-Ponty, *The Visible and the Invisible*, 199.

25 Adams quoting Merleau-Ponty, *The Visible and the Invisible*, 185.

26 Adams, "Nature's Participatory Psyche," 30.

27 David Abram, *The Spell of the Sensuous: Perception and Language in a More-Than-Human World* (New York: Pantheon, 1996), 33.

28 Abram, *The Spell of the Sensuous*, 66.

29 Christopher M. Aanstoos, "Psi and the Phenomenology of the Long Body," *Theta* 13.14 (1986): 49–51, at 49.

30 Michael Murphy, *In the Zone* (New York: Penguin, 1995).

31 Christopher M. Aanstoos, "Embodiment as Ecstatic Intertwining," in *Studies in Humanistic Psychology*, volume 29, ed. Christopher M. Aanstoos (Carrollton: West Georgia College Studies in the Social Sciences, 1991), 94–111.

32 Abram, *The Spell of the Sensuous*, 272–74.

CHAPTER TEN

1 Alfred North Whitehead, quoted in Arthur Koestler *The Roots of Coincidence* (New York: Random House, 1972), 111.

2   Erwin Schrödinger, *My View of the World*, reprint ed., trans. Cecily Hastings (Woodbridge, CT: Ox Bow Press, 1983), 21–22.

3   Robert G. Jahn and Brenda J. Dunne, *Consciousness and the Source of Reality* (Princeton: ICRL Press, 2011), 195–245.

4   J. S. Bell, "On the Einstein-Podolsky-Rosen Paradox," *Physics* 1.3 (1964): 195–200.

5   Robert Nadeau and Menas Kafatos, *The Non-Local Universe: The New Physics and Matters of the Mind* (New York: Oxford University Press, 1999), 65–82.

6   Erwin Schrödinger, "Discussion of Probability Relations between Separated Systems," *Mathematical Proceedings of the Cambridge Philosophical Society* 31.4 (1935): 555–63.

7   Nick Herbert, *Quantum Reality: Beyond the New Physics* (Garden City, NJ: Anchor/Doubleday, 1987), 230.

8   Vlatko Vedral, "Living in a Quantum World," *Scientific American* 304.6 (2011): 38–43.

9   N. David Mermin, "Extreme Quantum Entanglement in a Super-position of Macroscopically Distinct States," *Physical Review Letters* 65.15 (1990): 1838–40.

10  Menas Kafatos and Robert Nadeau, *The Conscious Universe: Parts and Wholes in Physical Reality* (New York: Springer, 2000), 71.

11  Nadeau and Kafatos, *The Non-Local Universe*, 65–82.

12  Nadeau and Kafatos, *The Non-Local Universe*, 2.

13  Kafatos and Nadeau, *The Conscious Universe*, 127.

14  Herbert, *Quantum Reality*, 214.

15  "Universe 101: How Old is the Universe?" *NASA*, accessed July 13, 2011, http://map.gsfc.nasa.gov/universe/uni_age.html.

16  Fred H. Thaheld, "Biological Nonlocality and the Mind-Brain Interaction Problem: Comments on a New Empirical Approach," *BioSystems* 70.1 (2003): 35–41.

17  Fred H. Thaheld, "A Method to Explore the Possibility of Nonlocal Correlations Between Brain Electrical Activities of Two Spatially Separated Animal Subjects," *BioSystems* 73.3 (2004): 205–16.

18  Vedral, "Living in a Quantum World," 43.

19 Brian D. Josephson and Fotini Pallikari-Viras, "Biological Utilization of Quantum Nonlocality," *Foundations of Physics* 21 (1991): 197–207.

20 Mark Anderson, "Is Quantum Mechanics Controlling Your thoughts?" *Discover Magazine*, January 12, 2009, accessed July 16, 2011, http://discovermagazine.com/2009/feb/13-is-quantum-mechanics-controlling-your-thoughts/article_view?b_start:int=0&-C.

21 Vedral, "Living in a Quantum World," 38–43.

22 Dean Radin, *Entangled Minds* (New York: Paraview/Simon & Schuster, 2006), 239.

23 Henry P. Stapp, "Quantum Physics and the Physicist's View of Nature: Philosophical Implications of Bell's Theorem," in *The World View of Contemporary Physics*, ed. Richard E. Kitchener (Albany: State University of New York Press, 1988), 40.

24 Brian Greene, *The Fabric of the Cosmos* (New York: Alfred A. Knopf, 2004), 84.

25 Greene, *The Fabric of the Cosmos*, 113.

26 Nadeau and Kafatos, *The Non-Local Universe*, 4–5.

27 Stuart Hameroff, quoted in Tom Huston and Joel Pitney "Finding Spirit in the Fabric of Space and Time," *EnlightenNext* (Spring/Summer 2010): 44–57.

28 Roger Penrose, quoted in Karl Giberson, "The Man Who Fell to Earth: Interview with Roger Penrose," *Science & Spirit* (March/April 2003): 34–41.

29 Robert G. Jahn and Brenda J. Dunne, *Margins of Reality: The Role of Consciousness in the Physical World* (New York: Harcourt Brace Jovanovich, 1987), 201.

30 Charles T. Tart, Interview with Renée Scheltema, *Something Unknown Is Doing We Don't Know What*, directed by Renée Scheltema (US, 2009), DVD, accessed July 17, 2011, http://www.somethingunknown.com.

31 Larry Dossey, "Nonlocal Knowing: The Emerging View of Who We Are," *Explore* 4.1 (2008): 1–9.

32 Larry Dossey, "PEAR Lab and Nonlocal Matter: Why They Matter," *Explore* 3.3 (2007): 119–96.

33 Larry Dossey, "Mind-Body Medicine: Whose Mind and Whose

Body?" *Explore* 5.3 (2009): 127–34.

34  Dean Radin, *The Conscious Universe* (San Francisco: HarperSanFrancisco, 1997).

35  Radin, *Entangled Minds*.

36  Jahn and Dunne, *Consciousness and the Source of Reality*.

37  Mari Sandoz, *The Buffalo Hunters* (Lincoln: University of Nebraska Press, 1954), 3–5.

38  Dylan Winter, *Starlings at Otmoor*, online video, accessed December 4, 2010, http://www.youtube.com/watch?v=XH-groCeKbE.

39  *Swarm: Nature's Incredible Invasions*, produced by John Downer (January 4, 2009; UK: BBC One, 2009), accessed July 14, 2011 http://www.youtube.com/watch?v=cIgHEhziUxU&feature=related.

40  "Swarm intelligence", *Wikipedia*, accessed December 3, 2010 http://en.wikipedia.org/wiki/Swarm_intelligence.

41  "Planes, Trains, and Ant Hills: Computer Scientists Simulate Activity of Ants to Reduce Airline Delays," *ScienceDaily*, accessed December 5, 2010 http://www.sciencedaily.com/videos/2008/0406 -planes_trains_and_ant_hills.htm.

42  Craig W. Reynolds, "Flocks, Herds and Schools: A Distributed Behavioral Model," *Computer Graphics*, 21.4 (1987): 25–34.

43  Peter Miller, "The Genius of Swarms," *National Geographic*, July 2007, accessed December 5, 2010, http://ngm.nationalgeographic .com/2007/07/swarms/miller-text.

44  "Caribou," *U.S. Fish and Wildlife Service*, accessed December 5, 2010, http://arctic.fws.gov/caribou.htm.

45  Karsten Heuer, quoted in Peter Miller, "The Genius of Swarms."

46  Captain A. H. Trapman, *The Dog: Man's Best Friend—A Book for All Dog Lovers* (London: Hutchinson & Co. Ltd, 1929).

47  Rupert Sheldrake, *Dogs That Know When Their Owners Are Coming Home*, reprint (New York: Three Rivers Press, 2000); There is abundant laboratory research on nonlocal knowing in a great variety of animals and organisms. For a review of the field, see Diane Dutton, "Clever Beasts and Faithful Pets: A Critical Review of Animal Psi Research," *Journal of Parapsychology* 73 (2009):43 ff, accessed January 22, 2011, https://

www.thefreelibrary.com/Clever+beasts+and+faithful+pets%3a +a+critical+review+of+animal+psi...-a0219588957; Susan J. Armstrong, "A Theoretical Inquiry into Animal Psi," in *Critical Reflections on the Paranormal,* eds. Michael Stoeber and Hugo Meynell (Albany: State University of New York Press, 1996), 133–58.

48  William James, "The Confidences of a Psychical Researcher," in *Essays in Psychical Research*, ed. F. H. Burkhardt (Cambridge: Harvard University Press, 1986), 375.

49  William James, "What Psychical Research Has Accomplished," in *The Will to Believe and Other Essays in Popular Philosophy* (London: Longmans, Green; 1910,), 299–300. Composed of segments originally published in 1890, 1892, and 1896.

50  Herbert, *Quantum Reality: Beyond the New Physics*, 249–50.

51  Radin, *Entangled Minds.*

52  Radin, *The Conscious Universe.*

53  Larry Dossey, *The Power of Premonitions* (New York: Dutton, 2009).

54  Stephen A. Schwartz, *Opening to the Infinite: The Art and Science of Nonlocal Awareness* (Buda, TX: Nemoseen, 2007).

55  R. Pizzi, A. Fantasia, F. Gelain, D. Rossetti, and A. Vescovi, "Nonlocal Correlation between Separated Human Neural Networks," in *Quantum Information and Computation II, Proceedings of SPIE* 5436 (2004):107–17, eds. E. Donkor, A. R. Pirick, and H. E. Brandt, accessed January 17, 2009, http://adsabs.harvard.edu /abs/2004SPIE.5436..107P.

56  Leanna J. Standish, Leila Kozak, L. Clark Johnson, and Todd Richards, "Electroencephalographic Evidence of Correlated Event-Related Signals Between the Brains of Spatially and Sensory Isolated Human Subjects," *Journal of Alternative and Complementary Medicine* 10.2 (2004): 307–14.

57  Leanna J. Standish, L. Clark Johnson, Leila Kozak, and Todd Richards, "Evidence of Correlated Functional Magnetic Resonance Imaging Signals Between Distant Human Brains," *Alternative Therapies in Health and Medicine* 9 (2003): 122–28.

58  Jiri Wackerman, Christian Seiter, Holger Keibel, and Harald Walach, "Correlations between Brain Electrical Activities of Two Spatially Separated Human Subjects," *Neuroscience Letters* 336 (2003): 60–64.

59 Gottfried Wilhelm Leibniz, quoted in "Gottfried Wilhelm Leibniz," *Stanford Encyclopedia of Philosophy*, December 22, 2007, accessed July 20, 2011, http://plato.stanford.edu/entries/leibniz/.

60 Erwin Schrödinger, quoted in *Quantum Questions*, ed. Ken Wilber (Boulder: New Science Library, 1984), 81.

61 Charles Darwin quoted in *The Life and Letters of Charles Darwin*, vol. 1, ed. Francis Darwin (New York: D. Appleton & Co., 1897), 81–82.

62 Philip Goldberg, *American Veda: From Emerson and The Beatles to Yoga and Mediation—How Indian Spirituality Changed the West* (New York: Harmony, 2010), 270.

63 William Blake, "Auguries of Innocence," quoted in John Bartlett, *Bartlett's Familiar Quotations*, 16th ed., ed. Justin Kaplan (Boston: Little, Brown and Company, 1992), 359.

64 Percy Bysshe Shelley, "Adonais," quoted in Bartlett, *Bartlett's Familiar Quotations*, 409.

65 William Wordsworth, "Tintern Abbey," quoted in Bartlett, *Bartlett's Familiar Quotations*, 373.

66 Samuel Taylor Coleridge, *The Statesman's Manual: Critical Theory Since Plato*, ed. Hazard Adams (New York: Harcourt Brace Jovanovich, 1971), 476.

67 Schwartz, *Opening to the Infinite*, 38.

68 Goldberg, *American Veda*, 346.

69 Walter Scott, *Hermetica: The Ancient Greek and Latin Writings Which Contain Religious or Philosophic Teachings Ascribed to Hermes Trismegistus*, vols. 1–4 (Boston: Shambhala, 2001).

70 Lynn Picknett and Clive Prince, *The Forbidden Universe: The Occult Origins of Science and the Search for the Mind of God* (New York: Skyhorse Publishing, 2011).

71 Picknett and Prince, *The Forbidden Universe*, 342.

72 Picknett and Prince, *The Forbidden Universe*, 339.

73 Samuel Johnson, *Quoteworld.com*, accessed July 24, 2011, http://www.quoteworld.org/quotes/7290.

74 Johnson, *Quoteworld.com*.

75  Albert Schweitzer, *Indian Thought and Its Development*, trans. Mrs. Charles E. B. Russell (New York: Beacon Press, 1934), 260.

76  Albert Schweitzer, "Albert Schweitzer," *Wikiquote*, accessed July 12, 2011, http://en.wikiquote.org/wiki/Albert_Schweitzer.

# Contributors

CHRISTOPHER M. AANSTOOS received his M.A. and Ph.D. degrees in phenomenological psychology from Duquesne University, under the mentorship of Amedeo Giorgi. Many of his publications are concerned with the philosophical and methodological foundations of psychology, including his editorship of the 1984 volume of the Studies in the Social Sciences series entitled *Exploring the Lived World: Readings in Phenomenological Psychology,* and the 1991 volume entitled *Studies in Humanistic Psychology.* He was also the editor of *The Humanistic Psychologist,* one of APA's division journals, and he has served as president of the Division of Humanistic Psychology of the APA. Aanstoos is a Professor Emeritus of the University of West Georgia, where he taught from 1982 until his retirement in 2018

JOHN H. BUCHANAN received his M.A. degree in humanistic/transpersonal psychology from West Georgia College and his doctorate from the Graduate Institute of the Liberal Arts at Emory University. He has been trained and certified as a Holotropic Breathwork practitioner by Stanislav and Christina Grof. Currently, he is writing a book based upon his continuing interests in process philosophy and transpersonal psychology. Dr. Buchanan also serves as president of the Helios Foundation.

JIM CARPENTER, PH.D., is both a clinical psychologist and a research parapsychologist. He is a Diplomate in Clinical Psychology, ABPP, and a Fellow in the American Academy of Clinical Psychology. He is a Clinical Associate Professor in the Department of Psychiatry of the University of North Carolina School of Medicine. Dr. Carpenter has published widely in psychology and parapsychology, with over 100 research articles, book chapters, and more popularly oriented pieces. For many years he has provided pro bono clinical consultation for persons who seek help with unpleasant experiences that they think of as psychic. He recently published a book developing a theory of psi, called *First Sight: ESP and Parapsychology in Everyday Life.* In 2012 he was awarded the Charles Honorton Award for Integrative Contributions by the Parapsychological Association; and he currently serves as president of that association.

JOHN B. COBB, JR. has held many positions including Ingraham Professor of Theology at the Claremont School of Theology, Avery Professor at the Claremont Graduate School, Fullbright Professor at the University of Mainz, Visiting Professor at Vanderbilt, Harvard, and Chicago Divinity Schools. He is often regarded as the preeminent scholar in the field of process philosophy and process theology, and is the author of more than forty books including: *Christ in a Pluralistic Age; God and the World;* and co-author with Herman Daly of *For the Common Good,* which was co-winner of the Grawemeyer Award for Ideas Improving World Order. In 2014, Cobb was elected to the prestigious Academy of Arts and Sciences.

LARRY DOSSEY, M.D., the author of twelve books and numerous articles, is the former Executive Editor of the peer-reviewed journal *Alternative Therapies in Health and Medicine,* the most widely subscribed-to journal in its field. He is currently Executive Editor of the peer-reviewed journal *Explore: The Journal of Science and Healing.* He has lectured all over the world, including major medical schools and hospitals in the United States, such as Harvard, Johns Hopkins, Cornell, the Universities of Pennsylvania, California, Washington, Texas, Florida, Minnesota, and the Mayo Clinic. In 2013, Larry Dossey received the prestigious Visionary Award by the Integrative Healthcare Symposium, which honors a pioneer whose visionary ideas have shaped integrative healthcare and the medical profession.

LEONARD GIBSON graduated from Williams College and earned doctorates from Claremont Graduate School in philosophy and The

University of Texas at Austin in psychology. He has taught at the University of Tulsa, Oklahoma, and Lesley College in Cambridge, Massachusetts. He served a clinical psychology internship at the Veterans Administration Hospital in Boston, Massachusetts and trained in Holotropic Breathwork with Stanislav Grof. Most recently he has taught Transpersonal Psychology at Burlington College. Together with his wife Elizabeth, he conducts frequent experiential workshops.

DAVID RAY GRIFFIN is Professor Emeritus of Philosophy of Religion and Theology at the Claremont School of Theology. His has published more than 34 books, primarily in theology, philosophy, and philosophy of religion, with special emphases on the problem of evil and the relation between science and religion. Some of his major works include: *Parapsychology, Philosophy, and Spirituality; Unsnarling the World-Knot: Consciousness, Freedom, and the Mind-Body Problem; Religion* and *Scientific Naturalism; and Reenchantment without Supernaturalism: A Process Philosophy of Religion*. He was also editor of the SUNY series in Constructive Postmodern Thought.

STANISLAV GROF, M.D., is a psychiatrist with more than fifty years of experience in research of non-ordinary states of consciousness. Currently, he is Professor of Psychology at the California Institute of Integral Studies (CIIS) in San Francisco, conducts professional training programs in Holotropic Breathwork and transpersonal psychology, and gives lectures and seminars worldwide. He is one of the founders and chief theoreticians of transpersonal psychology and the founding president of the International Transpersonal Association (ITA). In October 2007, he received the prestigious Vision 97 Award from the Dagmar and Václav Havel Foundation in Prague and in 2010 the Thomas R, Verny Award for his pivotal contributions to pre- and perinatal psychology. Among his publications are over 150 papers in professional journals and the books *Beyond the Brain; LSD Psychotherapy; The Cosmic Game; Psychology of the Future; When the Impossible Happens; The Ultimate Journey; Healing Our Deepest Wounds; H.R.Giger and the Zeitgeist of the Twentieth Century; Spiritual Emergency; The Stormy Search for the Self;* and *Holotropic Breathwork* (the last three with Christina Grof).

ROBERT MCDERMOTT, PH.D., is president emeritus of the California Institute of Integral Studies (CIIS) and chair of the CIIS program in Philosophy and Religion. Previously he was professor and chair of the

Philosophy Department at Baruch College, CUNY. His books include *The Essential Aurobindo* (1974, 1987), "Introduction" to William James's *Essays in Psychical Research* (1986), *The Bhagavad Gita and the West* (2009), *The New Essential Steiner* (2009), *American Philosophy and Rudolf Steiner* (2012), and *Steiner and Kindred Spirits* (2015). He was chair of the board of Sunbridge College in NY and of Rudolf Steiner College in Fair Oaks, CA, and served on the council of the Anthroposophical Society of America.

JOHN PALMER received his Ph.D. in psychology from the University of Texas in 1969. He was on the staff of the Rhine Research Center (formerly Foundation of Research on the Nature of Man) from 1984 to 2004, serving as Director of Research from 2000 to 2004. He was Director of Education from 1988 to 2004, in which capacity he was in charge of the 8-week Summer Study Program. He has been editor of the *Journal of Parapsychology* since 1994. He was President of the Parapsychological Association in 1979 and 1992. He has published numerous research articles in professional journals and is co-author of the book *Foundations of Parapsychology*. His research has focused primarily on psychological factors associated with ESP performance in the laboratory

CPSIA information can be obtained
at www.ICGtesting.com
Printed in the USA
LVHW081624261020
669852LV00043B/2601